THE NEW HINDU MOVEMENT
1886-1911

THE NEW
HINDU MOVEMENT
1886-1911

RAKHAL CHANDRA NATH
Kalyani University

SOUTH ASIA BOOKS
Box 502 : Columbia, Mo. 65205
U S. A.

in arrangement with
MINERVA ASSOCIATES (Publications) PVT. LTD.
7-B, Lake Place : Calcutta-700029
India

Printed in India by G. M. Ghoshal at The New Orion Press,
25, K. M. Naskar Road, Calcutta-700 040 and published by
T. K. Mukherjee on behalf of South Asia Books, Columbia,
Mo. 65205, U.S.A.

For my friend

SUHAS MAJUMDAR

PREFACE

THE PRESENT work is mainly concerned with the history of ideas that constituted the foundation of the New Hindu Movement, the so-called 'Hindu Revival' of the nineteenth century and the early decades of the twentieth. The Movement originated in Bengal, and the ideas following from it gripped the minds of the Indian people at large. This work might prove useful in understanding the Indian mind towards the beginning of the century in which we live and also the process of the growth of the nationalist consciousness. I have particularly emphasized the ideological roots of nationalism, which tend to be largely ignored in the recent studies on Indian nationalism. The scope of the work has been discussed at length in the Introduction.

To Professor Binoy Bhusan Chaudhuri, my teacher, my debt has been incalculable. It is small praise to say that he bore with perfect patience and courtesy my interminable visits to his place and my innumerable encroachments on his valuable time. But what Professor Chaudhuri and Mrs Chaudhri did for me was something far more precious. They received me with true affection and made each of my visits to their place an occasion of most delightful repose as well as the liveliest conversation. It is not only that whenever, in the course of discussing the ideas and events connected to my theme, I was carried away by a wholly uncritical admiration for their excellence, he exercised a healthy critical caution over my exuberence ; but that his whole method of supervision was to me the revelation of the mind of a truly critical historian. I shall not be far wrong in making the statement that if my work, as it now stands, can lay any claim to being a work of sober history, it is largely due to him. The deficiencies are wholly mine.

I thank my colleagues for their encouragement ; in parti-

(VIII)

cular I must mention the name of Dr Atmaram Ghosal, Professor Subhrendranath Majumdar and Professor Anil Roy. I acknowledge my debt to Shri Prabodh Kumar Biswas, Assistant Librarian, Presidency College, Calcutta, for his valuable help with books and journals. Professor Manas Kumar Bhattacharya and my younger brother Professor Paresh Chandra Nath have helped me in preparing the Index.

Shri Oroon Kumar Ghosh has kindly read my manuscript and made some valuable suggestions. My whole heart goes to thank him.

My thanks are due to Shri Tapas Mukherjee in undertaking the publication of a work by a wholly unknown author.

To my wife I am in debt so often that I usually end by not thanking her at all.

To my inspirer, I dedicate the book.

Rakhal Chandra Nath

'Nath Bhavan'
Central 'E' Road
Barrackpore 743101

CONTENTS

its own political progeny.

INTRODUCTION

DURING THE last quarter of the nineteenth century Bengal witnessed a religious movement which some critics have characterized as 'Hindu Revival'. The title has carried the implication that the movement sought to revive the superstitions and the many objectionable customs associated with Hinduism, which had begun to be looked upon as obsolete and otiose with the spread of the Western Enlightenment in India. A further implication has been the supposed undoing (by this alleged revival) of the many good things achieved by the reforming sects of the nineteenth century, notably the Brahmo Samaj, which had already rejected those customs and superstitions and had accepted the Enlightenment of the West as a basic ingredient of its creed.

Such criticisms, as noted later in this study, have been improper. The notion 'Hindu Revival' is of doubtful validity and a more appropriate title would be : 'The New Hindu Movement', - a phrase actually used by one of the sponsors of the movement, namely Bankim Chandra Chatterjee. Bankim coined the term 'New Hindu' to distinguish his interpretation of Hinduism from practises that were popular and orthodox; but the New Hindu spirit was in fact a pervasive one. It was in fact the informing spirit of the whole epoch designated by the more popular 'Hindu Revival' ; and the spirit was potent enough to outstrip the bounds of religion properly so-called and to irradiate at once the fields of Contemporary Literature, the Fine Arts, Music, History, Education and above all Politics. Actually, the New Hindu Movement had much to do with the Religious Nationalism of the Bengal Partition Movement (the Swadeshi Movement). Indeed, a clear understanding of Indian Nationalism requires a close study of the ideas that constituted the New Hindu Movement. The movement itself had a far larger scope—it was in fact the embodiment of a vision of the New India as it could be made. Seen in this light, the politics of the movement was only a by-product. Such a broad movement needs to be carefully studied.

The ideas that went to the making of the movement and those that justify the new title can be grouped under three heads : the idea of a Rational Religion, that of Personal Illumination through Religion, and that of an ancient Indian Civilization which was thought to be of paramount relevance to the India that was going the Western way.

(1) The spirit of rationalism transmitted through Western education coupled with the challenge of evangelism of the Christian missionaries had shocked the Hindus into an awareness of the imperfections of the prevalent Hindu religious customs and beliefs. Hinduism had been criticised as an accretion of external ceremonials and social conventions. The application of the rational approach towards religion had started with Rammohan Roy (1774-1833). Following his lead, later Brahmo leaders like Debendranath Tagore (1817-1905) and Keshub Chandra Sen (1838-84) had opted for a species of Intuitionism as the rational basis of the Brahmo creed of Vedantic Monotheism. But the doctrine that religious truths are intuitively self-evident had its pitfalls, as was evident from the career of Keshub Chandra Sen, in whose hands Intuitionism degenerated into a cult of subjective revelation apprehended by seers like Keshub alone—a reductio ad absurdum of Brahmo Rationalism and, by the end of 1860's, a new basis for religious faith was felt necessary. Also the Brahmo response to the challenge of European rationalism never faced the larger question whether religion had any satisfactory answer to the sort of rational scepticism that questioned the very basis of religion. Bankim (1838-94) was the first to grapple with this larger question. Bankim upheld that religion had a 'natural, a physical basis' and he approached the religious question from the standpoint of Humanism, that is to say, the doctrine that lasting happiness consisted in an organisation of

human faculties to a state of balance without any appeal to superhuman agencies. Bankim, taking his cue from the *Gita*, which preached a way of surrender of man's action, man's love, and man's knowledge to God as the best means to lasting happiness, and, interpreting this surrender as the most satisfactory statement of the doctrine of balance, attempted a humanistic solution of the religious question. The rationalistic approach to religion was thus vindicated by an appeal to purely Hindu sources and a version of Hinduism was offered which answered most of the sceptical questionings of religion seekers who had received the new education of the West.

The second idea was that of Personal Illumination through religion. The Brahmo way of interpreting Hinduism, while satisfying intellectual curiosity to a certain extent, had failed to answer a deeper need. The careers of Keshub Chandra Sen and Bijoy Krishna Goswami, both of whom had started as staunch champions of the Brahmo cause, illustrate most signally a phase in the religious quest of a people, in which a purely reforming creed, such as the Brahmo creed, comes to grief by failing to provide illumination to earnest religious consciences. Keshub ended by creating a private religion which he called "The New Dispensation." Bijoy Krishna leaned towards a Hindu cult (the cult of Chaitanya), but failed to carry his educated countrymen with him. Vivekananda, the disciple of Ramakrishna, wrested the initiative from Brahmo hands by investing the Vedantic doctrine of Personal Illumination with a new intensity by giving it a social message—the message of service as a sacrament but witholding none of its appeal as a way of spiritual enlightenment.

The third idea was the telescoping of a vision of Indian civilization into the present and the future. The vision of a glorious ancient civilization of India was conjured up by Bankim, Vivekananda and Rabindranath Tagore and they attempted to recapture the vision so as to re-enact it on the contemporary Indian stage.

Such ideas, which thus constituted the essence of the new movement, were not calculated to be passively contemplated by their recipients, but carried with them a positive activist message. Bankim's emphasis on Rational Faith and Vivekananda's emphasis on Personal Illumination, though operating on two very different planes, converged on a single point — that of service : in the first place, service of humanity as a sort of sacrament aiming at the realisation of the unity of all creation as preached in the Vedanta and in the second place the service of India through the sort of selfless (patriotic) action as preached in the *Gita*. The former, in its turn, led to the notion, of what Vivekananda called the 'raising of the masses' and of the womankind of India as the two foremost social programmes of the age ; the latter, to a new conception of patriotism which proved to be a vital force behind the Bengal Partition Movement. The vision of an ancient Indian civilization provided an ideology to the political aspiration of the age — the ideology of *Dharmarajya* (the Kingdom of Righteousness) — to be taken up, in due course, by Mahatma Gandhi in his formula of the Ramraj,— but without Mahatma's insistence on non-violence. *Dharmarajya* was sought to be founded by the method of 'revolutionary terrorism' of the Swadeshi days, but it actually fell a victim to the same 'terrorism' in its career of conspiratorial politics. The Partition of Bengal was annulled (1911), but the religious movement that considerably inspired the Swadeshi movement gradually died away.

This movement, in its successes as well as its failures certainly the most powerful religious movement of 19th century India, has yet had no authenticated history. The present work is an attempt at that. First of all, it is necessary to assign the chronological limits of the period we intend to study. The period covered here is 1866 to 1911.

The New Hindu Movement cannot be said to have really started before the year 1882, which witnessed the controversy on Hindu idolatry in the pages of the *Statesman* between Reverend W. W. Hastie (the then Principal of the General Assemblies Institution of Calcutta) and Bankim Chandra Chatterjee (under the pseudonym Ramchandra). The controversy created a stir among the educated Hindus of Calcutta, and it became clear that English-educated Hindus no longer regarded Brahmo theism as the only answer to their dissatisfaction with traditional Hinduism. Other writings of Bankim followed through the medium of two Bengali journals, *'Navajivan'* and *'Prachar'* ; and the publication in 1888, of his monumental *'Dharmatattwa'*, in which he gave the most systematic exposition of his version of Rational Hinduism, was followed by his no less monumental second edition of *'Krishnacharitra'* in 1892. In direct progression of these events came Swami Vivekananda's defence of Hinduism in the Chicago Parliament of Religions in 1893. The progress of the new movement was thus continuous from the year 1882 onwards. But actually the dissatisfaction of the English-educated Hindus with the religion preached by the reforming sects had come to the surface as early as 1866, when the Brahmo Samaj split into two distinct groups, the one emphasizing their Hindu identity and the other aiming at a clean sweep of the superstitions of Hinduism. The rift in the Brahmo Samaj resulting in the parting of ways between the 'conservative' Debendranath Tagore and the 'progressive' Keshub Chandra Sen was ostensibly on certain social questions like intercaste marriage and the wearing of the 'sacred thread' by Brahmo priests ; but there are signs that the disenchantment with the religion which considered worship without idols as the only test of a true religious life had already been widespread amongst the English-educated section. Consequently, 1866 may conveniently be looked upon as the year ushering in a new phase in the religious history of nineteenth century Bengal.

The year 1911 was the one of the annulment of the
partition of Bengal. This event marked the end of a phase
of political agitation in India ; and as that phase of political
agitation drew its inspiration from the religious ferment, and
as the new religious impulse seems to have totally exhausted
itself in the process of sustaining the political struggle, the
end of that struggle may also be said to have been the end
in a certain way of the religious movement.

In view of the usual characterization of this movement as 'the Hindu Revival', it is necessary to examine this.
Brahmo historiography and latterly, Atheistic school of historiography have been unanimous in treating this religious
'revival' as a term of derogation. With them, religious revivalism and social reaction are synonymous terms. According to Bipin Chandra Pal[1] (a one time Brahmo leader), to
whom we owe a great deal for our knowledge of the time,
this movement "set up a new defence of those social institutions and religious and spiritual tendencies that had pre-
viously been openly repudiated as false and harmful."[2] In
support of his argument, he explained how the Hindu revival
had put up a defence of 'Hindu idolatry', 'system of caste'
and 'child marriage.' Being inspired by its "revivalistic and
reactionary thought", he continued, "this movement declared
war upon all the fundamental progressive ideals of the
Brahmo Samaj," and "offered an effective check, for a time,
to the religious and social reform movements." The Missionary historian, J. N. Farquhar perceived in the Ramakrishna
Movement an attitude of apathy to social reform and an
illustration of 'full defence of the old faith'[3] in almost every
particular. In the opinion of a Marxist historian, R. Palme
Dutt[4], the movement was based on "the most antiquated
religion and religious superstitions" which held in high
esteem and veneration "every form of antiquated tradition."
To him, the movement was a retrograde one as the insistence
on orthodox religion and the "proclamation of the supposed
spiritual superiority of the ancient Hindu civilisation .. ..

inevitably retarded and weakened the real advance of the national movement and of political consciousness."

It is unnecessary to answer these criticisms author by author. We shall content ourselves by taking up the charges instead. The charge against idolatry implies a canon of criticism which is essentially Christian or Quranic. Such a canon is hardly called for by historical objectivity. From the standpoint of Judaeo-Christian (or Quranic) theology, idol worship is certainly crass heathenism. The New Hindus were at pains to point out that Hindu idolatry, unlike pagan idolatry, did not ever presuppose a multiplicity of anthropomorphic gods, but viewed the idol as embodying a certain attribute of the Deity. There is scarcely any evidence that in the fields of morality, education and politics the effects of the New Hindu Movement amounted to a negation of what had been achieved by the labours of the reforming sects of the preceding decades, notably the Brahmo sect.

As for social reforms like widow re-marriage etc., the New Hindu attitude to them was indifference rather than any concerted opposition to them. The New Hindu attitude was epitomised in Swami Vivekananda's assertion that the greatness of a people (or a religion) was not to be judged by the number of widows it allowed to remarry. This assertion was of a piece with Bankim Chandra Chatterjee's impatience with the contemporary idolization of 'reformers.' In his view, the New Hindus were to aim at the "moral and political regeneration" of contemporary Hindu society,—a work, which in his opinion, was the essential prerequisite to necessary social reforms. This attitude was hardly one of antagonism to social reform; it only emphasized a certain order of priorities—the priority of religious and political reforms over social reform. Actually, Swami Vivekananda's invectives against child-marriage—to take only one issue that agitated the minds of contemporary reformers were far more unequivocal than those of many of the reforming sects. The

precise natare of the New Hindu attitude to particular social
reforms was much too complicated to be treated adequately
in this introduction. But to condemn it as reactionary in
the sense in which the conservative opposition in the days of
Raja Rammohan was reactionry would be wrong. Certainly the New Hindus never founded an institution in the
manner of Raja Radhakanta Deb's (1784-1867) *Dharmasabha*[5]
set up (in January, 1830) with the express object of reviving
the custom of burning newly widowed women nor even one
to agitate against their re-marriage. If they had not agitated
either for the abolition of child-marriage—or any other social
evil for that matter—the reason must be sought elsewhere.

The New Hindu Movement was in essence a movement aiming at the resurgence of the whole Hindu society
and as such its primary concern was its spiritual awakening.
This they sought to achieve by purifying their own religion by
means of ideas derived from itself. These ideas included a new
conception of Bhakti, which included selfless action (Nishkam
Karma), for one's country and for humanity at large as a
central truth of religion; they included "love for all creation"
as the fundamental ethical truth of Hinduism ; and they
showed a way in which to attain "personal illumination"
through the practice of religion. They did not denounce
other religions as false but looked upon their own as true
enough and broad enough to include them all—in other
words, as being the most universal of them all. This was
the root idea behind Vivekananda's conception of 'aggressive
Hinduism' by means of which Hinduism was sought to be
propagated all over the world without attempting to suppress
any other religion. This was a programme far more ambitious in its scope than the programme of the reforming sects,
which at its best, was one of eradicating some particular
evils in Hindu society. Whatever verdict we may pass on
the success of this aspect of the New Hindu programme,
there is no way of underrating the fact that it was primarily
Vivekananda's preachings—anticipated by Bankim in such

essays as *"Bangadesher Krisak"* (The Peasants of Bengal)—
which roused the consciousness of the whole of India to the
two prime questions of reform in our national life : that of
'raising' the masses of India, and bringing the women of
India to the forefront of the national life. Whatever success
the New Hindu Movement may have achieved in the actual
working out of these programmes, it was primarily to its
credit that it released the Indian mind from its obsession
with petty social reform schemes and roused it to the consciousness of these larger programmes. It created a consciousness of national life and national needs which the reformers had failed to do.

In this connection, it must be remembered that Bipin
Chandra Pal covered in his work the period - 1880 to 1890,
thereby excluding Vivekananda from his discussion. He
also lumped together Bankim, the New Hindu with the
pseudo-rationalist Sasadhar Tarkachudamani who had come
to prominence during the period in question. He therefore
did have some justification for his charges, for Sasadhar's
approach to Hinduism was wholly reactionary as we shall see
in Chapter-1. What, however, Bipin Chandra Pal failed to
perceive (or what he perceived but faintly) was that Bankim's
true connection was with the rationalistic tendencies of the
Brahmo thinkers before him and Vivekananda after him.
It is true that Pal's criticism of Bankim was half-hearted
and not wholly disparaging but his failure to perceive
the distinction between the approach of such reactionaries
as Sasadhar and that of Bankim (and Vivekananda
after him), can only be explained by his obsession with
Brahmo reformism. As for J. N. Farquhar, he was a
Christian Missionary, and his whole work, devoted to the
religious movements of the nineteenth century, is presumably
wholly influenced by his particular attitudes to Hindu
thought in general and Vivekananda's thoughts in particular.
The same remark applies with more or less appositeness,
to R. P. Dutt, whose Marxist prepossessions against religion

prevented him from making a critical analysis of a complex
movement such as the New Hindu Movement (which movement he has never directly mentioned by name but contented
himself with the usual innuendos against the so-called 'Hindu
Revival'). He has made free use of such epithets as
'antiquated', 'obscurantist', 'reactionary', etc, in his characterization of the Hindu revival, but has furnished no single
instance of any truly reactionary action or thought of any
genuine New Hindu thinker. The assertion that the insistence on orthodox religion and proclamation of the
spiritual superiority of the ancient Hindu Civilization inevitably retarded and weakened the real advance of the national
movement and of political consciousness—will be examined
in our discussion of the Swadeshi Movement (chapter IX).

We now indicate how we have developed the arguments of this study. In the first chapter, we have explained
the religious scene in Bengal in 1870s. The period—1867
to 1882—marks a phase of acute religious uncertainty in the
history of the religious movements of the 19th century; this
unrest was something quite different from the mere revolt
against the abuses of Hinduism in Rammohan's time.
Keshub Chandra Sen and Bijoy Krishna Goswami were
representative figures of this phase of spiritual unrest.
Keshub Chandra Sen broke out from the Brahmo faith as
early as 1866. It was ostensibly on the ground of social
reform as to which Keshub sought to adopt a more radical
line than the Brahmos of the older generation. But by the
end of 1867, it was clear that Keshub was dissatisfied with
the earlier Brahmos' doctrinaire obsession with Vedantic
monotheism and what to him appeared their comparative
neglect of the deeper aspect of religion as a pathway to
personal illumination. Keshub thus became the central
figure of a phase in the religious life of Calcutta—a phase
which we have termed the 'Spiritual Unrest' of the 1870's
and which was characterised by some sort of a hesitant
deviation towards Hinduism on the part of some Brahmo

leaders of whom Keshub was the most influential.   Religious
chauvinism was another side of this unrest. Sasadhar
Tarkachudamani and his circle exemplified this side.   The
Arya Samaj and the Theosophical Society were straws in
the wind.

The second chapter explains the birth of a vision
which was telescoped into the future. With the publication
of Bankim's *Vanga-Darsan*, (in 1872) there began an assessment of the civilization of India, as a counterblast to the
wholesale rejection of it by the English-educated literati of
Bengal which had started with the founding of the Hindu
College (in 1817). Bankim's universalist approach precluded
any denigration of the European Civilization, but was actuated by a desire to counterpoise its obsessive hold on our
literati by reminding them of our heritage, which was portrayed in numerous essays on our ancient civilisation.

The third chapter explains the birth of the New
Hindu Movement in the context of the controversy between
Reverend W. W. Hastie and Bankim Chandra Chatterjee.
The fourth chapter gives an exposition of Bankim's ideas.
From 1882, till his death (in 1894) Bankim busied himself
with a rationalistic exposition of Hinduism. Brahmo rationalism had degenerated into 'Intuitionism' preached by
Keshub and the theory of "Jnanojjvalita Visuddha Hrdaya",
(a heart that was pure and that was irradiated by knowledge)
taught by Deverdranath. Bankim started from the basis of
Empiricism and instead of concentrating on points of doctrinaire theology (as the Brahmos had done) concentrated on
'conduct', and showed how the best conception of conduct,
conducive to 'lasting happiness' and arrived at empirically
from an analysis of man's faculties, called for the pre-
eminence of Bhakti over all other human faculties in order
to obtain a 'balance' of all these faculties,—a 'balance' which
constituted the perfection of 'manhood' and conduced to
'lasting happiness' even from the standpoint of empiricism.
But Bhakti, in the sense of the 'balancing' human faculty,

was Bhakti as explained in the *Gita*, which sought a balance of human 'actions', human 'love' and human 'charity' by means of Bhakti towards a pantheistic Personal God (Saguna Brahma) as distinct from the Transcendent Personal God of Brahmo and Christian Theology. It is not clear that Bankim quite succeeded in giving a rationalistic justification of this conception of God. But with this concession to doctrinaire theology, Bankim satisfactorily explained the basic tenets of Hindu ethics : (1) The 'Activism of the Gita' in the sense of service of humanity without any desire for the fruits of one's actions (Nishkam Karma), (2) love for all creation and love of one's country in so far as it was consonant with the former ; also charity to all creation. These and their connection to (3) the theology of Personal Pantheistic God were Bankim's contribution to the religious debate of the 19th century ; —and these three were the basic points of religion which were going to be discussed in the ensuing years. Brahmo obsession with Vedantic monotheism (ie., the doctrine of formless transcendent God) was not refuted, but was rendered otiose.

That Bankim's thoughts attracted general notice is proved by the stir created by the Hastie-Bankim Controversy (1882), the Brahmo's attack on Bankim (1884); the discussion in Ramakrishna's circle on Bankim's books and essays. The new interpretation of the *Gita* as a gospel of activism, which has since been generally accepted as the central doctrine of Hindu ethics and which has received general currency through the efforts of Tilak, Aurobindo and Mahatma Gandhi has to be ultimately traced to Bankim.

In the fifth chapter the Brahmo attack on Bankim is discussed. An attempt is also made to assess the extent of Western influence on Bankim.

The sixth chapter studies the inner life of Vivekananda and his teachings. Bankim's method was rationalistic. But meanwhile the spiritual unrest of the 1870's, symbolised in the career of Keshub Chandra Sen, which looked for 'personal illumination', irrespective of the social aspects of religion was getting intenser. Ramakrishna Paramahamsa, who harped on 'personal illumination' as the only end of religion came in contact with Keshub. Keshub's own development was towards creating a private religion of his own, which failed to survive its author (Keshub died in 1884). Ramakrishna's emphasis was on 'personal illumination' through mystical experience as taught in Hindu scriptures. The search for such 'personal illumination' was manifested in the career of Vivekananda with the greatest tragic intensity. An intense desire to serve humanity and to 'raise the masses and women of India side by side with a similarly intense desire for 'personal illumination' gave rise to a career of ceaseless travel through the world—spreading the message of the Upanisads, influencing men and women and literally wearing himself out to the uttermost limits of exhaustion. The message preached by Vivekananda was not un ke Bankim's, though reached through quite different methods. His argument was something like this : (1) Personal illumination through mystical experience presupposed the divinity of the soul which in its turn, presupposed an impersonal God (Nirguna Brahma) who was the sum total of all souls ; but who could as well be worshipped as a Personal God (Saguna Brahma) as a step towards reaching the Impersonal ; (2) the existence of such a God led to the ethical doctrine of love for all creation ; and (3) service through 'action' without any desire for its fruits purified the heart and rendered it fit for personal illumination.

The seventh chapter deals with New Hindu attitude towards social reform and their programme which followed from Vivekananda's thoughts consisted in the 'raising' of the (i) Sudras and of (ii) the women of India. This language was Vivekanada's, who impressed these programmes on the Indian mind, with irresistible force, by juxtaposing his schemes against those of contemporary 'social reformers', who had been clamouring for reforms like widow remarriage by means of (i) legislation or by invoking (ii) Shastric injunction. Vivekananda found fault with both these schools of reformers - the School of B. Malabari as well as that of Iswar Chandra Vidyasagar. Here again Vivekananda was anticipated by Bankim, whose objection to both these Schools was much more closely reasoned. Briefly stated, Bankim's objection to the Vidyasagar school was that it invoked Shastras, thereby rendering any rational progress impossible and keeping the door open for many objectionable Shastric injunctions. On the other hand, the reformers of the School of Malabari struck at the root of Hindu Society by representating the majority of Hindus as rapists and 'child-molesters', as Malabari had actually done while clamouring for the abolition of child-marriage. Bankim sought to replace 'reform' by 'regeneration' which implied reformation by the appeal to the essence of Hinduism. Thus Bankim pleaded for sea-voyage (as Vivekananda did) on the ground that even if it militated against 'Shastric' injunction, it was consonant with the essence of Hinduism which defined 'Dharma' as that which supported society and therefore could hardly be averse to such a vehicle of progress as sea-voyage. He approved intercaste dining and intercaste marriage in principle as the Hindu ethical creed of 'non-discrimination' amongst men and castes made room for such measures. But he would not make a reforming issue of them as such reforms led to the sort of 'sensationalism' which (amongst Derozians of an earlier generation) had seen in liquor-drinking the only way to India's salvation. Following the same line of thought, Bankim was content to raise the conception of 'womanhood' amongst Hindus, rather than plead after a contemporary fashion, for the so-called equality of men and women.

Bankim's creed of 'regeneration' was thus educative rather than legislative—an appeal to the essence of Hinduism, rather than to a call of fight for 'rights'. Vivekananda's creed of 'growth' was identical,—with this difference that his exposition of Hinduism would allow women the right to abstain from marriage if and when they chose to do so, and to participate in all expressions of the national life.

The eighth chapter deals with a significant aspect of the New Hindu Movement which was an attempt at vindication of the civilisation of India by a method which was more rigorous than the one tried by Bankim in his *Vanga Darshan* essays. This method was on the one hand that of historical research into the dawn of the Hindu Civilisation by Bankim himself and the discovery of a new 'canon of civilisation' by Vivekananda and Rabindranath Tagore, in the light of which they compared the civilisation of India with that of the West. In his '*Krishnacharitra*', Bankim sought to unfold a glorious period of India's civilisation—the period supervening between the age of the Veda and that of the Buddha. The characteristic feature of that civilisation was the building of a 'Kingdom of righteousness' by the King Yudhisthira under the guidance of Krishna. The ideal of that civilisation was the heroic Kshatriya ideal of fighting to the last for the sake of 'righteousness'. Bankim showed weighty reasons in favour of his belief that such a civilisation was no more figment of the poets' imagination, but had the support of good historical evidence. Vivekananda and Tagore modified the ideals preached by Bankim to a certain extent by taking in their sweep the whole length of India's history instead of confining their attention to a single epoch as Bankim had done. According to Vivekananda, the hightest ideal of India's civilization was monastic rather than Kshatriya, but the latter ideal had to be emphasized as well as the former in order that the balance which had been attained in the Mahabharata epoch could be restored. Tagore also spoke of such a balance but instead of seeing in the Indian historical ideal a balance between monasticism and Kshatriyahood, he sought it in the descriptions of the 'ideal of the forest' in the literature of ancient India. According to him the Kshatriya of the city and the Brahmin of the forest—these two together and in co-operation constituted the ideal of India's civilisation.

The ninth chapter studies the political results of the New Hindu Movement. The ideas as mentioned above, which in the case of Tagore as well as of Vivekananda, had no ostensible purpose expect that of increasing India's self-consciousness as to her heritage and of incorporating some noble elements of that heritage in the construction of a new Civilisation in India, proved to be of great political significance. The leading spirit in that direction was Bankim whose dissertation on the Civilisation of an ancient epoch had been interspersed with such phrases as 'political regeneration', which, in his opinion was Krishna's aim. In Krishnacharitra Bankim explicitly contrasted that aim with the contemporary social reformers' obsession with petty schemes of social reform. Against those schemes he pitted the programme of founding a 'Kingdom of righteousness' by means of a righteous 'war of restoration.' In the Swadeshi Movement this programme was taken up as a contemporary political creed. Bankim's secular writings attacking the policy of 'mendicancy' and 'loyal patriotism' pursued by contemporary political agitators paved the way for such a creed by being construed by such leaders as Aurobindo as a gospel of extremism. Bankim's novel Anandamath, in its turn, preached the theme of restoration in an Indo-British context. His rationalistic exposition made room for patriotism as a sacred duty and a part of religion. Aurobindo construed it as being the whole of religion. Bankim's doctrine of 'righteous war' was perverted to the creed of 'terrorism.' The creed of 'Swaraj' was closely connected to Bankim's doctrine of harmarajya (Kingdom of righteousness). Aurobindo and Bipin Chandra Pal developed the notion to a certain extent by incorporating some of Vivekananda's ideas. The creed of 'Swadeshi' was explained in Tagore's speeches and essays on the lines of his thoughts on the civilisation of India. The creed of 'National Education' followed from the thoughts of Bankim, Vivekananda and Tagore. The creed of boycott merged with the doctrine of terrorism. Thus the whole Swadeshi Movement (1905-11) was to a considerable extent an offshot of the New Hindu Movement. It achieved some sort of 'political regeneration' of the country. The partition was annulled. A far more important gain was the desire for political independence which began to be felt throughout the country and the stage was set for Mahatma Gandhi's arrival. The 'terrorists' set an example of reckless courage and the stigma of 'effeminacy' which had come to be attached to the Hindu name was effectively removed. But Dharmarajya was not founded; National Education failed; Swadeshi remained confined to some indigenous industrial undertakings; Boycott degenerated into political murder. The religious movement which had given rise to the political movement itself expired.

The last chapter attempts an assessment of the New Hindu Movement. The movement, on the plane of action, was only a partial success. The New Hindu thinkers by an interpretation of India's past civilization historicized the Indian past and stimulated a consciousness of history. They also discovered the essence of religion of Hindus. The movement again provided the ideology of social and political actions. What is more, the movement considerably contributed to the development of some aspects of Bengali culture.

A new litrature was evolved breathing new life into the language and into the conception of family life, vital with a new sense of beauty and with a new awareness of the possibilities of the old, taboo-ridden personal relationships in a Hindu family. There was a Renaissance of Art with new ideas quickening the artists' vision. The Ramakrishna

Mission, a New Hindu institution, gave expression to a humanitarianism which was raised to the level of a sacrament.

NOTES & REFERENCES

1. Pal, Bipin Chandra : *My Life and Times* : vol. I, Chapter XXII. Cal, 1932.

2. Pal, Bipin Chandra : *My Life and Times* : vol. I, p. 424.

3. J. N. Farquhar : *Modern Religious Movement in India*, New York, 1915, p. 186.

4. *India Today,* 2nd edition, 1970. Chapter XI.

5. Bagal, Yogesh Chandra : *Radhakanta Deb : Sahitya Sadhak Charitmala series-20* : Bangiya Sahitya Parishad, Calcutta.

CHAPTER - 1

RELIGIOUS SCENE IN BENGAL IN 1870s

DURING THE seventies of the last century, Bengal was in a state of religious ferment which differed in quality and kind from that of the earlier part of the century. The restlessness generated in Hindu Society by the impact of European Rationalism and Christianity on the one hand and the reforms prescribed by Rammohan Roy and the Brahmo Samaj on the other had been of a character quite different from the restlessness of this later period. In the first half of the nineteenth century English-educated Indians were so dazzled with the new light they received from the West, that in their zeal for reform they sadly overdid their part. In religion as in social customs and education, what was sought to be reformed and discarded was in most cases suggested by European critics of Hindu society, although except in education, the initiative in reconstruction generally proceeded from the Hindus themselves. Idolatry in religion, casteism and polygamy in social customs, (to name only two amongst the multitude of Hindu customs that offended the contemporary European conscience) were the items which they sought to discard. Also the study of Sanskrit language and ancient Indian learning in education began to be neglected. Vedantic Monotheism in religion, castelessness and monogamy in social customs, English language and English learning in education were the corresponding items embodying the proposed reconstruction. Confining ourselves to religious reformation which is our proper subject, the following extracts from Rammohan's works may be looked upon as embodying the whole of the religious impulse that dominated the religious scene in the half century that preceded the year 1870.

"My constant reflections to (sic) the inconvenient, or rather injurious rites, introduced by the peculiar practice of Hindu idolatry, which more than any other pagan worship, destroys the texture of society,.........have compelled me to use every effort to awaken (my countrymen) from their dream of error."[1]

"I regret to say that the present system of religion adhered to by the Hindus is not well calculated to promote their political interests. The distinction of castes, introducing innumerable divisions and sub-divisions among them, has entirely deprived them of patriotic feeling and the multitude of religious rites and ceremonies and the laws of purification have totally disqualified them from undertaking any difficult enterprises. It is necessary that some change should take place in their religion at least for the sake of their political advantage and social comfort."[2]

These extracts certainly mean that, with Rammohan religious reform was an instrument for social and political reform. The extracts, as they stand, can even be whole-heartedly supported by secularists and atheists. They advocate no positive religious doctrine, the denunciation of idolatry in the first extract being actuated by a motive which is wholly social and not particularly religious. But it must be remembered that this extract formed a part of Rammohan's preface to the Abridgment of the Vedant, a work in which he was pleading eloquently for Vedantic Monotheism. This was a positive religious doctrine, but even in its advocacy, Rammohan never allowed his love for the formless God of the Upanishads to get the better of his zeal for awakening his countrymen from their 'dream of error'. This dream was supposed to consist in their addition to idolatry and idolatrous rites and their support of the prevalent forms of Vaishnavism, particularly the sort of Vaishnavism that derived from Chaitanya.

It will not be a wrong summing up of the history of the Brahmo Movement upto the year 1866, (the year which saw the first schism in the Brahmo camp), to say that upto that year, in the religious controversies of educated Hindus, search for the meaning of religion and for a genuine religious life, played a part which was no more than secondary to the primary aim of combating European criticism by way of agitating for social reform on the lines suggested by that criticism and by denouncing the rites and beliefs practised and held by the generality of Hindus. This is not to deny the fact that there were amongst educated Hindus of that period, men like Devendranath Tagore, (1817-1905), who, as followers of Vedantic Monotheism dedicated their lives to the search for genuine spiritual illumination.[3] But such instances do not contradict our point that, till the year 1866, the religious discontent of educated Hindus was largely centred in a groove which was social rather than religious. The split in the Brahmo Samaj in that year, under the leader-ship of Keshub Chandra Sen, showed that something deeper was in the offing and the kind of spiritual unrest that we find in Keshub Chandra Sen is something unique in the recent religious history of Bengal. During the previous half century the uneasiness of conscience of the educated Hindus on the score of their social customs, held up to ridicule by Europeans (including Christian missionaries) had oversha-dowed their search for personal illumination.

(A) KESHUB CHANDRA SEN (1838-1884) :

It is notable that the parting of ways between Keshub Chandra Sen and Devendranath Tagore started with a ques-tion of social reform and involved nothing that could be called a genuinely religious issue. Keshub Chandra was in favour of intercaste marriage - a measure which to the cautious Devendranath seemed too sweeping and too prema-ture to be included in the social reform programme of the then Brahmo Samaj. Moreover, Keshub pleaded for the abolition of the Brahmanical thread worn by the Acharyas (i.e. priests) of the Samaj, and it was ultimately on this issue that he parted company with his leader to found a society on his own. To this he gave the name Bharat Varshiya Brahmo Samaj (1866).

But it soon began to be clear that social reform was far from the only reason of his parting of ways with Devendranath. In Keshub we are actually in the presence of a restless religious seeker, who, during the remaining years of his short life (1838-1884), would often part company with his dearest friends on issues which to a social reformer would seem trumpery, if not actually ridiculous. Thus in the very next year following his founding of a new Samaj, ostensibly with the intention of pursuing a more radical reform programme than that of the parent body, and thereby causing a more fundamental breach with Hindu society than Devendranath ever intended, Keshub gave clear indications of a proclivity for religious ecstasy which would seem offensive to the Brahmos of the earlier generation. To make matters worse, the outer forms adopted by Keshub and his followers in their desire for ecstasy, very nearly approximated the devices of Chaitanya. According to Keshub's biographer[4], the introduction of *Khole* and processional dancing and singing by way of invoking the name of God was something novel in the Brahmo Samaj. When Keshub's heart was filled with *Bhakti*, it yearned for things that would give full expression to this new impulse. He was moved with the desire for processional dancing and singing to the accompaniment of 'Khole.'

This 'influx of *Bhakti*'—a phrase used by Keshub himself at a later period in his life to describe the new impulse - was startingly revealed in an incident which occurred in October, 1867. To understand the full significance of this incident we must remember that Keshub had been a student of the Hindu College. The education imparted by this College was not only wholly secular and exuding, in an overpowering way, the exotic odour of European rationalism ; but at the same time, it was marked by an excessive antipathy to everything designated by the name 'Hindu'. Admittedly Keshub was not a Derozian ; and the historical accident of his separation (by about a quarter

of a century) from those early products of the Hindu
College, who bore that imposing title precluded him from
expressing his disgust with Hindu practices and manners by
so categorical an assertion as : "If there is anything that we
hate from the bottom of our heart, it is Hinduism."[5]   But
Keshub, in his revival of Hindu customs and practices, did
not have even the excuse of a Rammohan who had escaped
the influence of the Hindu College by having reached middle
age at the time of its foundation and a Devendranath who
had remained untouched by that influence by an exclusive
pre-occupation with religion and a crusading zeal against
Christian missionaries which at times seemed to border on
an antipathy to the founder of Christianity. Keshub's own
attitude to Christ was in striking contrast to that of his
erstwhile leader.   In lecture after lecture he sang the praise
of Christ in words of such passionate enthusiasm, that to this
day, scholars have been debating whether his whole life was
not after all dedicated to the mission of preaching an Indian
kind of Christianity.   Whether this opinion be true or not,
neither Keshub's education, nor the circle with which he
associated, nor his connection with the early Brahmo Samaj,
would give him much scope for retaining in his mind any
respect, not to say weakness, for any Hindu religious custom,
which the generality of the English-educated Bengalis of
the period looked upon as ridiculous if not actually
vulgar.

With this background of Keshub's upbringing in mind
we must examine afresh the significance of the incident that
occurred on the 5th of October, 1867. On that date the
citizens of Calcutta were regaled with the spectacle of a
religious procession with Keshub at its head, and a great
number of his followers bringing up the rear. All these
English-educated gentlemen were dancing together and
raising a chorus addressed to God with words of assurance
to all sinners to the effect that their salvation was certain if
only they were going to behave in a like manner. The

dancing and singing were of course accompanied with a vigorous slapping of *Kholes*, those spindle-shaped leather devices, the ridiculousness of whose shape was accentuated by their being made to dangle from the necks of those respected gentlemen. Keshub, the darling of Westernised Calcuttans, was, in short, leading a *Nagar-Sankirtan*—the favourite device of Chaitanya and his followers, intended to produce religious ecstasy of a communal kind.

Was Keshub turning a Hindu? Before answering this question we must note that the oddity of this incident had not been lost upon Keshub's followers, some of whom joined the procession only after some persuasion. Their reaction at the introduction of *Khole*, for example, has been quaintly described by Keshub's biographer in the following manner :

"Khole arrived, but the minds of Keshub's friends were not yet prepared for Khole."[6]

This reproachful statement on the part of one of the sincerest admirers of Keshub Chandra obviously conceals the fact that his English-educated friends were dismayed at their leader's fall from "progressive" Brahmoism into Hindu rusticity. Keshub was supposed to be much more progressive in his religious outlook than Devendranath Tagore. He had agitated for intercaste marriage, and broken with Devendranath on the question of the sacred thread worn by Brahmo priests, which the latter was unwilling to renounce. It was incomprehensible that this same Keshub would take to dancing in the streets and make himself ridiculous in a manner, which, even to a large number of Hindus seemed to be a sort of antic, devised by Chaitanya for the benefit of the illiterate masses. It was only Keshub's transparent sincerity and his conviction that in resorting to *Nagar-Sankirtan* he was being driven by an urge for higher spirituality, that his followers reluctantly joined the procession. But on that date was sown the seed of a second schism in the Brahmo camp.

We have dwelt on this incident in some detail with a view to making the point that one of the greatest minds in the Brahmo Samaj, in his search for spirituality, was no longer finding spiritual sustenance in the congregational worship of the formless God, introduced by Rammohan Roy and re-established by Devendranath Tagore by way of reforming the idolatrous religion of the Hindus.[7]   Obviously the efforts of Rammohan and Devendranath were completely lost upon Keshub. Their endeavours to free Hinduism from the cult of Hari and the cult of Divine Mother had back-fired, and the fire had consumed their most illustrious disciple.

It is only fair to add that Keshub did not recognise such acts and such beliefs of his as militating against the Brahmo conception of formless God. He was prompt in asserting that he was not reviving the idolatrous cults of Hari and of the Divine Mother. He would justify himself, quite sincerely, by saying that he was only adopting the popular idolatrous forms of Bhakti, to the worship of the formless God of the Brahmo Samaj. But this answer would hardly convince the progressives in his own faction, not to mention the followers of Devendranath Tagore.

The remaining acts of Keshub's life have to be viewed in the light of the clue furnished by the incident of October 5. In 1868, he became the centre of a new controversy, in which he was publicly accused of intending to revive the Hindu doctrine of incarnation and claiming to be an *Avatar* in his own person. He had actually been seen receiving salutation from some of his followers, who had publicly prostrated themselves before him in a manner which bespoke the sort of humility to which only *Avatars* were entitled. Public ridicule in the form of written denunciation of his conduct from the followers of Devendranath as well as a few of his own brought from Keshub the reply that while he was far from making the claim of *Avatarhood* in his own person, he held such gestures of humility to be quite proper in devotees as an aid to higher spirituality. The critics amongst his own followers were silenced but it became clear that progressivism in India could hardly count upon Keshub as one of its champions.

The next two acts of Keshub were as unpredictable as any of his former acts had been. His enthusiasm for Christ had earned him many English admirers and his visit to England in 1870 was accorded the distinction of his being received by the Queen herself. But his Christian friends began to be gradually estranged from him on learning that he was not going to recognise Christ as a mere man of God as the Unitarian Christians believed, and that, with all his enthusiasm for Christ, he was not ready either to subscribe to the orthodox Christian doctrine of Christ's being a member of the Trinity. In short, he alienated Unitarians and Trinitarians alike.

Even the extent of his supposed deviation was revealed in 1872. In that year was passed the Brahmo Marriage Act, which required an explicit declaration of being a non-Hindu, from any one performing the marriage sacrament with rites that did not wholly conform to those customary in a Hindu marriage. Keshub had been at least partially instrumental in the promulgation of the Act, and he did not flinch from its implication in regard to Brahmo marriage rites. He renounced Hindu society with a bang, and seemed to imply, in the most unmistakable manner that the mockery of clinging to the Hindu fold as Devendranath and his followers did cling to that fold whilst the generality of Hindus were vociferous in repudiating them, was not for him.

The 'progressives' in his camp were in a dilemma. Was not this last act of Keshub a supreme act of progressivism? He had given the lie to his accusers' calumny of being unduly partial to Hinduism. He had taken the final plunge, from which even the most radical amongst them had flinched. Would he remain steadfast in this stance of progressivism? Would he go on championing their cause? The progressives in Keshub's faction became bemused.

But in 1875, Keshub was introduced to Ramakrishna

Paramahamsa. The 'Saint of Dakshineswar' was a rustic, in whose upbringing English education had no role whatsoever to play. But he was a man of God all right. He preached the truth of all religions, whilst remaining true to his own in a manner, to which even the most orthodox amongst Hindus could not object. The discussion on religion and how to lead a religious life dedicated to the one aim of realising God, was his only pastime. Indeed, it was his only occupation, from which he gained no worldly advantage, apart from receiving his meals by the generosity of the trustees of the Dakshineswar Temple, who paid for his keep as a sort of a permanent guest. He performed no miracles, and in fact, professed his inability to perform any. He spoke the sweetest Bengali, but not without a generous sprinkling of rustic words. He went into innumerable fits of Samadhi, the trance like state in which the devotee was supposed to remain in God's presence, as long as the fit persisted. But whether in Samadhi or in the consciousness of the waking state, Ramakrishna seemed to be equally in God's presence— singing, dancing and gossiping away his waking hours by discussing God and the life of religion. He was childlike in his simplicity, cheerful in the manner of gay Bohemians, tender as a mother to young disciples, and sombre as a Hebrew prophet in his denunciation of worldliness. Even Devendranath Tagore had been sufficiently impressed by him to invite him to a Brahmo festival, but had withdrawn the invitation at the last moment out of a fear that Ramakrishna would disgrace the distinguished gathering by appearing in his scanty Bohemian clothings.

Keshub immediately took to this extraordinary man in the manner a 'dope - addict takes to another'[8], and there grew up between them a friendship which lasted until Keshub's death. Keshub wrote of Ramakrishna in the columns of his English paper and made the rustic saint's name famous amongst the English educated public of Calcutta.[9]

Keshub's progressive followers did not grasp the significance of this friendship at once. The significance, indeed, was not easily understandable, and, to this day, it has remained controversial how far Keshub was influenced by Ramakrishna and how far the latter's celebrity and the course of events it brought in its wake were due to the publicity he obtained amongst the English-educated public through Keshub's influence. It is possible that but for Ramakrishna's connection with the Brahmo Samaj Narendra Nath Datta, later Swami Vivekananda, would never have met him. It is possible that, but for this connection, Mahendranath Gupta, the chronicler of Ramakrishna's later days would never have heard the saint's name. What would have remained of Ramakrishna and his name, if we allow for these possibilities, is anybody's guess. One thing is, however, certain. Keshub was gradually drifting away from public life, into the solitude of his own self, the self of a religious seeker absorbed in the contemplation of his saviour. It is fruitless to enquire how far Ramakrishna was responsible for this.

However an event occurred in 1878, which brought about the second schism in the Brahmo Samaj and Keshub's reputation as a progressive social reformer became permanently damaged. In that year Keshub gave one of his daughters in marriage to the Maharaja of Cooch-Behar. The girl was of minor age, and it was against well-known Brahmo principles, avowed by Keshub himself on many occasions, to arrange the marriage of minor children. By this act of his, therefore, Keshub not only violated one of his own principles, but it was further alleged that he had allowed the marriage to get polluted by a mixture of Hindu and Brahmo rites. The allegation was possibly not wholly true. What had actually happened during the marriage ceremony seemed to be a case of forcible imposition of some Hindu rites by the members of the Rajah's family. However, the incident was enough to provoke the long-suppressed anger of Keshub's

progressive foliowers to the bursting point.   They raised a
hue and cry in the columns of their newspapers and accused
Keshub of allowing his interest to get the better of his
principles.   Keshub rejoined by asserting a clean conscience
that took orders from God alone and was inspired by an
'inner voice' that guided him in every action. not excluding
his daughter's marriage.   The 'progressives' at once broke
off all connection with him and fonnded the Sadharan
Brahmo Samoj, which was set up on vigorous and unfailing
progressive principles, with a democratic constitution, an
elaborate apparatus of rules - in short, with anything and
everything that was in strict conformity with the most fastidious radical conscience.

At all events, the doctrine Keshub began to preach
from now on was far more concerned with spiritual culture
and mystic communion with God than with social reform.
This doctrine he called 'the New Dispensation', implying, by
this somewhat pompous title, that it was a direct revelation
from God and was not to be confounded with the rationalistic worship of a formless God advocated by the generality
of English-educated Brahmos.   The severe strain involved in
preaching this new doctrine and rallying behind him a new
band of followers,—now that his most eminent disciples had
deserted him,—broke his health, and Keshub died prema-
turely at the age of forty-five years (January, 1884).

Before concluding this brief summary of Keshub's life,
we should say a few words as to its significance in the
context of the religious movements of his time.   Keshub
Chandra Sen symbolised, to a pre-eminent degree, the
spiritual unrest of the religious seekers of the 1870s.   Starting
his career as a social reformer in the conservative—or rather,
cautiously reformistic—Brahmo Samaj of Devendranath
Tagore, he was in the end repudiated by conservatives and
radicals alike owing to his gradual absorption of ideas
and practices which were repugnant to the spirit of European
Rationalism imbibed by the English-educated Calcuttans of

his age. Keshub's was restless mind,[10] and the New Dispensation, which was calculated to be the finished edifice, embodying all the materials he had collected during a whole life-time, was a hotch-potch of disconnected ideas - an inchoate mass of spiritual divinations, which failed to survive their author.[11] The eclecticism which combined the worship of the formless (unitarian) God of the early Brahmos with Vaishnavite methods of rousing religious ecstasy and, at the same time, advocated sort of divinity for Christ, failed to be convincing because of its own extravagance. Not content with the multifariousness of this fare Keshub accentuated the extravagance by adding to these constituents the doctrine of Inspiration or Inner Voice, the theory of a new species of Yoga, the creed of an order of Saints or Great men, and many more dogmas of the same kind. Keshub's religion was a conglomeration of diverse religious beliefs derived from diverse religious sources, and met the fate common to all such eclectic religions. But the uniqueness of Keshub's religion lay in this ; the coat of many colours he strove to weave during his life time was not tailored to suit the whims of a restless intellect, but was dyed by a burning 'private' vision whose hunger for all the colours of the religious spectrum seemed to be imperious and insatiable. This was the reason why he gripped the imagination of his contemporaries with such irresistible force, and this again was the reason why he was forgotten so soon after his death. Keshub Chandra Sen represented an interregnum of acute religious uncertainty, which, if it were not to be followed by a period of stability, would bring in its wake consequences that could be disastrous to the rising generation.

(B) BIJOY KRISHNA GOSWAMI (1841 - 1899) :

If Keshub Chandra Sen, in the unpredictability of his continuously developing religious viewpoint and the inconclusiveness of the conclusions reached by a life-time effort primarily represents the religious uncertainty of the seventies,

Bijoy Krishna Goswami represents the force of the orthodox tradition in a strikingly unorthodox manner. Keshub's work may be viewed as a continuous protest against orthodoxy,— not alone the old time-honoured orthodoxy of pre-historic Hinduism but also the orthodoxy of Rammohan's religion as well as the temporary orthodoxies punctuating his own religious life. Bijoy Krishna Goswami, despite his apparent resemblance to Keshub in the restlessness of his religious quest was a man of a very different stamp. Like Keshub, he certainly changed his religious ground oftener than is congenial for consistent seekers, but unlike Keshub, his shiftings were not motivated by a thirst for variety in religious experiences but by a steadfast desire for union with God. Born in an extremely conservative Vaisnav family of Santipur tracing its descent from Sri Chaitanya's celebrated friend and disciple Advaitacharya, Bijoy had reached adolescence in an atmosphere of extreme orthodoxy. But the Vedantic study of the Samkara School demolished his old faith in popular Hinduism and the worship of the popular Hidu Gods and Goddesses could not appeal to him any more. But this school also failed to offer any solace to his struggling soul athirst for a loving communion with his Maker. He became exceedingly restlesss. He was drawn at this stage to the Brahmo Samaj by some of his old acquaintances. The atmosphere at the Samaj attended by a host of devotees engaged in prayer, recitation and singing of hymns devoutly touched him very much. He listened to a sermon delivered by Devendranath Tagore and returned home a new man.[12]

But this new man came into conflict with the sanctified traditions of his family, his caste and his community. He threw away his Brahmanical thread in the belief that wearing a sacred thread was contrary to the Brahmo principle of castelessness. Of course, the penalty he received was severe —he was excommunicated by his relatives at Santipur. There was a good deal of persecution, but he bore it all with modesty and humility and not with the arrogance common amongst persecuted social reformers.

But, none the less, Bijoy's career upto the year 1878, was a story of a number of significant reforms in the best style of progressive social reformers. He was possibly the first Brahmo to sacrifice his Brahmanical thread. He was certainly the first to agitate against Devendranath Tagore's propensity to compromise with Brahmo priests who were stubborn in retaining such threads. He was the first among Keshub's associates to protest against their leader's inclination towards Avatarhood. It was possibly his initiative more than anyone else's that gave rise to a democratic opposition in the years when Keshub tended to rule his congregation like an autocrat. Last but not the least, it was his voice which rang the loudest in declaiming against Keshub's compromise with child-marriage when the child concerned happened to be his own daughter. But side by side with these reforming acts, Bijoy from his early days had been giving indications of a burning desire for communion with God. The psychological state which Vaishnavas of the school of Chaitanya designate as *Arti* (passionate longing for communion with God) had been evident in him on more than one public occasion when the English-educated congregation had been started by his heart-rending cries for his remaining divorced from his God. Bijoy's true bent,—shut out of sight by years of devotion to the casue of social reform,— came out in the open no sooner had he started work as a preacher (Pracharak) in the Sadharana Brahmo Samaj. The sermons he delivered from the pulpit of the Brahmo Samaj were becoming occasions of an unprecedented religious ecstasy. Bijoy would often end a sermon by a passionate address to the Mother of the Universe, and his cry : "Mother, oh Mother" would affect his listeners with its profound intensity. This was bad enough. But what was infinitely worse was the visit to Bijoy's pulpit by a Sannyasin. His conversation with Bijoy ended by making the latter lost to the cause of Brahmoism.   Bijoy became restless to make the Sannyasin his *Guru.*

The Sannyasin declined.   "It is pre-ordained that you'll meet your *Guru* elsewhere"—he said mysteriously. Bijoy now began to roam from place to place in search of his pre-ordained *Guru.* He visited Darjeeling and met a sage who had pierced the six chakras, but was again rebuffed by the same mysterious reply.   He visited Gaya, a place sacred to both Hindus and Buddhists, and prostrated himself before the celebrated *Babaji* of Akashganga Hill.   The Babaji was not his pre-ordained Guru.   But he was impressed enough by Babaji's longing for God's communion to donate him his own solitary retreat for spiritual culture.   In this retreat Bijoy lay unconscious in his restlessness on a certain day, to be roused by the touch of a stranger, who startled him by sundry revelations about his own life, and thereupon gave him spiritual lessons that would lead him direct to his God. The stranger, it appeared, was in his subtle body, coming all the way from Tibet, to give solace to the bleeding heart of Bijoy.   He was, in short, the pre-ordained *Guru.*

From this day on opened a new career for Bijoy, in which the occurrence of many miracles of the sort foreshadowed in the above incident, has made the scientific historian's task difficult in treating his later development with any amount of confidence.   However, Bijoy now gathered around him a flock of disciples, most of them Hindus and only a handful of them Brahmos.   He was expelled from the Sadharan Brahmo Samaj in 1886.   The charges against him were, firstly, his insistence on Gurus as spiritual guides; secondly, his encouraging the habit of prostration before idols and particular individuals; thirdly, his practice of referring to the love of Radha and Krishna as an ideal of the worshipper's devotion to his God; fourthly, his propensity to baptise people by uttering *Mantras*, and finally, his uncritical acceptance of certain doctrines or rules of conduct because of the supposed sanctity of a book or a person prescribing such doctrines or such rules of conduct. Bijoy defended his conduct by asserting purity of motive and explaining away all the charges by a somewhat liberal interpretation of the Brahmo creed but tendered his resignation as a preacher (Pracharak) of the Samaj all the same. His following was already large enough to start him on an independent religious career of his own.

Bijoy's subsequent activities can be briefly described. Without actually enrolling himself as a member of the school of Chaitanya, he practised the mode of spiritual culture known as *Madhura Bhava* (in which the devotee looks upon his God as the Divine Spouse) and ended his days by unremitting spiritual labour for the liberation of his disciples.[13]

In summing up the life and works of Bijoy Krishna Goswami, we should note that he was very much a child of the seventies in the unrest of his soul which no existing sect or creed could extinguish. This gains added significance from the fact that unlike Keshub, Bijoy had never received the benefit of an English education. Thus his break with his orthodox past indicated a deeper spiritual craving than was the case with the generality of the English-educated Hindus, whose dissatisfaction with their ancestral religion was actuated more by a desire to look civilised to their English masters than by any spiritual urge of their own. What is more significant still, is the fact that Bijoy Krishna, to the end of his days, remained steadfast in acknowledging his debt to the Brahmo Samaj. This makes the marked Hinduisation of his later development a much more remarkable phenomenon than it would ordinarily be. In his own words, the association with the Brahmo Samaj, salutory as it was, "failed to quench the thirst of his soul." His later Hinduisation has therefore to be viewed as no nostalgia for the fold he had wilfully deserted. Indeed, it is questionable whether he returned to the fold at all, considering the conflicting claims made by his Hindu and Brahmo disciples in regard to the significance of his later development. His Hinduisation was actually a prelude to a higher synthesis—a synthesis that was evolving slowly and steadily during his later years.

(C) RELIGIOUS CHAUVINISM :

SASADHAR TARKACHUDAMANI (1851-1928)

A significant aspect of the religious scene in the 1870s was the efforts of Sasadhar Tarkachudamani and his circle towards the defence of orthodox Hinduism. Briefly stated, the movement instituted by Sasadhar and his circle was an apology for Hindu orthodoxy, clothed in a pseudo-religious, pseudo-historical garb. It was the contention of this circle that orthodox Hinduism had possessed everything that was supposed to be the gift of the 'advanced' civilisation of the nineteenth century West. The following extract from a lecture delivered in the Albert Hall in 1875, will indicate the method of Tarkachudamani and his disciples : "Many people believe" so runs the extract, "that the ancient Indian heroes appeared in the battlefields with bows and arrows, swords and clubs and other devices of a primitive sort.They presume that the science of warfare in which our forefathers were instructed is to put to shame when judged by the standard of modern artillery and the sophisticated arms employed in modern wars. But readers of the Ramayana know better."[14]

It is obvious that here we are face to face with a type of mentality which confused religion with national glory and conjured up visions of national glory by playing upon emotions rather than by sober accounts of authenticated history.

Pandit Sasadhar was born in an orthodox Brahmin family. His education was of the orthodox Brahmanical type, being wholly free from the contamination of English or Western ideas. When he was twenty three years old he was appointed Pandit in the pay of Annadaprasad Roy, zamindar of Kasimbazar. It was under the patronage of this zamindar that Sasadhar started his career as a preacher of Hinduism.

It is said that 'his heart cried out' at the spectacle of his religion and society being ridiculed and reviled by some of his own correlegionists whose judgement, he assumed, was perverted by a little English education. They had been declaring that the customs and rites of the Hindus were superstitious and barbarous. Sasadhar happened to be at Monghyr sometime during the latter half of 1870s, where he made the acquaintance of another gentleman, whose heart in its turn, (so we are told) was 'crying out' like Sasadhar's and for a similar reason. He was no other than Paribrajak Krishnaprasanna Sen, later Sreemat Krishnananda Swami. They started lecturing in Calcutta and surrounding places, founding, to begin with, the *Arya Dharma Pracharini Sabha* in Monghyr. In district and sub-divisional towns, in villages, and, in fact, in every possible place they set up societies for the protection of religion (the so-called *Dharma Rakshini Sabha*) and other societies of a similar nature.[15]

Posterity has failed to remember Sasadhar and Krishnaprasanna as well as the movement started by them. Considering the commonplace nature of their ideas and their hostility to the new religious conscience which was profoundly influenced by English education, the judgement of posterity seems but natural. But Sasadhar and Krishnaprasanna, between them evidently held the Calcutta religious stage for a period, however short. Rabindranath Tagore, in his *Jeevan Smriti,* refers to Sasadhar and his rise to fame. Characteristically Tagore does not mention any date. Bankim Chandra Chatterjee refers to Sasadhar's movement in 1884. Navin Chandra Sen, the celebrated Bengali poet of the age, devotes a whole section of his autobiography to the mode of Sasadhar's preaching. We are told explicitly by a disciple of Sasadhar's that his movement started with their (his and Krishnaprasanna's) joint collaboration in the religious preaching at Monghyr,[16] from where the wave spread to Calcutta which was thereupon made the headquarters of the movement. The same disciple also tells us that the movement

lasted for about ten years.[17] We can put the date of
Sasadhar's work in Calcutta, with some confidence between
the years 1875 and 1885.

The movement launched by Sasadhar and his circle
created a considerable stir. It gave rise to much uneasiness
amongst the Brahmos. Rajnarain Bose, the then President
of the Brahmo Samaj led by Devendranath Tagore thus wrote
to his counterpart of the Sadharan Brahmo Samaj : "If you
do not preach your religion in accordance with Hindu ideals,
the events of Monghyr will be repeated elsewhere : the Arya
Sabhas will supersede the Brahmo Samaj everywhere."[18]
Again, Sasadhar was in great request amongst the contemporary English-educated intellectuals of Calcutta like Jogendra
Chandra Bose, Indranath Banerjee,   Bhudev Mukherjee,
Akshoy Chandra Sarkar, Chandranath Bose, Ramendra
Sundar Trivedi. The saint of Dakshineswar who was daily
growing in fame in those days paid him a visit on his own.[19]
But the most notable event in Sasadhar's career was his
acquiantance with Bankim Chandra Chatterjee, the doyen of
the English educated intellectuals of Nineteenth century
Bengal. Sasadhar's introduction to English educated Bengal
is said to have been due to Bankim.[20] It has even been
suggested by some latter-day admirers of Sasadhar that
Bankim's own religious views were influenced by Sasadhar's
rationalistic discourses.[21] Whether this be true or not, the
courtship between the orthodox Pandit and the English-
educated intellectual appears to have been a short-lived one.
In the opening number (1884) of *Prachar*, Bankim's organ
for expressing his religious opinions, occurred a foot-note
which purported to convey Bankim's profound disagreement
with Sasadhar's mode of interpreting religion and his conviction that such a mode could have no lasting influence.[22]
Bankim's remark happened to be prophetic. The first
volume of *"Dharma Byakhyya"*, his magnum opus, was
published in the same year and from the evidence left to us
it appears that the projected second volume never saw the

light of the day.

Two other events of Sasadhar's career deserve our
attention. Sometime in 1884, Romesh Chandra Dutt, who
was engaged in publishing his translation of the Rigveda,
wrote in a Bengali periodical an article which vindicated the
European Indologists' view of the earliest literary production
of the Hindus as being a work of human agency, incorporating the history of a people in the infancy of its civilisation.
This article roused Sasadhar's orthodox conscience and he,
in his turn, took up the pen to denounce Romesh Dutt for
his apostacy and his skepticism regarding the revealed nature
of the Vedas. Sasadhar's article had unforeseen consequences. Without any prompting from Romesh Dutt a
number of progressive youngmen took up his cause and
manhandled the orthodox preacher in the middle of a lecture
he was delivering in the Sanskrit College of Calcutta. As for
Sasadhar, the incident put a damper on his religious
enthusiasm and he allowed his movement to die a natural
death. But not before a gigantic attempt at revival in 1891
when he mounted a country-wide agitation to prevent the
acceptance of the Age of Consent Act. He lived for many
more years but his public life came to a close with this event
of 1891.

What was this method of religious interpretation[23]
which made Sasadhar temporarily so popular even amongst
the English-educated Hindus ? One of Sasadhar's disciples
has called it 'the scientific interpretation of Hinduism.' He
has found fault with Bankim Chandra Chatterjee's repudiation of Sasadhar's 'method', because, in his opinion, Bankim
himself in his religious writings followed the same method.
We shall discuss Bankim's method in its proper place, but as
regards Sasadhar it has to be noted that as this Pandit of the
old School was innocent of science and its method his
method should more properly be called 'rationalistic.' It
was in fact pseudo-rationalistic as we shall try to show below,
but Sasadhar did seem to his admirers to be engaged in an

attempt at rendering the doctrines and rituals of orthodox
Hinduism acceptable to reason without any appeal to the
'supersensible.' Thus he sought to justify the religious
fasting observed by orthodox Hindus on every 11th lunar
day (Ekadasi) by an appeal to considerations of health. This
was, no doubt, puerile since the argument, while it might
serve the cause of hygiene, hardly served the cause of
religion. But English-educated Hindus were fascinated by
Sasadhar's naturalistic definition of religion, which did not
base the validity of religious truths on scriptural revelation,
but sought to define religion as a sort of 'humanism.' The
analogy used by Sasadhar in this connection was that as the
Dharma of water was liquidity and that of fire its ability to
burn, so the *Dharma* of man was a property of his
'humanity'. It appears that it was this definition which had
appealed to Bankim Chandra's rationalistic temperament and
urged him to make the Pandit's acquaintance. Obviously it
was a definition in keeping with the spirit of European Rationalism, but Sasadhar's articulation of the 'method' revealed
its barrenness. Just as Krishnaprasanna, in his Albert Hall
lecture had sought to find the most prodigious scientific
achievements amongst the Hindus of the Ramayanic Age, so
did Sasadhar discover Darwinism in an aphorism of Patanjali.
This was plain chauvinism, but Sasadhar phrased his argument
in a form which seemed to involve much philosophic reasoning and proceed from an acutely logical intellect. The nature
of Sasadhar s 'pseudo-rationalism' will be clear from an
analysis of his proposition that "the complete man can be
born in India alone."

Sasadhar sought to establish this chauvinistic proposition by a bit of geographical reasoning. We in India have
six whole seasons, with Spring coming in the wake of Winter,
Summer following upon Spring, Summer in its turn being
followed by the Rains, the Rains preceding Autumn, and
Hemanta (late Autumn) coming after Autumn completing a
cycle of the most various seasonal fluctuations. According to

Sasadhar the European nations have no notion of such variety in the seasonal spectrum. How, under such deprivations, can those nations produce the complete man ?, asks Sasadhar and ruefully shakes his head.

This is a weird piece of reasoning but Sasadhar the logician anticipates the skepticism of his dull listeners and goes on to make his mighty thought-process transparent : "The cycle of the six seasons involves a continuous transformation in all the modes by which nature and the five sense (of man) act and react upon each other. It is therefore reasonable that the five senses (of the Indian man) should have an all-round development", and thereby produce the complete man who cannot help being an exclusively Indian phenomenon. It is in this manner that Sasadhar renders his reasoning fool-proof.

But Sasadhar does not stop here. To rub the lesson in, he resolves the all round development of the Indian man into its constituent parts and goes on explaining this mighty process of development : "The sweet and unobtrusive heat of Spring, the intense heat of high Summer, the languishment brought about by the cold of early Winter, and the violent shakings of the limbs produced by the cold of mid-Winter—all these varieties of heat have gone towards developing our tactile sense. But what hope is there of such finished development of the tactile sense in countries where there are only two seasons—Summer and Winter ?" Clearly not much, implies Sasadhar but refrains out of modesty from openly saying so.

But Sasadhar continues to sing the glory of India and he now takes up the Indian man's auditory sense. "Look", he says, "the sharpness you will find in the Indian man's auditory sense is something you will never find in any other nation, whether it be the English nation or the French. It is due to this completeness of the auditory sense that the science and art of music have reached such heights in India."

We have said that Sasadhar's orthodoxy appealed to the English-educated generation of the Seventies by its rationalistic pretensions. Contrariwise, it did not receive unqualified approbation from any and every member of the orthodox school despite its fight for the cause of orthodoxy. Kalibara Vedantabagish was a scholar of the orthodox school and he was skeptical enough of Sasadhar's 'method' to give expression to his doubts by bringing out a rejoinder to Sasadhar's *Dharma Byakhya*—namely the treatise which contained such precious gems as the proposition about the completeness of the Indian man. He applied the resources of his superior scholarship to demolish the theory of the supposed Darwinism of Patanjali. He opposed the naturalistic definition of religion as given by Sasadhar on the ground that religion was religion only because its authority derived from extra-human sources—else it would be conditional on the subjective whims of every individual man. He poured ridicule on the hygienic interpretation of Ekadasi, and asserted that the custom was useless apart from its religious sanction. Besides Sasadhar's prolix exercise in pseudo-rationalism Kalibar's short work stands out as a monument of scholarship and good sense. But at the same time it represents orthodoxy in its determined stand against the rationalistic temper of the times.

From the above analysis, we can discern two distinct trends in the religious scene in Bengal in 1870s. The first was an acute spiritual unrest affecting some of the best minds of the generation. It was characterized by a profound dissatisfaction of an earlier generation with orthodox Hinduism now spreading all along the line and becoming quite general. In particular, the dissatisfaction now involved the Brahmo creed itself. In the minds of religious seekers like Keshub Chandra Sen the need was felt for a faith that would show the way to personal illumination. By the end of 1870s even the question of social reform was relegated to the second place by those with whom the religious quest superseded all other questionings.

The second trend of the religious scene was represented by Sasadhar Tarkachudamani and his circle. Their activities were chauvinistic as their movement was an apology for Hindu orthodoxy, clothed in a pseudo-religious, pseudo-historical garb. Even scientific discoveries of the most variety were sought to be associated with an obscure Hindu past.

Mention should here be made that Arya Samaj and Theosophy were straw in the religious wind of the time. But, while Arya Samaj had an appreciable impact in Western India, its impact in Bengal was negligible. Theosophy also created a stir amongst the educated community in Bengal only for a short time. But as these movements bear little or no influence or connection with the New Hindu Movement in Bengal, we refrain from a detailed study of these movements in this work.

NOTES & REFERENCES

1. Preface to the translation of an *Abridgment of the Vedant*, 1816, English Works, vol. 1.
2. Letter to James Silk—Buckingham, 1818.
3. The spirit of Western rationalism, disseminated through the teachings of the Hindu College, proved inadequate to solve Devendranath's spiritual problems and the result was a period of almost intolerable spiritual agony and unrest. His autobiography amply testifies to his search for 'personal illumination'.
4. Upadhaya Gour Gobinda Roy : *Acharya Keshub Chandra* : Keshub Centenary, Allahabad Series, p. 400.
5. Sibnath Sastri : *Ramtanu Lahari O Tatkalin Banga Samaj,* Chapter IV.
6. Upadhaya Gour Gobind Roy : *Acharya Keshub Chandra :* Keshub Centenary, Allahabad Series, p. 400.
7. Keshub Chandra Sen : *Jeevan-veda* : translated by Jamini Kanta Koar : Nababidhan Trust : 3rd edition, 1969. Chapter VII, 'Influx of Bhakti.'
8. The simile is from Ramakrishna. He compared the religious man's craving for religious companionship to the hashis-addicts.
9. "We met one (a sincere Hindu devotee) not long ago, and were charmed by the depth, penetration and simplicity of his spirit. The

never ceasing metaphors and analogies in which he indulged, are most of them as apt as they are beautiful. The characteristics of his mind are the very opposite to those of Pandit Dayananda Saraswati, the former being as gentle, tender and contemplative as the latter is sturdy, masculine and polemical. Hinduism must have in it a deep source of beauty, truth, and goodness to inspire such men as these." (Keshub in the *Indian Mirror,* 28 March, 1875). Quoted by Dr Prem Sundar Basu in *Life and Works of Brahmananda Keshub.,* p. 318.

10. Sir Henry Maine had said that the creed of the Brahmos lacked stability ; he had ascertained this by frequent conversations with Mr Sen, their leader. P. C. Mojumdar : *Life & teachings of Keshub Chandra Sen,* p. 157.

11. In a letter to Sophia Dobson Collet (May, 31, 1881), Rajnarayan Bose by way of criticising Keshub wrote : "Keshub Baboo prides himself on his New Dispensation. There is not, however, the least originality in the idea as the name implies. The New Dispensation consists in merely jumbling up the doctrines & dogmas, the forms and ceremonies of different religions explaining the fancied a legorical meaning contained in those doctrines & worshipping saints & great men. The idea is not a new one in our country."

12. Bipin Chandra Pal : *Saint Bijoy Krishna Goswami,* First edition, Calcutta, p. 23.

13. Bipin Chandra Pal : *Saint Bijoy Krishna Goswami,* First edition.

14. *Paribrajaker Patrika :* Compilation of lectures by Krishnananda Swami.

15. Societies with titles as *"Sunity Sancharini Sabha"* (Societies for the inculcation of good morals), *Balyasram* etc.

16. "Both Swami Krishnananda and Sasadhar Tarkachudamani pioneered religious discourses at Monghyr.............Later Chudamani left Monghyr and started preaching and exposing Hindu scriptures making Calcutta his centre." *Brahman Samaj :* Falgun, 1334, B. S , pp. 241-242.

17. *Ibid.*

18. Quoted in *Paribrajaker Patrika.* 3rd edition, 1332 B. S. The first edition of the book was published in 1816 Saka, i.e. 1894 A D.

19. Sri 'M'. *Ramakrishna Kathamrita :* vol. I, Chapter 19, (Passin).

20. Nabin Chandra Sen : *'Amarjiban.'*

21. *Brahman Samaj :* Falgun, 1334 B. S. vide essay by Panchanan Tarkaratna.

22. Bankim Chandra : 'Hindudharma', *Prachar* I.

23. Tarkachudamani, Sasadhar : *Dharmabyakhya.*

CHAPTER-II

THE BIRTH OF A VISION

IN CHPATER - I, we explored the religious scene of the 1870's and discovered in it a new spiritual unrest, of which an important feature was a quest for personal illumination symbolised in the career of such leaders of the English-educated public of Calcutta, as Keshub Chandra Sen. In this chapter we intend to argue that the quest for a glorious ancient civilisation of India was as powerful a factor in shaping the imagination of the same public during the same decade. The New Hindu Movement was a product of a combination of both these quests.

CIVILISATION OF INDIA :
THE ORIENTALIST AND THE OCCIDENTALIST VIEW

The impact of the West on India was in a sense more fundamental than would appear from the evidence of the events we have narrated in Chapter - I—a confrontation of civilisations rather than a conflict of certain religious beliefs contending for ascendancy over the Hindu mind. It is true that during the first wave of self-criticism generated in the Hindu mind by the Western impact, European rationalism, no less than Christian propaganda, had shocked the Hindu into an acute awareness of the imperfections of his own religion. This awareness, in its turn, led to the attempt at religious reformation initiated by Rammohan Roy. But the problem of the aforesaid confrontation of civilisation had its deeper aspect—it raised the question of reformation of civilisation also. And reformation of civilisation, if it was contemplated at all by English - educated Hindus previous to the year 1870, was to a considerable extent contemplated on the lines suggested by Macaulay's celebrated formula, and was thus more a programme of transplantation, (that is to say the cultivation of an exotic plant on the indigenous soil), than of resuscitation (that is to say, the

revitalisation of a dying plant of native origin by infusing
new life in it). Of course prior to Macaulay, there had been
a school of Orientalists who had been speaking favourably
of the ancient civilisation of India, but the Indians themselves
had remained practically unaffected by the researches
of such scholars as William Jones and H.T. Colebrooke. To
understand the new Indian awareness of this indigenous
ancient civilisation, it is relevant for us to know something
of those researches as well as of the school of British thought
on India, of which Macaulay was a product and for this
knowledge we must go back by a whole century from the
period we are investigating.

European discussion of India had started as early as
the second half of the 18th century. Books on India had
begun to multiply, and as a result, European understanding
of Hinduism and Indian Civilisation had started proceeding
on two lines. First, the positive and active ideology for
the government of India was based on three schools of
English political thinking : Utilitarianism, Evangelism and
Whig Liberalism. All these were hostile to the beliefs
and customs of the Hindus which they regarded as stagnant
and obscurantist.

The utilitarians gave a dismal view of ancient India,
indicted that the ancient Hindu polity, perceived in the
remote Hindu past was a barbaric society, censured her conservative institutions like priest-craft and caste system.
Charles Grant, Parry, and Wilberforce, the leading Evangeli-
cals, in their writings and speeches depicted Indian Civilisation as barbaric, Hinduism as degarding, rotten to the core
and incapable of any sort of restoration or reform. Practically the same line of criticism was adopted by Whig Liber-
als amongst whom, we need only mention Macaulay. In his
zeal for the cultural conquest of India by England Macaulay,
though totally ignorant of ancient India, went to the length
of making a foolish remark such as the following :

"A single shelf of a good European library is worth

the whole native literature of India and Arabia." So, his own proposal was that Indians should thoroughly assimilate themselves to British culture, arguing that there was no other road to modernity.

The second line of thinking was pursued by the British Orientalists who upheld that India's golden period as culture lay in a remote, uncharted period in world history.

On the other hand, the Orientalists, in their study of Indology pursued two objectives—Sanskrit language being the grand repository of the religion, philosophy and history of the Hindus, they turned first, to the cultivation of Sanskrit studies and translation of great Sanskrit Works ; secondly, they undertook to reconstruct the history of the Hindus. The Orientalists had their golden period during the time of Warren Hastings. Earlier isolated individuals in the Company's service—such as Alexander Dow and J. Z. Holwell had acquired an intellectual appreciation of Indian Civilisation, but such appreciation had been isolated and was not based on adequate scholarship. Warren Hastings was the first great administrator to adopt a cultural policy which, coupled with 18th century European climate of thought and opinion, favoured the growth of genuine Orientalist Movement. This growing interest in Oriental learning gave birth to the Asiatic Society, a great landmark in the history of Indian culture. William Jones particularly rendered the greatest service by his remarkable discovery of a common source of the language of the Indo-European peoples. He linked Sanskrit to the European language family and maintained that Sanskrit was the fountainhead of many languages : "The Sanskrit language, whatever be its antiquity, is of a wonderful structure, more perfect than the Greek, more copious than the Latin, and more exquisitely refined than either, yet bearing to both of them a stronger affinity both in the roots of verbs and in the form of grammar, than could possibly have been produced by accident,...there is a similar reason, though not quite so forcible, for supposing that both the

Gothick and the Celtick, though blended with a very different idiom, had the same origin with the Sanskrit ; and the old Persian might be added to the same family..." [1]

This was not all. The Orientalists devoted their attention to the translation of the Sanskrit works. Wilkins translated the *Bhagavadgita* (into English) in 1785 under the patronage of Warren Hastings himself, deciphered several Sanskrit inscriptions, published a translation of the *Hitapodesa* (1789) and also a grammar of Sanskrit language (1808). J>nes translated the *Sakuntala* (1789), the *Gitagovinda* (1789), the *Manusamhita* (1794) and the *Hitopadesa* (published after his death) and edited the *Ritusamhara* (1792). His plan to prepare a digest of Hindu and Muhammedan Law after the model of Justinian's code was endorsed by Lord Cornwallis in 1788, but Jones did not see the completion of the work. The work of Wilkins and Jones was continued by Henry Thomas Colebrooke and Dr Horace Hayman Wilson. Colebrooke translated Jagannath Tarkapanchanan's famous work on Hindu Law, the *Vivadadhangarnava*, into English under the title of the *Digest of Hindu Law on Contracts And Succession* (1798). His work on Sanskrit grammar and a learned account on the Vedas were published in Calcutta in 1805. He also published a critical edition of the famous Sanskrit lexicon the *Amarkosh* in 1808. Dr H. H. Wilson translated the *Meghaduta* (1813), compiled a Sanskrit-English Dictionary (1819), and had the eighteen principal Puranas translated into English with the help of some pundits.

Side by side with the study and translation of Sanskrit works, the Orientalists provided the beginning of the excellent Indological study continued later by both European and Indian scholars in Bengal. Though interpretations vary and later researches have shown gaps in his exposition, most writers have attributed to William Jones[2] the phenomenal discovery of the Aryan golden age. To him ancient Hindus were a "people with a fertile and inventive genius." In his discourse "On the Hindus", Jones starts with the

emphatic assertion that—"how degenerate and abased so
ever the Hindus may now appear, that in some early age
they were splendid in arts, and arms, happy in Government,
wise in legislation, and eminent in various knowledge."[3]   He
went on to explain his statement by referring to four aspects
of Ancient Hindu Civilisation—its language and letters,
Hindu philosophy and religion, the actual remains of their
old sculpture and architecture and the written memorials of
their sciences and arts.   But, Jones laments, the civil history
of the Hindus is involved "in a cloud of fables" and the
present-day Hindus behave very differently from the ancient
Hindus.   Again, in his discourse entitled "Asiatic Society,
Civil and Natural", Jones identified through Greek sources
Patibothra as Pataliputra and Sandracottus as Chandragupta.

The broad generalisations of Jones about ancient
India were supplemented by H. T. Colebrooke. His primary
research interest was about the Vedic age and the principal
discoveries were monotheism and widow remarriage etc.
Having explored the grammatical treatises and the commen-
taries, the philosophic systems and the immense literature
of the Vedic period, Colebrooke depicted the Indo-Aryan
period as a golden age. But the present deterioration of
Hinduism, according to him, was due to misunderstanding
of numerous texts by the modern Hindus.   He asserts emphatically of the Vedas : "Most of what is there taught, is
now obsolete ; and in its stead new orders of religious
devotees have been instituted ; and new forms of religious
ceremonies have been established. Rituals founded in the
Puranas and observances borrowed from a worse source,
the Tantras, have in great measure......(replaced) the Vedas."

As a leading Orientalist in India, Colebrooke's successor was H. H. Wilson, who with the assistance of several
Bengali intellectuals, notably Tarachand Chakraborty and
Ram Comul Sen, did his best work in translating, describing
and analysing the Puranas. Wilson's research interest included the whole range of post-Vedantic Indian history and he

derived his materials both from literature and inscriptions. Under his guidance, the Asiatic Society became the real repository of historical and archaeological sources in India. While Wilson attempted to demythologize and give historical substance to the legendary heroes of the Hindus, he encouraged the younger generation of British Orientalists to make a serious study of non-Aryan, non-Vedantic cultures, and to reconstruct the Hindu histories on a regional basis during the early medieval period. Under his patronage and encouragement, the first authentic histories of Nepal, Orissa, Rajputana and Kashmir, based on inscriptional and written records, were written. Such researches in the 1820s paved the way for the significant developments of the 1830s. It should be remembered that in 1831, Sir Alexander Cunningham arrived in India and the archaeological work of the Asiatic Society of Bengal began in earnest. In 1837, James Princep, the then Secretary of the Asiatic Society, finally unravelled the mystery of the Brahmi Script and was able to read the edicts of the great Emperor Ashoka. The Maurya civilisation became now for India what Rome and Greece had become for Europe.

The final and possibly the greatest Orientalist achievement during the years previous to 1870, was Max Muller's publication of the *Rigveda* together with his many writings on the Vedic Age. The works of Jones, Colebrooke, Wilson, Prinsep and Max Muller, combined together, provided sufficient information testifying to the fact that India's past by no means corresponded to the picture of unrelieved gloom painted by Mill, Grant and Macaulay. If anything, the ancient Indian civilisation in many respects compared favourably with ancient Greece and even with contemporary Europe.

The question is : how did these discoveries react on Indians ? The answer, at any rate upto the year 1850, is that Orientalism was by and large a European affair, the Indians themselves appearing to ignore it altogether. Certain-

ly this statement could hardly be true in an absolute sense
as regards men so enlightened as Rammohan Roy, Dwarakanath Tagore and Devendranath Tagore not to mention tradi-
tionalists like Ram Comul Sen and Raja Radhakanta Deb,
Tarachand Chakraborty's association with Wilson has already
been noticed. But the writings of these men give little countenance to the assumption that in their reforming efforts
they made very considerable use of the findings of the
Orientalists regarding the ancient civilisation of India. David
Kopf, in his *British Orientalism and the Bengal Renaissance*
has argued that Rammohan was influenced by the writings
of Jones and Colebrooke in propagating his creed to Vedantic Monotheism as the religion of India's Golden Age,
Even if this be true—Mr Kropf's findings are not adequate
enough to warrant this view as anything more than moderate-
ly probable—Rammohan's interest in Orientalist findings
could not but be confined to the religion of ancient India to
the utter neglect of her civilisation with its achievements in
politics, literature, the Fine Arts and the Sciences. In vain
do we look for an echo of the praise of *Sakuntala* mouthed
by Rammohan's elder contemporary Goethe, in Rammohan's
own writings. Radhakanta Deb was a great Sanskritist and
a regular correspondent of Wilson's, but his primary interest was in lexicography ; and his monumental *Sabdakalpa-
drum* could hardly be regarded as an adequate attempt to
recall the glories of India's past civilisation. Lexicography
passed muster with pandits of the old school, but to the
rising generation of the Hindu College literati it was the
veritable bugbear.

The fact of the matter was that Orientalism—in the sense
of any full-blooded enthusiasm for things ancient—was far
from a pervasive sentiment amongst Indians previous to the
fifties of the 19th century. The older generation of the
English-educated Bengalis were much too preoccupied with
the spread of English education in Bengal, (with which their
reform schemes as well as their prospects of advancement in

the new regime were inextricably connected) and largely tended to ignore the glories of their own tradition that were being gradually uncovered by the painstaking labours of their European contemporals. Rammohan actually pleaded against founding a Sanskrit College in Calcutta, ostensibly on the ground of the obsolescence of the traditional system of education, but, all the while remaining obstinately silent as to the labours of the Orientalists. The Derozians actually subscribed to the creed propounded by Macaulay and went the whole hog in denouncing everything Indian. Even Vidyasagar started his literary career by translating English text books and by rendering a Hindustani production into the Bengali he was doing so much to create and beautify. In such a climate, Orientalism amongst Indians could hardly be contemplated as a serious proposition—it simply did not exist.

As regards the Brahmo Samaj, it has also to be remembered that it laboured under the initial disadvantage of having its prospects inevitably tied up with the Anglicising generation. It was only amongst people with some amount of English education that it could look for converts. True, the same English education was the only passport to the researches of the Orientalists,—but to ask people to combine together in their hearts, a love of India's past with a dissatisfaction of the traditional religion, was no easy task. In the event, the family of the Tagores was the only Brahmo group that sought to represent itself as a group of Orientalising Brahmos—the group headed by Keshub Chandra Sen and, later still, the group that went by the name of Sadharan Brahmo Samaj inevitably opting for a predominantly Westernizing posture. In this connection, it is significant that Rabindranath, in all his writings on Rammohan, has tried to represent the latter as a champion of Orientalism, at the same time insisting that the tenets of Brahmoism did represent the religion of India's Golden Age. Significantly, Rabindranath nowhere mentions Rammohan's displeasure with the founding of a Sanskrit College in Calcutta. In the light of what we have said concerning the extent of Rammohan's Orientalism, it is not necessary to contradict Rabindranath, nor to wholly discountenance the claim put forward in favour of the family of the Tagores. Our only point is that neither Rammohan nor the Tagores of the first two generations represented by Dwarakanath and Devendranath appear to have shown much interest in the ancient Civilisation of India apart from the religion of the Upanishads. Reverence for the glories of India's historical past was a dominant feature with the Tagores of the next generation, Rabindranath himself proving to be the greatest Orientalising Brahmo that ever lived. But in 1850, he was not even born.

The general Brahmo position (if we exclude the Tagores of the third generation) regarding India's past civilisation comes out most clearly in Sivnath Sastri's *Ramtanu Lahiri O Tatkalin Banga Samaj* with its tell-tale omission of the names even of so eminent an Indologist as Rajendralal Mitra as well as that of Ramesh Chandra Dutt, the famous Bengali translator of the *Rigveda Samhita*. Sivnath's book, which sets out to give short life sketches of all 19th century Bengali luminaries especially in the fields of religion, social reform and polite learning, and is on that account regarded as the standard work on Bengal Renaissance includes, amongst other things, the life-sketches of an eminent homeopath, of a not-so-eminent barrister, and of many other lesser worthies, but it fails to include the name of a single Orientalist, Western or Indian, who flourished during that age. This is not to deny the merits of Sivnath's work, but the fact that both Rajendralal Mitra and Ramesh Chandra Dutta were men of far greater eminence in the intellectual life of 19th century Bengal than, for example, Barrister Monmohan Ghosh, their omission from Sivnath's work, probably suggests a certain kind of prejudice of Brahmo leaders like Sivnath against Orientalism. Of course,

Sivnath's work was written at the turn of the century, but there is no reason to believe that the prejudice was not of much longer standing.

After 1850, significant developments occurred. Rajendralal Mitra started publishing his Indological works. Vidyasagar began collecting Sanskrit works and popularising such works as *Sakuntala* by rendering them into his own beautiful vernacular. The *Mahabharata* was translated by Kaliprasanna Singha. Sanskrit texts began to be published and translated. A climate was created in which the new English-educated literati were prompted to look back to their own ancient heritage with interest and even with reverence.

But this newly grown, inchoate interest in India's ancient civilisation amongst English-educated Indians was not the only fact that operated in favour of Orientalism (more properly Hinduism as we shall see in due course) in the years preceding 1870. The field of Medieval Indian history had already begun to be explored by British historians. Tales of Rajput and Maratha chivalry had begun to stir the imagination of English educated Hindus. Tod's *Annals and Antiquities of Rajasthan* (1829) had already become a classic. And by the beginning of the seventies the stage was imperceptibly being set, in the minds of Bengali Hindus, for the appearance of a vision of a historical India, which was great in peace as well as in war, in the arts as well as in the sciences, in religion as well as in secular civilisation—in short in anything and everything that constituted the greatness of a people that was latterly considered the most degenerate of all living races.

THE VISION

It is a debatable question whether the findings of the Orientalists as well as those of the historians of Medieval India constituted anything near a total picture of India's past. Far more debatable is the question whether that past

was as glorious as it began to be represented in India by
Indians from the beginning of the 1870s. This is the reason
why we have given the present Chapter the title "The Birth
of a Vision". The findings of European Orientalists merely
formed the background of the Vision, and as we shall see
presently, the vision itself, as constructed by thinkers like
Bhudeb and Bankim, was by no means a mere restatement of
Orientalist findings in a compendious and attractive form.
It was a true vision in the sense that it sought primarily to
capture the minds of the new generation, and at least in the
case of Bhudeb, dispensed with all demands of historical
criticism by telescoping in the future an apparition of India
of the past. As to the historicity of Bankim's picture, we
shall discuss that question at the end of this chapter. Here
we shall only remark that for as long as the half century
that elapsed between the dates 1870 and 1920, educated
Hindus of Bengal were very much pre-occupied with the
vision of an ancient Hindu civilisation of unexampled
magnificence and they were trying all the time to recapture
the vision so as to re-enact it on their own stage. Indeed,
it will not be too much to say that for a certain space of time
the Biblical saying was as true of the sons of Bengal as of the
sons of Israel : "I will pour out my spirit upon all flesh,
and your sons and your daughters shall prophesy, and your
old men shall see visions, and your young men shall dream
dreams." Bengalis in the course of that half-century did
in fact prophesy; their old men did see visions; their young
men did dream dreams. Minor poets sang out and held the
audience spell-bound by the note of unconquerable conviction
in their voice when they said,

> "Speak out ye, speak out in a cadence
> emulating the sound of a hundred instruments :
> A new Sun shall arise on this old Eastern Sky."[4]

The same poets thrilled their listeners by conjuring up a
vision of the special glory of their land, a glory that was
not recorded in the annals of any other nation, and one

which on closer analysis turned out to be totally insubstantial and by that very reason appealed to one as being all the more imperishable :

"What shall I sing here, oh what song !
—Here, where the sound of
     the deep—throbbing OM and
the cadence of the divine Sama
used, in old days, to send a quiver
     to abodes in the distant firmament ?"[5]

Thus it is clear that if the new arrival on the Bengali stage was only a vision and not a real discovery of an ancient civilisation, the vision was powerful enough to grip the Bengali mind for a whole half century. This vision originated in the minds of Bhudeb and Bankim.

BHUDEB'S VISION

Bhudeb Mukherjee's short work *A Vision of Indian History as it appeared in a Dream* was published in 1875.[6] Ostensibly it set out to describe the possible course of Indian history after the third battle of Panipath following a hypothetical Maratha victory. But as it is very much in doubt that the Marathas were capable of such farsighted statesmanship as Bhudeb would credit them with, his narrative should be looked upon as the description of a state of affairs, not as they might occur but as Bhudeb would wish them to occur. His picture is in fact an idealised one—a vision of a high Hindu civilisation as it appeared to an orthodox nineteenth century Hindu with a mind well-versed in the best thought of the East as well as the West.

In ten chapters, Bhudeb presents a blue-print of a civilisation in the making. The Hindu-rajya founded by a descendant of Shivaji excels in its policies. It follows a religious policy of strict equality as between Hindus and Muslims. It is a system of absolute monarchy with an extremely centralized defence but with generous scope for decentralization in every other department — particular emphasis being laid on largely autonomous village communities. The new regime aspires to inculcate a spirit of adventure amongst Hindus by sending them overseas, not in indiscriminate violation of the Hindu ban on seafaring but by restricting sea travel to able-bodied intelligent youngmen who would travel for instruction and knowledge and for the service of their motherland. They would learn Western sciences and spread the knowledge in their own land. The new regime would cautiously eradicate the seeds of subversion engineered by foreign missions but would not interfere with the free propagation of thought, subversive or otherwise. The new regime would witness a true Hindu renaissance—a revival not merely of ancient learning but an efflorescence of culture embracing all sorts of intellectual activities. The new regime has two intellectual centres—Kanauj, the centre of ancient learning and Benaras, the centre of new learning. The most important classical languages are taught in Kanauj, Sanskrit being recognised as the chief of them but Greek, Latin and Arabic, in their respective order being taught with equal enthusiasm. The most distinguished researches are held in Universal history; books of astonishing originality are produced in great number; the most renowned Sanskrit scholar is employed in writing the epic of Indian revival. In Benaras, original researches are conducted in all the modern sciences; wonderful astronomical discoveries are made; physics makes splendid strides ; wonderful advances are made in military science. Not only that, trade and commerce would also flourish. Festivals in the new regime will be occasions of charity as also the demonstrations of the sense of national unity. Bhudeb contemplates high praise for the new regime by foreign observers.

The importance of Bhudeb's work lies in the fact that it is the first document of its kind. Here we have a full-length description of a civilisation in the making, all its elements being ingredients of a strictly Hindu society which is Hindu in the accepted sense of the term. It is a concep-

tion neither harking back to a hypothetical Vedic prototype,
nor contemplating a shadowy Ram-rajya, too good to be
wholly credible. Bhudeb does not denounce caste or child
marriage. He envisages no programme for remarrying Hindu
widows. He does not even allow Hindus to undertake
pleasure trips across the seas. Far from making a clean
sweep of idolatry, he remains shamelessly attached to it. In
short, his vision contains nothing to which even the most
inveterate preacher of Hindu orthodoxy can object.

But this is only a partial view of the matter. A closer
view suggests that Bhudeb is a true visionary, and his
acceptance of contemporary Hinduism is only a natural
set-off to a rising civilisation whose future glory has to be
made credible by the very facts of its present decline. This is
clear from a consideration of the three basic features fundamental in Bhudeb's contemplated Hindu regenerations,—his
conception of a Renaissance of Hindu Letters, his idea of
Hindu Imperial Expansion and his scheme of a Rising
Brahmanical Order. These ideas run like a silver thread
through Bhudeb's argument and raise his book from the level
of a tract for the cause of orthodoxy to that of a tract for
the times.

Bhudeb, however, was writing a historical parable, not
a true work of history. Though all the elements of his
contemplated Hindu civilisation arose from historical
Hinduism, not excluding the doctrine of Hindu Imperial
Expansion, Bhudeb, in the eighteen seventies, was not reviving a chronology of past historical facts but telescoping a
quasi-historical vision into the future. More important than
this, his vision was not such as to have any immediate impact
on Indian society, either in the direction of practical politics
or in the actual cultural activities in which the educated
public of the time were engaged. We now turn to another
thinker whose disquisitions on the Hindu past were going to
have more practical consequences.

The monthly journal *Vangadarsan* was founded in

1872 and was edited by Bankim Chandra Chatterjee during the years 1872 (April-May) to 1876 (March-April). It was not purely literary journal, nor a pure journal of ideas. It was an omnibus production—the sort of periodical, in fact, whose scope includes 'all knowledge as its province.' Right from the opening number there began to appear articles whose subject was the civilisation of the Hindus,—and these were not articles written by pedants with an antiquarian interest. They were full-blooded articles, and even when they were not written by Bankim himself, his guiding spirit was very much in evidence behind them, breathing into them a soul which is what transforms antiquarianism into something more into a piece of vital writing.

The very first article of the first number[8] sought to remove a long-standing stigma on the Hindu name. British writers had been portraying Hindus as a cowardly race. Was this picture truthful, or was it a scandal spread by the British to make Hindus believe that their current subjugation had nothing accidental about it but was conditioned by a history that was as inglorious as it was drab ? The author of the article referred to the work of Indologists who conceded achievements of some notable things by our ancients, —but who contended that all these achievements had been confined to the fields of art, literature, and kindred matters,— the infamy of cowardice in the field of battle being a perennial characteristic of the Hindu race. About the question whether there was any historical evidence to justify this belief the author argued that in the absence of historical writings left by Hindus themselves and in view of the whole of the information in our possession being derived from accounts given by their enemies, namely- the Mahomedans and the Greeks—the case of the Hindus was going by default. But even the evidence of enemies, whatever its worth, would tell us a very different tale, if properly interpreted. The author took up the case of Muslim invasion and asked his readers to compare the Indian experience of the Arabs with their experience elsewhere. After the death of the Prophet, it took the Arabs scarcely a quarter century to found a world Empire, and, whether it was Egypt or Syria, Africa or Spain, Persia or Turkistan, Arab arms proved irresistible everywhere. The common belief is that they were checked only in the West, thanks to the valour of Charles Martel. But what are the facts concerning the Arab invasion of India ? The Arabs could obtain hardly a foothold there. Even that tiny foothold, in remote Sind, did not survive the death of the conqueror, and was eventually recaptured by Rajputs. The invincibility of Arab arms was tested in the land of the Hindus, and it was at the end of full five hundred years, from Mohammad Bin Kasim, the Arab to Sehabuddin Ghori, the Afghan,—after wave upon wave of Muslim hordes had impinged upon the citadel and failed to bring it down—that Hindu resistance was finally crushed. The resistance again was notably not the resistance of a united India, but of the fragmented, decrepit and ramshackle India of the post-Harsha era. It was not the India upon which the world-conquering Macedonian had hopelessly to turn his back, and in which Seleucus Nicator had to swallow the bitter pill of defeat. That was an India whose prowess her sons never chronicled, but of whose glory her would - be conquerors, in recounting their own valour, left enough indication for a startled posterity to ponder upon, and for a subjugated race to recapture in its mind's eye.

This was the note on which *Vangadarsan* started—a note of unconquerable assurance as to a glorious Hindu past. The interesting point about the Vangadarsan articles, however, was a complete absence of chauvinism. This is evident even in the opening article, which, while conjuring up an image of Hindu military greatness, by no means absolves the ancients of responsibility in causing the contemporary decline. Hindus had never had any sense of national unity, nor even any commonly held desire for political independence, and, in default of these all their military greatness as ultimately of no avail. It was the British conquest and Western Learning that were making us conscious of these public virtues. This was the vein in which Vangadarsan set off the declining Hindu present against the glorious Hindu past. On close analysis, this furnishes a clue to the proliferation of Indological articles in Vangadarsan, in face of the professed intention expressed in its introductory article of making the journal a vehicle of the New Learning. Indology, as conceived by Bankim, was very much a part of the New Learning ; it was in fact the testing ground for the latter. To understand this let us refer to "The Peasants of Bengal", a very famous essay published in Bhadra, Kartick, Pausa, Falgun, 1279 B. S. numbers of the journal, discussing the contemporary condition of the peasantry in Bengal. In this article there was little scope for an excursus into Indology, but here again the author, with a flourish of the rationalistic teachings of the New Learning, sought the peasantry's contemporary decline in a past phenomenon,— that of an early civilisation owing its birth to a temperate climate and exceptional fertility of soil. These conditions while giving an early rise to civilisation in India, inevitably caused its decline,—first, by multiplying the labour force too speedily without the safety valve of colonisation to arrest over-crowding, then by driving that labour forces owing to its superfluity in numbers, to the level of subsistence and thereby denying its harsh and competitive existence any leisure for mental improvement,—in the process, converting it into a drag upon the higher classes, involving the latter in its doom the doom of a numberless multitude of submissive and semi-barbarous peasantry dragging, in its very submission and sheep-like subservience, the superior classes to its own inglorious level. What the lower orders lost in mental vigour, the Brahmans lost in religion. They became priests of a pseudo-religion, spreading an ever-expanding cobweb of shastric instructions over Kshatriyas, Vaisyas and Sudras. The cobweb spread, entangling and ensnaring the flies—depriving them of locomotion. The fate of the deceiver is self-deception, and the cobweb spread by Brahmans ultimately trapped their own souls : the rich soil of their intellect became an arid desert[9]. Here, again, we are face to face with a post-mortem of the Hindu decline, but here the dissection involves another part of the corpse.

To a careful reader a review of the Vangadarsan articles would suggest two things regarding their character. Their most notable characteristics were their universalism and the predisposition towards a comparative study of civilisations with a view to fixing up the bearings of the declining Hindu civilisation in the light of other civilisations, past and present. The former characteristic suggests a broadness of outlook which made the Vangadarsan writers emphasise the universal rather than the particular qualities in the civilisation of ancient India. As example of this characteristic we may mention the article on 'Eloquence' published serially in the first two numbers of the journal. In the author's opinion it is eloquence that rouses the nations of the world to historical actions that may be called truly great,—and it was during the great ages of eloquence that India achieved her true greatness. But historical India has largely been an ineloquent race with a peculiar fondness for solitude and reflection. In the author's judgment it is this strain of reflectiveness in our character that has given us Bengalis a fire that can only smoulder into lyrical effusiveness; but cannot burst into the conflagration of soul-stirring eloquence to lead us to mighty public events of good or evil. The author compares the classical age of India with the age of the epics, and points out how the prodigious eloquence of the heroes and heroines of the epics degenerated into sentimental effusiveness in the characters[10] of classical literature.

Side by side with this search for universal qualities in the civilisation of ancient India, the Vangadarsan writers began a comparative study of civilisations. A good example of this is the article entitled : "How the Nations of the World Achieve Greatness ?[11]", published in the second number. The author starts on the assumption that "the histories of the nations that achieved greatness in the past or are achieving greatness before our eyes, almost invariably exemplify a general law. These nations follow, in each case, a particular bent, set their hearts on making that bent all-powerful, staking even their lives on it,—in a word, going the whole hog in its pursuit. This is the law, though the bent itself may vary according to variation of time, place or race." The author illustrates this thesis by historical examples, attributing the greatness of the Greeks to their burning desire for excellence in every human pursuit and that of the Romans to their desire for military glory and an indomitable acquisitive instinct. He points to the indifferent state of the Arabs before the birth of the Prophet despite their courage and fierce independence of spirit and describes how the religious bent instilled into them by Mahomet made them, in the space of a few years, the mightiest nation on earth. He cites the case of England and illustrates how the mere commercial spirit, if pursued with determination can bear down all opposition and make a handful of islanders the lords of the seas and arbiters of the fate of far bigger nations. The author does not forget his own land, whose ancient glory he attributes to the unquenchable thirst for knowledge exemplified in the lives of the Brahmanas, who renounced everything even the merest pursuit of happiness, common to all classes of men of whatever race or religion in the pursuit of knowledge.

Another very revealing article published in the last three numbers of the journal is the one entitled, "Indian Women"[12]. It is obviously intended to glorify Indian Womanhood by glorifying a few women famous in literature and the religious lore. But in sharp contrast to the usual run of such essays it draws up the debit side of the balance sheet with an unusual candour. "Indian women have had no freedom and consequently they have been totally deficient in the faculties that derive their strength from freedom." This indictment is followed by the remark that "such mental faculties as owe their growth and development to the quickening touch of freedom are conspicuous by their absence in the woman of India." This is disparaging enough, but the author goes on to suggest that (owing to this want of freedom) "Indian women have been lacking the piety which has made a large number of European women so deservedly famous. No Indian woman has, for example, been known to have acted in the manner that Mrs. John Howard did. She has never accompanied her husband to distant lands and passed her life by dedicating it to the service of others."—Such is our author's judgment on the character of the female species in 'spiritual' India when contrasted with its counterpart in the 'materialist' West.

It is doubtful whether in point of originality and output of new information, the Vangadarsan writers outstepped the limits of Indological discoveries made by European Indologists during the earlier parts of the century. Some of the articles were in facts no more than mere popularisations, and fragmentary ones at that of a far more elaborate European research. But here was a popular platform erected by a man of genius, intent upon making all that was known and discovered about his country's ancestry available to the reading public of Bengal. Here was a man who was not cramped by the narrow nationalism, who would glorify one's own ancestry at all costs, but who, like all educated men of his generation, admitted the superiority of contemporary European civilisation—merely protesting that his own country's decline had nothing preordained or perennial about it but was only a falling off from an original state of greatness and glory. If Vangadarsan achieved anything of lasting value, apart from the influence it exercised on the growing literature of Bengal—it was this that it made ancient India contemporaneous, to the extent that it made

Hindus conscious of their civilisation. It gave them a pattern worthy of emulation, which in some ways, despite its ancientness, was nearer to them than the high contemporary civilisation of the West. Actually this nearness of the ancient civilisation was of the crucial importance : it was of the same order as the contemporary West's nearness to ancient Greece. The nineteenth century awakening of Bengal has been compared with the Renaissance of the Western countries that began in the 15th century. In this context the term Renaissance has been loosely construed to mean any sort of reawakening,—the crucial significance of the West's discovery of the ancient world being glossed over in the case of Bengal, and her contact with contemporary West has been made by most historians to do duty for a stimulus that rightfully belongs to ancient India. This explanation of the Bengal Renaissance is largely true, at least during the period previous to 1870. But with the publication of Vangadarsan we enter a new era in which the term Renaissance has gained a new significance—which is far more akin to the sense in which historians of the West apply it.

This is not to deny the Western contribution to this Renaissance and, in fact, the Vangadarsan writers themselves would be the first to repudiate such a view. In their search for an identity in a glorious Hindu past, they erred on the side of Anglomania rather than Indomania, if by Indomania is meant the acceptance of all that is Indian to an exclusion of all that is non-Indian. The greatest achievement of Vangadarsan and Bankim was possibly this : he raised from the bottomless depth in which it had fallen the stock of the Hindu civilisation without depreciating in any manner that of the Western.

Vangadarsan also introduced a vogue which persisted for a considerable length of time during the succeeding decades. From now on Indological speculation were going to occupy a large amount of space in the periodical literature of Bengal as a matter of course. That this was an achievement of high order becomes clear when we remember the Orientalist-Anglicist controversy in Macaulay's time. When in 1835, Macaulay superseded the Orientalist demand for a system of education in India that would proceed on indigenous lines, he did so against the opposition of a handful of British scholars, the Indian reaction being one of absolute silence. The ignorance of Indians about ancient India was, at that time, so prodigious that their silence could not even be interpreted as a sort of opposition to the Orientalist scheme, —they simply failed to divine the implications of the controversy. That controversy was now a matter of past history. The debate on National Education, which will be discussed later, showed that the controversy was very much open at the turn of the century. Was Western education without an indigenous element in it the right sort of education for Indians ? asked the proponents of the National Education scheme. Vangadarsan did not start the controversy, but it indicated the ways along which the later arguments on this question took shape and developed. Vangadarsan was supposed to represent the progressive literati of nineteenth century Bengal, and it was expected that it would reflect the reforming zeal of the generation. It must be admitted that Vangadarsan did not wholly belie that expectation. In his celebrated essay on "Equality" (published in *Vangadarsan* in 1281 B. S.) Bankim praised the efforts of Vidyasagar and the Brahmo Samaj for widow remarriage and female emancipation. But as early as the spring of 1873, Vangadarsan had attacked Vidyasagar's method of fighting polygamy in Hindu society. Modern critics have misunderstood Bankim so much as to accuse him of a desire to retain that vulgar custom. But we have the latter's positive statement to the contrary. What Bankim was trying to impress upon his readers was that the recourse to the 'Smritis' for social reform was a course fraught with dangerous possibilities. It was in fact a double-edged sword, which, by sanctifying the Smritis with all its customs, good

9

and bad, was furnishing the reformer with a weapon that could recoil on him. This was the substance of Bankim's argument, but actually the argument foreshadowed the whole of the New Hindu approach to the question of social reform. Here it suffices to say that the New Hindus deprecated social reform in the Brahmo manner, and looked upon the raising of the lower orders by educational and economic reforms as the surest means of reforming Hindu society. This was also, by and large, the Vangadarsan approach to the same question.

NOTES AND REFERENCES

1. P. J. Marshall (ed.) *The British Discovery of Hinduism in the 18th century* : (Cambridge). William Jones "On the Hindus", p. 252-53.

2. For a detailed study, S. Mukherjee : *Sir William Jones : A study in eighteenth century British Attitude to India,* Cambridge, 1968.

3. Op. cit. P. J. Marshall, p. 251.

4. Atul Prasad Sen : "বল বল বল সবে শত বীণা বেণু রবে

   নব-দিনমণি উদিবে আবার পুরাতন এ পূরবে"

5. Rajani Kanta Sen : "সেথা আমি কী গাহিব গান ?

   যেথা গভীর ওঙ্কারে সাম ঝঙ্কারে

   কাঁপিত দূরবিমান ?"

6. It was published in the *'Education Gazette'* of the same year.

7. This doctrine probably arose from a consideration of Hindu co'onisation in the past. The colonisation, in ancient times, of some places in the Far East, notably Thailand and Cambodia, had probably been effected on the lines prescribed by Bhudeb in any future scheme of colonisation.

8. *Vangadarsan*, Baisakh, 1279 B. S. "Infamy of India."

9. *Vangadarsan* : Falgun, 1279 B. S.

10. The author compares the classical Sakuntala of Kalidas with her original in the Mahabharata and is not particularly pleased at the transformation of the fiery heroine of the epic into the civilised goody-goody of Kalidas's making.

11. *Vangadarsan,* Jaistha, 1279 B. S. "মনুষ্যজাতির মাহাত্ম্য কী সে হয় ?"

12. *Vangadarsan :* Magh. Falgun, Chaitra, 1282 B. S.

CHAPTER – III
THE BIRTH OF A MOVEMENT

THE CONTROVERSY between Reverend W. W. Hastie and Bankim Chandra Chatterjee in the columns of the *Statesman* constitutes a significant landmark in the history of the development of the ideas of the New Hindu Movement. On the 20th of September, 1882, the *Statesman* of Calcutta published an account of a grand *Sradh* ceremony that had taken place in the ancestral house of the Rajah of Sovabazar on the 17th. The Sovabazar family was one of the richest, and at the same time, the most influential, families of 19th century Calcutta. It was well-known that this family was a pillar of Hinduism, and a great advocate of the cause of Western enlightenment insofar as that enlightenment did not strike at the roots of orthodoxy. It is one of the paradoxes of the social history of Nineteenth Century Bengal that orthodox Hindus like Dewan Ram Kamal Sen and Raja Radhakanta Deb were no less instrumental in the spread of Western enlightenment than thinkers like Rammohan Roy who considered orthodoxy as the root of all social evils in India. Actually the role of the former was possibly of greater effectiveness as the researches of historians like David Kopf[1] and Ramesh Chandra Majumdar are making abundantly clear. These researches show the incorrectness of the popular opinion which would give all the credit for the spread of Western enlightenment in India to the enemies of orthodoxy. What the 'orthodox camp' of the advocates of Western enlightenment lacked was this : It failed to give a rational explanation of their orthodoxy insofar as such rational explanation was rendered imperative by their own acceptance of Western enlightenment. This failure was as true of the enlightened members of the Sovabazar family as of every other member of the 'orthodox camp' of the advocates of Western enlightenment.

Radhakanta Deb (1794-1867), the illustrious member

of the Sovabazar family, defended Hindu idolatry on the ground that, for the masses in India, it served the same purpose as dolls served for children,—for it prevented those masses from getting addicted to practices that were blatantly immoral. It was with such feeble arguments, conceding almost the whole point to the enemies of idolatry, that members of the 'orthodox camp' of the advocates of Western enlightenment in India preserved in their idolatry, and it was this ambivalence of their attitude that rendered them fit targets for attack by Brahmo as well as Christian propagandists. The Sradh of 1882 was open to attack on an identical reasoning : it would have possibly gone unnoticed had there been not a large gathering of English-educated Hindus in the ceremony,—some of them well-known for their enlightened views on social and religious questions. But to Rev. Hastie the Sradh seemed to furnish a classic example of what to him was an undesirable combination of Hindu orthodoxy and Western enlightenment and it was this combination that, in his view, made the ceremony doubly intolerable. To understand the missionary's wrath let us quote the *Statesman* account of the ceremony as summarised by Jogesh Chandra Bagal[2] : "The spacious quadrangle of the Rajbari, the various articles, requisite for the Dansagar Sradh, the family idol *Gopinathji* placed on a silver throne, all these were duly noticed (in-the Statesman account). The presence of nearly four thousand Brahman scholars (Adhyapakas) and other guests from all sections of the community was specially mentioned. There was a long list of the English-educated Bengalis who were present at the ceremony. This list included men like Maharaja Jotindra Mohan Tagore, Kristodas Pal and Dr. Rajendra Lal Mitra."

There is little doubt that it was this display of the idol of Gopinathji and the apparent approval of that display by some of the most illustrious members of the Hindu community, otherwise engaged in spreading the enlightenment of the West in India, that irritated W.W.Hastie. As

Principal of the General Assembly's Institution, he must have felt that the mantle of Alexander Duff, his more illustrious predecessor and founder of the Institution, had fallen upon him, and he lost no time in opening his attack. This was a strange mixture of Christian indignation against an idolatrous ceremony, bountiful commiseration for the lot of fallen Bharatvarsha and a respect for the Hindu receivers of Western enlightenment, whose attendance in such a ceremony proved, in the missionary's view, a gross betrayal of that enlightenment. His letters began to be published one after another : the first[3] questioning 'the supposed necessity of idolatry,' the second[4] inveighing against its 'alleged harmlessness' and the third[5] demolishing 'the ultimate philosophy of Brahmanism.' The supposed necessity was given in Radhakanta Deb's words[6] and was demolished by two arguments, one historical and the other rational. The historical argument was the example of the aboriginal Tribes of India converted to Christianity, who were raised "in a single generation from the grossest idolatry up to the purest worship of God." "If objection be taken to Christian examples" Hastie hastened to cite the case of the Mohammedan masses of India, who dispensed with the necessity of idols without any visible inconvenience. Hastie's rational argument against idolatry consisted in the alleged existence, even in savages, of a "supersensuous reason" which made the necessity of worship through sensible idols superfluous. In the second letter Hastie went a step further, and rejected altogether the alleged harmlessness of the superfluity and blamed on it "all the demoralisation and degradation of India." In the third letter was proposed the demolition of the "inner citadel" of Hinduism which in the missionary's view was the philosophy of Vedanta, especially that version of it which was associated with the name of Shankaracharya. Rev. Hastie thought he had found no less than four unanswerable objections to this philosophy.[7] It was a negative idealism "giving no satisfactory explanation of the existent world and its stable order"; the negativism as a cosmological theory, in its turn, extended to the sphere of morality and practical action ; it bred despair and gave "no hope, being without God in the world"; last but not least, it led to the "dogmatic Nihilism of Buddha." Rev. Hastie concluded his third letter by hinting that the only hope of Hindus lay in embracing Christianity.[8] At this moment Bankim Chandra Chatterjee spoke out.

The rejoinder of Bankim, (under the pseudonym Ramchandra) when it was published, was as truculent as Rev. Hastie's provocation was gross. We reproduce the letter the first of a series, in full :

THE MODERN ST. PAUL

Sir,

Will you allow me to suggest to Mr. Hastie, who is so ambitious of earning distinction as a sort of Indian St. Paul, that it is fit that he should render himself better acquainted with the doctrines of the Hindoo religion before he seeks to demolish them ? As matters stand with him, his arguments are simply contemptible; and I think the columns of the *Statesman* might have been more usefully occupied by advertisements about Doorga Puja holiday goods than by trash which renders the champion of Christianity contemptible in the eyes of idolaters. This may be harsh language, but the writer who mistakes Vedantism for Hinduism and goes to Mr. Monier Williams for an exposition of that doctrine, hardly deserves better treatment. Mr. Hastie's attempt to storm the 'inner citadel' of the Hindoo religion forcibly reminds us of another equally heroic achievement—that of the redoubted knight of La Mancha before the windmill.

Let. Mr. Hastie take my advice, and obtain some knowledge of Sanskrit scriptures in the ORIGINAL. Let him study then critically all the systems of Hindoo philosophy—the *Bhagabatgita*, the *Bhakti-Suka* of Sandilya, and such other works. Let him not study them under European Scholars, for they cannot teach what they cannot understand; the blind cannot lead the blind. Let him study them with a Hindoo, with one who believes in them. And then, if he should still entertain his present inclination to enter on an apostolic career, let him hold forth at his pleasure, and if we do not promise to be convinced by him, we promise not to laugh at him. At present, arguments would be thrown away on him. There can be no controversy on a subject when one of the controversialists is in utter ignorance of the subject matter of the controversy; and if under such circumstances the 'olympians: only yawn' and do not assert, Mr. Hastie has only to thank his own precipitate ignorance.

Ramchandra

It is unnecessary here to pursue the controversy in detail. We would do well to bring out the important points emphasized. Rev. Hastie resented Bankim's suggestion that he should take lessons under a Hindu and roundly declared "that both the Sanskrit language and Sanskrit literature are much better understood at this moment in Europe and America than in India."[9] He poured abuses on Ramchandra for trying to belittle the scholarship of European Sanskritists and for what seemed to him a disparagement of the 'intellectual superiority of Europe.'

Bankim, in two elaborate letters, tried to establish the essential irrelevance of all missionary and in fact, all European criticism of Hinduism and outlined his own sketch of what he called 'rational Hinduism.' Actually, without making any verbal assertion to that effect, he announced the birth of the New Hindu Movement. Bankim gladly conceded the intellectual superiority of Europe but asserted that the 'intellectual superiority alone' could hardly 'enable one to dispense with the essential conditions under which alone knowledge can be acquired'.[10] He pointed out that European

scholars had no adequate conception of the rich and
varied field of Indian philosophy like Nyaya or Vaishnava.
Bankim multiplied these examples by mentioning many
other branches of study, and while admitting without 'hesita-
tion' "the decided superiority of the European enquirer in
the fields of Vedic literature" he asserted that the "Vedas
(did) not represent the living religion of India." Bankim
felt, the intellectual superiority of Europe' could only make
a desperate bite at the husk' of Hinduism 'but could not
arrive at its kernel.'

Bankim next explained what he called 'rational
Hinduism', in other words, its kernel without its husk.' In
his opinion, "Hinduism like every other fullyd eveloped religious system, consisted of, *first*, a doctrinal basis or the
creed ; *secondly*, a worship or rites ; and lastly, a code of
morals more or less dependent upon the doctrinal basis."[12]
"This was the whole field of study" of which idolatry
"formed only a subordinate part of the second division" (i. e.
worship or rites). According to Bankim, the doctrinal basis
consisted of dogmas formulated in a mass of philosophical
literature and of Puranic legends growing out of these dogmas. It was however in the 'depths' of the philosophy that
the 'foundation of a modern Hinduism' were laid, broad and
solid. He was at pains to point out that the philosophic conception of the duality of Nature and Soul was at the basis
of worship and it was their union—"the love for all that
exists"—that formed the Hindu's religion. The conception
of the trinity arose from discriminating in the Universal Soul,
the three qualities of love, power and justice. Of the legend
of Krishna, Bankim upheld that "Krishna is soul, Radha is
Nature" and the religion of the Hindu consisted in glorifying that union, because it was this union that was the source
of "all love, truth and beauty."

On idolatrous worship, Bankim said that it hardly
stood in need of the sort of apologetic defence proposed by
Radhakanta Deb. "The true explanation (consisted) in the

even true relations of the subjective Ideal to its objective Reality." As the ideal in beauty found expression in human art, so the ideal of the Divine in man received a form from him and that from an image.[13] This to Bankim was the intellectual basis of idolatry and he pointed to the rituals of *Pran Pratishtha* and immersion of the image which distinguished Hindu idolatry from the worship of sticks and stones. Moreover, this idolatrous worship was by no means compulsory for all devotees. He summed up with the assertion : "A man may never have entered a temple and yet be an orthodox Hindu." Regarding the ethics of Hinduism, Bankim said that "the Hindu ethical system (sought) to regulate the conduct of individuals as well as the conduct of society".

It would be in order here to note a curious feature of the controversy which ensued—the complete silence of both the contending parties in regard to Brahmos or Brahmoism. In the beginning of Chapter-II, we referred to the Brahmo-Christian conflict as having held the stage in the religious drama till the year 1870. The attack on Rammohan Roy by Serampore missionaries during the early twenties in the wake of his Vedantic publications, the tract of Devendranath bearing the title 'Vedantic Doctrines Vindicated', published in the early forties, Rev. Dyson's attack on Keshub Chandra Sen during the early sixties—all these and many other similar missionary attacks and their rebuttals by Brahmos bear testimony to this strange phenomenon of a secondary event coming to overshadow the primary one. For the Brahmo-Christian conflict was, of course, an offshoot of the Hindu-Christian conflict. It had to be so if only because the Brahmos, even in the period of their greatest ascendancy constituted no more than a fringe of the Hindu society in point of numerical strength. But the importance attached to them by Christian missionaries was understandable. It arose from the fact that the secular education of the West imparted by the Hindu College, and later—since the publication of Macaulay's celebrated Minute, by all

10

educational institutions sponsored by the Government and
most such bodies set up on private initiative, had a curious
effect not wholly anticipated by Christian sponsors of that
education. It certainly subverted the basis of the traditional
faith in the minds of its recipients. This was predicted by
Macaulay in a letter to his father, but he was sadly deluded
in his hope that out of the ruins of the traditional faith in the
minds of the Hindu recipients of Western education, would
sprout the resplendent sapling of Christianity, gradually to
overspread the whole of India. The consequence of the subversion of traditional faith turned out to be not a conversion to
Christianity, but a leaning towards Brahmoism, very often
resulting in actual conversion to that faith. This was the
background of the missionary attack on Brahmoism—a fact
which has to be clearly remembered if we want to understand
the historical significance of the Hastie-Bankim controversy.
The essential point of the controversy was this : It was the
first missionary attack directed against the English-educated
public of Calcutta that ignored the Brahmos altogether.
Clearly, to Rev. Hastie, the bolt of Brahmoism was shot, and
it no longer possessed the credentials of a worthy antagonist
to Christianity.

The same must have been the feeling   Bankim
Chandra Chatterjee whose silence regarding the Brahmos has
to be interpreted in the same manner. It however differed
from the missionary viewpoint in this : whilst the latter was
ignoring the Brahmo-Christian conflict in the changed historical context of the early eighties, Bankim was ignoring the
Hindu-Brahmo conflict. That this was not actuated by a
desire to avoid unpleasant sectarian wranglings becomes clear
when we consider the essential point of Bankim's new exposition of Hinduism. His insistence on the 'kernel' of the Hindu
faith as distinguished from the mere 'husk'—in which category he included the Hindu practice of idolatry and the institution of caste, points to an essentially new direction in
Hindu thought,—and this new direction indicated not an

antagonism to the faith of the Brahmos, but to its redundancy in the changed historical circumstances. Bankim's discrimination of the kernel of Hinduism from its 'husk'—the 'non-essential adjuncts', as otherwise called the external forms of Hinduism,—foreshadowed his whole later doctrine as also that of Swami Vivekananda, who, as we shall see later, started as Bankim had done years before him from the 'eternal verities' of Hinduism as his point of departure. The departure is brought into sharper focus if we compare Bankim's defence of idolatry with that of Mrityunjay Vidyalankar, the orthodox adversary of Rammohan. Mrityunjay's tract of 1817 was intended to demolish the Vedantic monotheism of Rammohan by appealing to the orthodox argument that Vedantic worship was for Sannyasins,—the worship of idols being the basis of the religion of all householders. Bankim's argument was of a totally different order, since he pleaded that no mere form of worship constitued the essence of Hinduism,—that essence was the doctrine of the Soul's union with Nature and the ethical corollary of that doctrine—the code of *'love for all that exists.'*

The method of discovering that kernel was Rationalism,—and in this regard Bankim's application of the phrase 'rational Hinduism' was of the highest significance. What he meant by the epithet 'rational' is not made sufficiently clear in the *Statesman* letters. But this rationalistic method was Bankim's chief contribution to the religious debate of nineteenth century Bengal.

Bankim's rationalistic method sharply differed from that of European Rationalists and he argued that the adoption of the rationalistic method was quite compatible with the retention of basic religious beliefs. Bankim stressed it particularly in view of the fact that in Europe spread of rationalism tended largely to undermine religious beliefs. Since the introduction of English-education in Bengal, it was evident, all along the line, that young people who received that education were apt to become atheists. The Brahmo response

to the challenge of European Rationalism remained confined
to that part of the challenge which involved a question of idol
worship, but never faced the larger question whether religion
had any satisfactory answer to the sort of rational skepticism that questioned the very basis of religion. Bankim was
the first to grapple with this larger question. In the third
letter to Rev. Hastie he made the significant statement :
"Hinduism does not consider itself placed on its defence...
And on the bar of Christianity, *which itself*[14] *has to maintain
a hard struggle for existence in its own home,* Hinduism also
pleads want of jurisdiction."

This statement is extremely significant, although Bankim
in 1882, did not elaborate on the facts that had given rise to
'the hard struggle' he attributed to Christianity 'in its own
home.' Bankim's rationalism was calculated to furnish
religion (not merely the Hindoo religion or the religion of
Europeans, but any and every religion whatever) with a
weapon that might lead the battle to a successful issue.
Needless to add, Bankim wanted religion to come out
victorious in this struggle. But the battle with rationalism
required arms that would themselves draw upon the resources
of the rationalist's arsenal. It was primarily to this end that
the development of Bankim's religious thought was directed.
We shall devote the next chapter to an exposition of that
development.

NOTES AND REFERENCES

1. Kopf, David : *British Orientalism and the Bengal Renaissance.*
2. *Bankim Rachanavali :* Sahitya Samsad, editorial notes.
3. *The Statesman,* September 23, 1882.
4. *The Statesman,* September 26, 1882.
5. *The Statesman,* September 29, 1882.
6. "As you Europeans give dolls to your children, so do we Hindoos
   give these idols to our children, to our uneducated women and
   common people, who cannot do without them, but we do not
   eally worship them ourselves."

7. Hastie's letter, *the Statesman,* September 29, 1882.

8. "And as I may yet endeavour to show, a truer and profounder philosophy is demonstrating the all-important fact, that it is only Christianity, with its revelation of the Divine Personality in all the fulness of His self-existent thought and eternal purpose, that can rationally take the place of the falling Brahmanism, so as to reconcile the soul of India in a pure and blessed life, to the universe around them and to ourselves."

9. Letter dated October 7, 1882.

10. Letter dated October 28, 1882.

11. Bankim's letter : *The Statesman,* October 28, 1882. 'The Intellectual Superiority of Europe.'

12. *Ibid.*

13. *Ibid.*

14. Emphasis added.

CHAPTER - IV

RATIONALISM AND RELIGION

(A) VARIETIES OF 19TH CENTURY RATIONALISM IN REGARD TO RELIGION

IN CHAPTER Three, we used the phrase 'rationalistic method' to characterise Bankim's approach to religious questions. We shall see now that the application of this method to religion in general and to Hinduism in particular was Bankim's most significant contribution to the religious debate of the Nineteenth Century; and it was also productive of the most lasting consequences.

As noted in the previous Chapter, this method consisted in a rationalist attempt to answer the rationalist objection to all religions—the objection, that is to say, not against idolatrous Hinduism alone, but against the general religious position. The course of the history of rationalism in Europe since the 18th century has shown that there have been two broad phases in that history. The first was the pre-Darwinian phase in which the rationalist objection to religion was directed against the two pillars of orthodox religions,—scriptural revelation, and church. But the general rationalist position in the eighteenth century was not atheistical, but a plea for some sort of Deism. This is not to deny that some of the philosophers of the French revolution, and a few other philosophers,—the most noted among whom being David Hume, were thorough going atheists. But as a general statement of the eighteenth century rationalist position in regard to the religious question, this description is largely true. Rationalists in the eighteenth century denied the authority of the church and the truth of scriptural revelation, but they felt that the existence of God was a 'necessity of reason', as the elaborate mechanism of creation seemed to point to a supremely intelligent artificer. This was the celebrated 'argument from design' for the existence of God. Also, the need for some system of morality in the organisation of all societies seemed to point to a Supreme Moral Being.

This eighteenth century approach to religion underwent a complete change since the publication of Darwin's monumental work.[1] The design in the creation was now seen to be a work of evolution, and with this last prop of supernatural existence removed from the hands of the religiously-minded, religion itself ran the hazard of being brushed aside to make room for total atheism. This, in a nutshell, was the post-Darwinian rationalist position in regard to religion—a position that has persisted to this day.

The consequence of these movements of thought in Europe was not confined to Europe alone. The introduction of English education in India was a vehicle of transmission of this influence to India and this made the new generation of Indian students profoundly influenced by these currents of thought. It was certainly not a widespread trend during the earlier half of the century, but it can not be denied that a section of the young Bengal Group (the so-called Derozians) was affected by it. It has been said that the Brahmo-Movement was an answer to the challenge of European Rationalism and that of Christianity to Hindu religious beliefs and Hindu social customs. In Chapter-I, we referred without criticism or coment to this popularly held theory of the origin of Brahmoism. To appreciate thes ignificance of Bankim's work, it would be pertinent to discuss, at this point, the specific Brahmo position in regard to rationalist criticism of religion. We quote below some passages, one by Rammohan Roy and the others by Keshub Chandra Sen to illustrate that position.

Rammohan writing in 1820, in his preface to his work, "The Precepts of Jesus", thus refers to pre-Drawinian Rationalism : "A notion of the existence of a supreme superintending power, the Author and Preserver of this harmonious system, who has organised and who regulates such an infinity of celestial and terrestrial objects : and a due estimation of that law which teaches that man should do unto others as he should wish to be done by, reconciles us to human nature, and tend to render our existence agreeable to ourselves and profitable to the rest of mankind- The former of these sources of satisfaction, viz., a belief in God, prevails generally ; being derived either from tradition and instruction, or from an *attentive survey of the wonderful skill and contrivance displayed in the works of nature* "[2]

This extract, especially the italicised words, clearly indicate that Rammohan was not averse to using the so-called 'argument from design' to prove the existence of God. But his reference to 'tradition' and 'instruction' is a clean indication of his approval of scriptural revelation.

It was left to Devendranath Tagore to discard the notion of scriptural infallibility altogether. It will not however, be true to say that he advocated the thorough-going rationalist position of the pre-Darwinian era. He did not expound his beliefs as a 'necessity of reason', but sought their sanction in "a heart that was pure and that was irradiated by knowledge". This somewhat vague terminology was replaced in Keshub Chandra Sen's writings by the term 'Intuition'.

Keshub, writing in September, 1860, in the fourth number of his "Tracts for the Times" (thus) described, what according to him, was the "Basis of Brahmoism." "Its basis is in the depths of human nature. Brahmoism is founded upon those principles of the mind which are above, anterior to and independent of reflection, which the variations of opinion cannot alter or affect. It stands upon intuitions."[3]

He went on to explain the meaning of the term : "Intuition denotes those cognitions which our nature immediately apprehends. To take (an) example,............How do you come to know the reality of the external world ? Is it not true that logic can never give you this knowledge ? The mark of intuition is immidiacy. Intuitive truth is directly cognizable; it is seen face to face."[4]

In another place he wrote : "Are their other religious truths besides the intuitive ? Yes : truths derived from experience."[5]

He examined possible objections to the Doctrine of Intuitions and cited a host of philosophers who had spoken in favour of intuition. He dismissed the objections as proceeding from "the convenient system of empiricism."

"(Some people) thoroughly ignore the intuitive or *a priori* element in human knowledge and regard it as a capricious sentimentality or at least a derivative cognition. That these prejudices are generally the result of superficial views and indicate a tacit acquiescence in the convenient system of empiricism can hardly be disputed."

If we examine these extracts a bit closely, we notice that they certainly embody a species of rationalism, but it hardly corresponds to the predominant rationalist position of the 18th century philosophers in regard to the truth of religious beliefs. Keshub's Intuitionism was hardly in consonance with the empirical spirit of the age; and his somewhat derogatory reference to the "convenient system of empiricism" gave his position away. The real danger of Keshub's 'Doctrine of Intuition' lay in this : the so-called 'objective' intuition of the philosophers ran the hazard of becoming far more 'subjective' and arbitrary than book revelation.[6]

From Keshub to Bankim the chronological interval was small—both were born in the same year—but in the world of ideas they had very little resemblance. Bankim must have noted with care how the progress of Brahmoism towards the rationalist creed, first, by renouncing book revelation, then by appealing to the universal, objective intuition of the philosophers gradually sank into the quagmire of the subjective intuitions of Keshub's later career. What is certain is that, in his search for the 'basis of religion' he was careful to exclude any appeal to the sort of 'intuitionism' preached by philosophers, but devoted himself to a consideration of the

11

view-point of science—the so-called 'convenient system of empiricism' mentioned by Keshub Chandra Sen. Extracts from Bankim's writings will make this clear.

Referring to the general run of Brahmans, Christian, Musalmans and Jews who subscribed to the doctrine of revelation and distinguishing from these a second class of thinkers amongst whom he counted himself, Bankim wrote :[7] "The second class of thinkers say that there is no adequate ground for the belief that any religion or any religious scripture is revealed. Such is the opinion held, for example by thinkers of the Schools of Buddhists, Comteans, Brahmos and New Hindu thinkers; they recognise no revealed scripture. But this denial of Revelation faces them with the onus of proving that religion has natural, a physical basis. In default of that, religion loses all support,—on what then will it stand ? This physical basis of religion is not an imaginary insubstantial conception; even those thinkers who recognise some religion as revealed by God are not debarred from acknowledging such physical basis.

"The present writer, like a great many latter day interpreters of Hinduism chooses to belong to this second class of thinkers. I do not recognise any religion as made or revealed by God. I hold that religion has some natural, some physical basis."

The importance of this extract derives from the fact that it is by far the clearest statement of the rationalist creed from the pen of a nineteenth century Bengal writer. Although Bankim is content to enlist himself in the class of religious thinkers who include, amongst others, the thinkers of the Brahmo School, the phrase 'physical basis of religion' sufficiently set him apart from those who subscribed to the 'Doctrine of Intuition'. Again this phrase was not to be interpreted as indicating a merely Deistic profession in the manner of eighteenth century rationalists. It did not exclude that, because in another place Bankim made much of the 'Argument from Design' but was careful to note that : "According to (John Stuart Mill) the mechanism of creation points to a creator of the Universe. This is of course an old argument and is far from being an incontrovertible one. There were valid answers to this argument even before the publication of Darwin's theory. But, now Darwin has shown that the design in creation occurs from itself."[8]

This was written in 1875 (B.S. 1282), that is to say, seven years before the controversy with Hastie. Bankim's rationalist position, at the start of his religious career, was thus the post-Darwinian position of scientific agnosticism. We know from some of his autobiographical references that it was in fact more than that. Actually he had passed through a long spell of atheism and when, at last, he began to have glimpses of the truth of religion, it was not through a sudden flash of divination of the 'supersensible', or the electrifying touch of a divinely inspired Guru, but through a rigorous, painstaking logical analysis of human existence, avoiding the futility of all species of logical analysis only by the touch of an insight—human again, and not mystical — developed by a life-long habit of seeing life deeply and 'seeing it whole'.

(B) THE HUMANISTIC APPROACH TO RELIGION

That which Bankim accepted as the 'natural', the 'physical' basis of his religion was not the existence of God or of a supernatural order as a 'necessity of reason,' but something else which marks him out as a thinker much before his time. He approached the religious question from the standpoint of Humanism. Humanism is an old doctrine. As an ethical system aimed at regulating men's lives so as to secure them the highest happiness by rousing all their faculties to the fullest extent, it is as old as the Greeks. But neither the Greeks, with their system of anthropomorphic gods, nor any other people with their diverse religious faiths succeeded in erecting the doctrine of Humanism as a full-fledged substitute for religion. It is only in our own times—

times in which faith in all creeds not amenable to the test of human experience has all but disappeared—that Humanism is fast coming to be recognised as a serious and perhaps the only (scientifically) admissible alternative to religion. Bankim was one of the first thinkers to recognise this. Certainly he was the first to show that a religion of love and devotion was not incompatible with the humanistic approach.

He started with the definition of religion : "That which makes for the highest development of man—a development that is at once physical, mental, and social—that constitutes teligion."[9]

We shall see in the course of the next chapter how this definition of religion brought on its author the bitter animosity of the Brahmos, who promptly condemned the supposed atheism of Bankim. Actually, what galled them most, was not so much the secularity of Bankim's definition as the fact that Bankim in his definition totally ignored the controversy regarding the superiority of a certain form of worship, (in this case, the monotheistic worship advocated by Brahmos) as the crux of the problem of religion but put all the emphasis on conduct. The history of the Brahmo movement during the half-century that elapsed between the years 1828 and 1878, had shown that the questions of worship and social reform were the crucial issues behind all its schisms, and all its religious efforts. Bankim's emphasis on conduct seemed to render that controversy otiose by totally ignoring the question of worship. Actually, Bankim was not ignoring it, he was only relegating it to its proper place by recognising worship as part of conduct,—but his humanistic approach left him no alternative but to start from the basis of conduct, the only possible secular foundation of religion to a mind that accepted the scientific objection to all species of the supersensible. Let us quote another extract to illustrate the secular orientation behind Bankim's search for the essence of religion : "I do not profess to make any one religious by raising the bogey of future existence.........As far as possible, I am excluding the notion from my exposition of religion.   I cannot hope to raise the edifice of religion on the foundation of something which does not subsist in your mind. Moreover, it seems to me that the exclusion of future existence does not necessarily leave religion without a foundation."[10]

What was the foundation then ?   The answer was : the secular pursuit of happiness in which human conduct expressed itself.   But an analysis of happiness showed that it was not a matter of uncultivated sensation as it was usually supposed but the result of applying certain faculties—bodily or mental, as the case may be, to the attainment of certain ends, the faculties themselves being refined by a certain process of culture.[11]   The highest happiness of man, therefore, required the fullest development of his faculties—physical, intellectual, active and aesthetic.[12]   Having reached this step of the argument it was but natural to pursue the notion of the fullest development of the faculties,—and Bankim devoted all the preliminary chapters of his systematic exposition of religion to the clarification of that notion.

Obviously all this was nothing but pure Humanism, reminding us of Plato's educational theory explained in the *Republic* and summed up in the formula 'gymnasium for the body and music for the soul.' More striking was the similarity of Bankim's Humanism to that of Aristotle. It all but approximated to the conception of the 'virtuous man' elaborated in Aristotle's "*Nicomachaean Ethics*."   The parallelism was even more striking in Bankim's doctrine of 'balance' which was almost identical with Aristotle's doctrine of 'mean' and very closely resembles the general Greek notion of 'harmony.' Put in a nutshell, Bankim's conception of 'balance' was that of controlling device for faculties like 'lust' and 'anger', lest they should negate such faculties as 'charity' and 'love for fellow-beings.'   It is, however, to be noted that Bankim derived his doctrine from Hindu sources tracing his whole conception to the verse in the Gita.[13]

"Ragadvesavimuktaistu Visayanindriyaiscaran ।
Atmavasyairvidheyatma prasadamadhigacchti ॥"

"He who seeks pleasure by means of sense, that have been made free of lust and revulsion and rendered subject to his own direction—that man of self-control (Vidheyatma) attains peace." This according to Bankim was the Hindu version of the Greek doctrine of 'harmony' just as the Hindu doctrine of 'regulating the senses' was the basis of his scheme for developing all the human faculties by a 'system of culture.' The question, however, was not how far this scheme was derivable from the scriptures of the Hindus, but how far it constituted a religion at all. Was it not a system of ethics essentially naturalistic and atheistical ? It was indeed a version of a godless glorification of man—an overweening presumption of Man's fragile humanity to shine forth as the 'measure of all things.'

The answer to this question, as furnished by Bankim, was a very simple one, transforming (as in a flash) his tract on Humanism into a work of deep and all-absorbing piety. In essence his answer was that the balanced development of the faculties was unattainable except by turning them all towards God, or,—to put the matter in more naturalistic terms—except by making all the faculties subservient to the faculty of *Bhakti* (reverential love). In his own words : "The condition in which a person's intellectual faculties get directed towards God, the active faculties are dedicated to Him, the aesthetic faculties flourish in the enjoyment of His beauty and the physical faculties apply themselves to His work—I call that condition *Bhakti*."[14]

Again "the true harmony of all the faculties is in their subservience to *Bhakti*."[15]

It is obvious that with this idea, wonderful as it is, Bankim goes beyond the limits of strict humanism and introduces a certain non-human element into his religion. He introduces God as a supremely perfect Personal Being who pervades the whole universe[16] and acts as a rallying point[17] of all human faculties, which thereby get harmonised and become the perfect instruments for the noblest type of human action imaginable. It should not be thought for a moment that with the introduction of God, Bankim abandons 'humanism', but with this introduction follows an exposition of a naturalistic ethics which is as profound in its simplicity as it is magnificent in its comprehensiveness.

Briefly, it is this. *Bhakti*, though directed towards a non-human personal Being, is nevertheless the quintessence of all human activities seeking expression in action that is purely human because the Divinity is in essence "a Being pervading the whole universe and work aimed at Him is work aimed at the world."[18] According to Bankim, such work constitutes the best worship, popular worship, idolatrous or otherwise, being essentially secondary and aiming at the worshipper's own purification of heart.[19]   Bhakti is therefore humanistic worship *par excellence*, and this doctrine must be regarded as Bankim's answer to the main point of all Brahmo and Christian criticisms of Hinduism (the criticism that Hindu worship was aimed at stocks and stones).

(C)   MONOTHEISM AND PANTHEISM

Bankim makes much of the fact that the love that embraces the whole world is a logical corollary of the Hindu conception of God as the "soul of the world " Humanitarianism is thus of the very essence of the Hindu's religion. Since God pervades all humanity—and indeed all *creation*, Bhakti towards God of necessity includes love for everything that exists. Bankim contrasts this pantheistic conception of God with the monotheism of Christianity and Brahmoism. Without anywhere mentioning the Brahmos by name, he obviously intends to make this point as a serious criticism of their doctrine. As he puts it : "The God of the Christian is beyond the world. No doubt He is its lord, but just as the king of Gemany or Russia is a person essentially different from the mass of his German or Russian subjects, so is God of the Christian ...... To love Him one has to make (an attempt at a) special expansion of one's faculty of love as in the act of loving a temporal king.

Not so the God of the Hindu. He pervades all creation ...... He is in me. When I love myself, I love Him. If I do not love Him I do not love myself either ...... If I do not love all humanity, I would not be loving Him, I would not be loving myself ...... Thus love of the world is in the very foundations of Hinduism."[20]

This is not to suggest that he intends to depreciate the humanitarian work done by either Christians or Brahmos. Indeed, in the next section we shall see that it was Bankim's contention that the doctrine of humanitarianism had remained virtually a dead letter amongst the Hindu for ages past and that the revival of that doctrine was one of the chief aims of the New Hindu Movement. But the criticism implicit in the contrast of the humanitarianism of the Pantheist with that of the Monotheist was doubtless a way of winning over converts to Brahmoism to the Hindu fold.

But there is an implication of this criticism which is of greater importance from the standpoint of Bankim's rationalism. We have just seen that the basic point of his criticism of Christian—(we should say Judaeo-Christian)—monotheism is this : Such monotheism presupposes an External God, a God "who is beyond the world". The notion of such a deity is of course foreign to the spirit of science, which would have nothing of an entity that lies essentially outside the domain of experience. Not only that. His distance from humanity, renders it difficult for love towards Him to flow spontaneously. Neither of these defects are operative in the case of the sort of Personal Pantheism professed by Hindus.

Bankim thus attempted to find some natural, some physical basis of religion in consonance with the spirit of the post-Darwinian rationalism of 19th century Europe. His natural basis consisted of the following steps :

1) He started from the universal natural urge to happiness and showed that happiness was not a matter of uncultivated sensation but presupposed a stage of development in certain faculties aiming at certain ends.

2) This led him to the doctrine of the fullest development of the faculties.

3) As the faculties themselves clashed among themselves, he was led to the doctrine of balance.

4) The balance could not be attained except by directing the faculties to some rallying point, a non-human Personal Being, who allowed them the fullest development by curbing some and letting the others run their full course.

5) Such a Personal Being was God in the Hindu conception, that is, a Being who pervaded all creation.

6) The direction of the faculties to God implied their balance in their fullest development. It implied the resolution of the conflict of self-regarding impulses with other-regarding ones. It implied the resolution of the conflict between self-love and love of humanity. It caused the fullest development of the active faculties by being aimed at God who was in all creation[21] ; and of the intellectual faculties by requiring knowledge of the most comprehensive kind to get a proper understanding of God, because knowledge of God involved knowledge of all creation, of the nature of the God-seeking soul and of God's relation to both.[22] The same was true as regards the faculty of love. The direction of the faculties to God necessitated the fullest development of the faculty of love so that it could embrace all creation.

7) Thus the humanistic pursuit of happiness, on analysis, led to the three ultimate aims of Humanism : Bhakti to God, love to humanity and peace in heart. These in their totality constituted the 'whole virtue of man' in his humanness. These alone made for lasting happiness.[23]

Such was the rationalistic structure of Bankim's 'Natural Religion'. The special results were :

First, the new doctrine of Hindu worship which in its

12

best form consisted in self-less action that aimed at the
service of humanity. The controversy as to the idolatrous or
non-idolatrous worship was resolved by relegating them both
to a secondary position. It is only necessary to add that such
selfless action was preached in the Gita. Thus Bankim's
rationalism led him to the doctrine of Nishkam Karma.

Secondly, Humanitarianism was seen to be of the
essence of Hinduism—which partly distinguishes Hinduism
from Christianity or Brahmoism.

Thirdly, the comparison of Judaeo-Christian monotheism with the Personal Pantheism of the Hindus pointed
to the superiority of the latter from the standpoint of Reason
as well as that of Bhakti,

(D)   THE ACTIVISM OF THE GITA

In emphasising the 'natural basis' of religion and its
rationalistic structure as constructed by Bankim, we have refrained from giving a proper summary of his religious views
in their totality. In particular, we have said nothing as to
their political implications. In 'Dharmatattwa' Bankim in-
corporated certain doctrines about political action as direct
corollaries of his conception of "action aimed at God."
These were of the highest significance in providing the ideological framework of what has been called Religious Nationalism. We shall discuss them in their proper place when we
come to explain the nature of that nationalism. We discuss
here his doctrine of action, the so-called Activism of the
Gita, which is an important aspect of New Hindu doctrines.
It was a doctrine of the profoundest significance, forming
as it were, the essence of the teachings of Swami Vivekananda, Lokamanya Tilak and Mahatma Gandhi. It will be
hardly an exaggeration to say that with the introduction of
this doctrine the whole conception of Hinduism has undergone a permanent change. The religion that was concerned
with 'personal salvation' alone throughout its past history
and in its social aspect included a mass of obsolete and

obstructive social customs was shown capable of a social significance which its past adherents had done nothing to exploit and little to understand.

This social significance was attributed to the doctrine of 'action' as explained in the *Gita*. But before explaining that doctrine let us listen to Bankim's own words regarding the traditional, theological interpretation of that doctrine and how the decline of the Hindus was sought in such an interpretation of their religion.

Referring to Verse 2/47 of the *Gita*, where action is praised and perfect indifference to the fruits of the action is impressed upon the religious seeker, Bankim says : "Some of the commentators of Hindu scriptures have confused the meaning of this verse (by an interpretation which is absolutely unwarranted). Thanks to them, we have been led to believe that karma (action) in this and similar contexts means sacrifices prescribed in the Vedas......According to this view, the verse prescribes Vedic sacrifices but speaks against desire for heaven which is the end of such sacrifices."[24]

Elsewhere Bankim discusses the influence of such interpretation on Hindu history : "The greatest men in India had, in their religion, taken to the 'path of knowledge.' They had decided that action was not for people who followed the path of knowledge, and, in that belief they held action in great contempt. Their example was followed by the whole of India, rendering her lost to all desire for a life of action. The result of all this was a vast over-crowding of never-do-wells in the land leading to its present state of decline."[25]

This historical view of the traditional doctrine of action led Bankim to press the doctrine in its secular sense ;—in his view, this was the sense in which *the Gita* had preached it. He pointed out with great force that the Verse 3/5 and 3/8, where the *Gita* was asserting how it was impossible to exist even for a moment without some sort of action could hardly be interpreted by taking action to mean Vedic sacrifice but obviously intended it as a Law of Life. Bankim elaborated this theme of Action as a Law of Life, and connecting it with his humanistic treatment of religion, showed that the *Gita* had been preaching the sort of action that was aimed at God, who was not a Being outside the world but one who pervaded all creation.[26] In other words, (as we pointed out earlier) the action preached by the *Gita* was aimed primarily at the service of all creation and only secondarily at ritualistic worship.[27]

We have only to compare Bankim's commentary on the 'Doctrine of Action' with that of Mahatma Gandhi to understand the revolution in Hindu thought brought about by Bankim's interpretation of that doctrine. Regarding the same doctrine the Mahatma says : "I look upon *Chapter-3 of the Gita* as the key to its meaning ; and what I regard as the essence of that chapter is this : Life is for service, not for pleasure."[28]

Again, "the usually accepted notion of a Bhakta is that of an indolent man who counts his beads…He will lift his hand from his beads only to take his food. He won't do so to work a machine or to do some service to the poor. (But) the *Gita* explicitly says : 'Success (in religion) is not to be had without action.'[29]

We see in these extracts a perfect identity with Bankim's view. It is true the Mahatma is referring to the traditional notion of a Bankim, whereas Bankim's objection was to the traditional notion of 'a man of knowledge',—but the two views only add up to the fact that 'men of religion' in India were 'men of inaction.' This identity of views inevitably leads us to the question ; From which source did the Mahatma derive his interpretation of the Gita's doctrine of action ?

It is not wholly impossible that he got it direct from Bankim. The Mahatma's commentary had its origin in the studies he had undertaken during his years of imprisonment in connection with the Non-cooperation Movement. It is, however, unlikely that he had gone through Bankim's commentary for that commentary does not seem to have been translated into Gujrati (or English). But among the books the Mahatma went through in prison there is an explicit mention of a Gujrati version of Bankim's *"Krishna-charitra."*[30] In that book occurs the specific atement :

"The doctrine of action had been current even before Krishna's time. But according to the accepted view of that doctrine 'Karma' meant vedic sacrifice. In the religion that was current (before Krishna's time) the word 'Karma' was not employed to mean the totality of acts which the Westerners designate by the title 'Duty', and which a man is required to do during the course of his life. It is only in the *Gita* that we see the word 'Karma' to have shed its accepted meaning and to have taken up (the extended sense).[31]

But did the Mahatma derive his interpretation from a study of this passage ? It is certainly possible that he did, but there is no positive evidence to suggest that this was in fact the case. It is far more likely that he got the hint from his study of Tilak's commentary. From which source then did Tilak get the idea ?

It is well known that there was a traffic in ideas from Bengal to Maharashtra right from the days when Keshub Chandra Sen founded the Prarthna Samaj in Bombay (1867). It is also well known that the vogue for the *Gita* in Bengal amongst her English-educated public started with Bankim's commentary.[32] The Maharastrian fervour for the *Gita* and its doctrine of action could well be the result of a transmission of ideas to Maharastra from Bengal.[33] It is a distinct possibility that Tilak was one amongst the many who were in the receiving end of that process of transmission. But again the evidence is not conclusive. For all we know Tilak may have hit upon his interpretation of the 'doctrine of action' in the same manner as Bankim did—by some original impulse of his mind. There was of course an element common to both : the temper of the time was decidedly against a ritualistic interpretation of the scriptures.

But whatever the influence exercised by Bankim's commentary on the *Gita* on the long line of commentators including such distinguished names as Tilak, Aurobindo and Mahatma Gandhi, it is clear that Bankim was the first in the line to propound the doctrine of action in its currently accepted sense. He was also the first Hindu to break the tradition of sectarian interpretation of such ideas as 'Svadharma' (one's caste duty) by giving to that expression the rendering of 'duty assumed by oneself voluntarily.' This—if nothing else—places Bankim securely in the front rank of the religious thinkers of Modern India.

E) THE NEW CONCEPTION OF BHAKTI

It must also be mentioned that the new humanistic conception of Bhakti as the balancing faculty of all other faculties, which is to be considered Bankim's most original contribution to religious thought of Bengal at the time had its origin in some verses of the *Gita*. Bankim mentions in particular the verse (Gita 3/30) in which Krishna urges Arjuna to dedicate all his actions to God. The *Gita* does not speak of such actions as are accepted by all to be otherworldly—but all sorts of action including the soldier's action in the battlefield. Also in another place Krishna urges Arjuna to dedicate not only his actions, but all his human efforts from the taking of food to the giving of alms.[34] It is from such hints as these that Bankim reaches his own conception of Bhakti. It was from this new conception that the idea of serving one's country as an act of worship ultimately derived. This idea exercised a great influence on our national struggle. In the Swadeshi Movement this idea was given practical shape, though in that movement it was perverted enough to produce in some young minds the conviction that even the killing of Englishmen if undertaken without any thought of personal gain, could be considered an act of worship. We shall discuss the causes of this perversion in its proper place. But here we must mention that the same idea was propagated in a purer form during Mahatma Gandhi's movement. Here again Bankim must be looked upon as a pioneer.

NOTES AND REFERENCES

1. Charles Robert Darwin (1809-82) : *Origin of Species*, 1859.
2. *The Life and Letters of Raja Rammohan Roy* : Sophia Dobson Collet, edited by D. K. Biswas, 1962, pp. 109-110. p. 16.
3. *Life and Works of Brahmananda Keshav* : Prem Sunder Basu, p. 16.
4. *Ibid.* p. 16.
5. *Ibid.,* pp. 30-31.
6. "Revelation is subjective, not objective." Prem Sunder Bose : *Life and Works of Brahmananda Keshab.* p. 31
7. *Bankim Rachanavali*, Samsad, vol. 2. pp. 791-92.

(কোন পথে যাইতেছি ?)

8. *Ibid.,* p. 273. ত্রিদেব সম্বন্ধে বিজ্ঞানশাস্ত্র কি বলে ?
9. Devatattwa O Hindu Dharma: *Bankim Rachanavali, vol.* 2. Sahitya Samsad p. 778.

cf. I yield to none in the firmness of my conviction in the existence of the great Author of Nature and my trust in his Providence...... (But I am not one who think that a belief in God or in a number of Gods or in a future existence or in anything else which does not admit of proof constitutes religion. But when such belief or any belief whatever, furnishes a basis for conduct—for the conduct of the individual towards himself as well as towards others, when by becoming a common faith and therefore furnishing a common basis of conduct, it becomes a bond of union between man and man, a standard by which human existence individual and aggregate, comes to be regulated, it is religion. : "Letters to Hinduism" : *Bankim Rachanavali* Sahitya Samsad, vol. III, p. 237).

10. Bankim Chandra : *Dharmatattwa* Chapter VII.
11. *Ibid.* Chapter-II : what are the elements of happiness ? First, the cultivation of mental and physical faculties and their development and refinement brought about by such cultivation. Second, the balance of the faculties with one another. Third, their satisfaction in that balanced state of development and refinement.

12. *Ibid.* Chapter-V.
13. *Srimatbhagbat Gita*, 2/64.
14. *Dharmatattwa :* Chapter-XI.
15. *Ibid.*
16. *Dharmatattwa* : Chapter XXI. See the comparison between the conception of Hindu God and Christian God.
17. See the discussion in Chapter-V on August Comte's influence on Bankim. The expression 'rallying point' occurs in Comte's naturalistic definition of religion. See also Appendix-B, *Dharmatattwa*.
18. *Dharmatattwa* : Chapter-XX.
19. *Ibid.*
20. *Dharmatattwa* : Chapter-XXI.
21. *Dharmatattwa* : Chapter-XIV.
22. *Ibid.* Chapter-XV.
23. *Ibid.* Chapter-XI.
24. *Srimatbhagbat Gita* : Vide Bankim's Commentary on verse 2/47.
25. *Ibid.* Commentary on verse 3/21.

> "Yad yadacarati Sresthastattadevetars janah /
> Sa yat pramanam Kurute lokastadanuvartate //

(For whatsoever a great man does, that very thing other men also do, whatever standard be set up, the generality of men fo low the same.)

> "কর্ম্মণ্যে বাধিকারন্তে মা ফলেষু কদাচন ।
> মা কর্মফল হেতুভূ'মা তে সঙ্গোহস্তকর্ম্মনি ॥

26. *Srimatbhagbat Gita* : Bankim's Commentary on verse 2/47. Also *Dharmatattwa* Chapter-XIV.
27. *Dharmatattwa* ; Chapter-XX : Teacher : I advise you to dedicate yourself to work for the sake of God.
Disciple : But is that not puja or homa or some sort of sacrifice.
Teacher : No, that is an error. These are not work for the sake of God. They aim at the seeker's own benefit. Even if you perform them for the increase of Bhakti (and not for any concrete benefit that may accrue to you), even then they aim at your own benefit. But as God pervades the whole world,......that which aims at it the benefit of the world properly constitutes the sort of work which Krishna (i.e. God) calls my work."

It may be noted in this connection that just as Bankim humanised the *Gita* doctrine of action by delivering it from the traditional ritualistic interpretation put to it by the long life of commentators from Sankaracharya to Sridhar Goswami, in the same manner he recovered the Hindu notion of charity from the same narrow ritualism serving the interest of a selfish class of priests. Referring to the Gita verse 17/20 on charity which commended the sort of charity of which the receiver was to be one from whom no return was to be expected and which satisfied the criteria of being meant for the right sort of receiver and for the right sort of occasion or place, Bankim pointed out how so self-explanatory an injunction was interpreted by traditional commentators to indicate something quite different from the obvious humanitarian intent of the Verse. 'Right sort of receiver' was interpreted by both Sankar and Sridhar to mean "Brahmans of high Scholarship" ; 'right occasion' was interpreted as some auspicious day of the lunar calendar ; and 'right place' was interpreted as a place of pilgrimage. Bankim asserted that as the verse contained nothing to suggest so fantastic a notion of charity, but obviously enjoined it for the needy sweeper as much as for the needy Brahmin. We have to guard against ortho-dox commentators who often transformed the lofty religion of the Hindus into a narrow, dogmatic pseudo-religion of the priests.

28. M. K. Gandhi : *Gitabodh,* Chapter 3.
29. *Preface to Anasakti Yoga : Gandhiji's Commentary on the Gita.* p. 21.
30. *Gandhi Rachanasambhar* : vol. 3. Gandhi Centenary Samiti (West Bengal), Chapter XI (My Study).
31. *Bankim Rachanavali :* Sahitya Samsad : "Krishnacharitra" p. 533.
32. Ramendra Sundar Trivedi writing twelve years after Bankim's death (i. e. 1906) says : "Gita was not widely read by the English-educated people when Bankim Chandra started his commentary on it. But when Bankim is at the root of anything it gets wide publicity". *Charitkatha.*
33. Nabin Chandra Sen in his autobiography says in regard to the enthusiasm for the Gita in Calcutta during the eighties : "It was Bankim's genius that produced a craze for the Gita in Calcutta". *'Amar Jiban'.*
34. *Srimatbhagbat Gita* : 9/27-28

13

CHAPTER - V
THE BRAHMO REACTION

AN IMMEDIATE consequence of the labours of Bankim and Vivekananda was a considerable weakening of the hold of Brahmoism on the minds of the English-educated Hindus of Bengal. That it was the New Hindu Movement which was the most powerful factor in the decline of Brahmoism has to be emphasized because Brahmo historians, and following in their footsteps, the generality of the historians of the atheistic school, have sought the cause of that decline in the rise of Revivalism. As they have used it, 'revivalism' is an omnibus expression under which they have chosen to include beliefs and practices so diverse as those held by different schools such as the schools of Sasadhar, the pseudo rationalist, Annie Besant, the Theosophist, Bankim, the humanist-rationalist and Vivekananda, the Neo-Vedantist. It is relevant here to point out that contemporary Brahmos clearly understood the nature of the threat created for this movement by the ideas propagated by Bankim and Vivekananda. The charge they levelled against Bankim was not one of revivalism. On the contrary, they called Bankim an atheist —a positivist of Auguste Comte's school. As regards Vivekananda, they refrained from attacking his ideas, but sought the more convenient expedient of character-assassination.[1] It is only fair to add that the Brahmo Samaj which included men so famous and great as Rammohan Roy, Devendranath Tagore and Keshub Chandra Sen,—not to mention a host of other persons of unquestioned piety and purity of character, could not as a whole be guilty of such scurrility which was confined to small sections of the Brahmo public. But the infamous libel on Vivekananda's character was spread by no less a person than Pratap Chandra Mozoomdar, the biographer of Keshub Chandra Sen and the leader of his congregation since his master's death. Shibnath Sastri, likewise, in his celebrated historical work on the Bengal

Renaissance (*Ramtanu Lahiri O Tatkalin Banga Samaj*), introduced a sentence, which insinuated that in point of excellence of character, Bankim fell short of Keshub Chandra Sen, who was Sivnath's erstwhile spiritual guide, and also of Dwarakanath Vidyabhusan, who was his (Sivnath's) uncle. Needless to add, Sivnath did not care to substantiate his charge by citing any actual instance of Bankim's deficiency. Clearly, Brahmoism was in desperate straits and was in search of scapegoates on whom to blame its own dying influence on the new generation of educated Hindus seeking spiritual sustenance in the writings of Bankim and Vivekananda. An opinion has gained ground, that Bankim and Vivekananda, were, in some unethical way, instrumental in the weakening of the hold of Brahmoism. The truth is just the reverse. Brahmoism had been dying a natural death since the promulgation of the Native Marriage Act in 1872, when it professedly dissociated itself from the Hindu fold. The ideas of Bankim and Vivekananda destroyed its claim to intellectual superiority and severely weakened it. The attacks on Bankim and Vivekananda in a way recoiled on Brahmoism and hastened its downfall. We chronicle below some of these attacks on Bankim in the actual order they had taken place.

A) THE ATTACK ON BANKIM

Since the time of Rammohan, the Brahmo religious views and activities came in opposition to those of the orthodox Hindus. From Rammohan to the establishment of the Sadharan Brahmo Samaj, the Brahmo movement had undergone many doctrinal changes through successive stages, their rallying points being the monotheism of the Vedas and the Upanishads and the attack on Puranic religion and idolatry with all its elaborate rituals and sacrifices. As we pointed out, the theoretical basis of Brahmoism was Intuitionism as expounded by Keshub and adumbrated in Devendranath Tagore's formula of 'a pure heart irradiated by knowledge'

as the basis of religious truths. Bankim's exposition of 'a natural, a physical' basis of religion was powerful enough to al-
arm them.

It is interesting to note that the Adi Brahmo Samajists
responded at once to the writings of Bankim. Not to speak of
the other group of the Brahmos, even the orthodox Hindus
did not welcome Bankim's interpretation. The Adi Brahmo
Samaj led by Debendranath Tagore and Rajnarain Bose had
so long been steering a middle course in their attempt to res-
tore national glory as well as to follow a policy of reform.
They had no radical programme of social reform. They concentrated on Vedantic monotheism and eradication of idolatry believing that the Brahmoism they followed and preached,
was in consonance with true Hinduism and, that this should
be followed by all enlightened Hindus. Thus, they argued
they were the real preservers of all the glories of the Hindus.
Both the new reformists and the old conservatives, according
to them, were equally in the wrong. That was why no anti-
Hindu ceremony or ritual would get their approval or patronage. They neither supported Keshub Chunder's Intercaste
Marriage Bill nor approved of widow remarriage that
Vidyasagar tried to introduce. Despite all these, new Hindu
thinkers like Bankim did not recognise their claims to be the
preservers and followers of true Hinduism. While reviewing
Rajnarain Bose's treatise *Hindu Dharmer Shresthatta* in
Vangadarsan, Bankim showered praises on the author and
welcomed such writings, but (he) differed on the main purport
of Rajnarain. Bankim wrote[2], "It can be easily inferred
that the author should make an attempt to establish the
superiority of what he himself considers to be the Hindu
Religion. Hindu Dharma, according to him, consists in the
worship of Brahman and therefore, worship of Brahman is
the best Religion, and his end in view must be to establish
the superiority of this Dharma and it cannot be his aim to
establish the superiority of the Dharma (or Religion) in
general of the country. He says, Hindu Dharma is the best

Dharma, but he does not agree that the religion as it is extant among the people in general is not the best religion. The worship of Para Brahma—the Highest Being, is the very essence of all religions."

Bankim continued, "The Religion, he (the author) upholds, is to be found deep down in the Hindu Sastras and there is no doubt about it. But, that is only a part of Hindu religion and a small part of it. To equate the part of a thing with the whole of it is anything but truth. Almost all things have something of it that is praiseworthy. The Worship of Brahman alone cannot be termed as Hindu Dharma."

Evidently, Bankim did not accept the monotheism of the Vedanta as preached by the Brahmos as the essence of Hinduism. Hence a clash between New Hindu thinkers and the Adi Brahmo Samajists was inevitable. It came about some twelve years after the publication of Bankim's review of Rajnarain's work.

The immediate occasion for such a controversy was supplied by the publication of two periodical papers *Navajivan* and *Prachar*. 'Navajivan' was edited by Akshoy Chandra Sarkar, a writer of some fame and a friend of Bankim. In the opening number of *Navajivan*, Bankim contributed an article under the caption 'Dharmajijnasa' (An enquiry into the Meaning of Religion), clearly indicating his preference for a humanistic definition of Religion, and quoting with approval the definition[3] proposed by Auguste Comte, the founder of Positivism. In *Prachar*, likewise, he wrote an article entitled 'Hindu Dharma' (The Hindu Religion), in which, following the same humanistic approach, he asserted that 'that alone was true religion which furthered the cause of human development—physical, mental and social', According to Bankim, the essence of Hinduism (and not everything that currently passed for Hinduism) approximated to this definition closely enough to necessitate a re-examination of the *Shastras* in the light of that definition. The only sentence in this article that might provoke the Brahmos

—although the sentence was not provocative at all—was
this : "Brahmoism is only a branch of Hinduism, and it be-
trays no symptom that could make one presume that it would
in future be generally accepted as a social religion."[4]

It does not seem to be provocative in tone, however
it did provoke the Adi Brahmo Samaj leaders so much as
to make them start a regular campaign against Bankim in
which sober criticism was mixed with vulgar vituperation.
The sober criticism was furnished by Dwijendranath Tagore,
Devendranath's eldest son and the then editor of *Tattwabodhini*. Dwijendranath questioned the humanistic approach
to religion and argued that furtherance of happiness, which
in Bankim's approach, was to be the ultimate test of religious
truth was not an adequate test. Incidentally Dwijendranath
attributed atheism to Bankim and said, "According to
Bankim Baboo God and Life after death have no necessary
connection with Religion."

This is sober criticism, though it is clear from what
we have seen in Chapter-IV, that Dwijendranath was misled
by Bankim's humanistic approach to suspect him of atheism
which was furthest from the case. But Dwijendranath was
hardly to be blamed, because, his criticism, being based on
the first instalment of Bankim's contributions to *Navajivan*,
could not anticipate the complete development of Bankim's
humanistic approach. But Dwijendranath's sober criticism
was accompanied (in the same number of *Tattwabodhini*) by
an article by Rajnarain Bose, the then President of Adi
Brahmo Samaj, which was far from sober criticism. It is interesting that Rajnarain accepted Bankim's humanistic test of
a religion ("that which contributes to man's development—
physical, mental and social"), with (his) whole heart[5] but
claimed that Brahmoism alone passed that test fully. But he
accused Bankim of being a follower of Comte and reviled
him with the title "an infamous follower of Comte" (an alternative meaning of this expression is "a follower of Comte's
infamous doctrines.") Also he called Bankim an 'atheist'.

Very soon Rajnarain was followed by an article in *Navya Bharat* by Kailash Chandra Sinha, the Assistant Secretary of the Adi Brahmo Samaj at the time. Kailash Chandra's article was thoroughly scurrilous. In fact, it seems to have been inspired by malice since it did not criticise the religious views of Bankim at all, but attacked a historical piece 'Infamy of Bengal' contributed by Bankim to *Prachar*. But the undercurrent of religious hostility was betrayed in Kailash Chandra's slighting reference to *Vangadarsan*, *Navajivan* and *Prachar*. Kailash Chandra's vituperative style reached the limits of virulence in the concluding passage of his article where he addressed Bankim thus : "Oh Bengali writer ! if you intend to write history, first of all study thousands and thousands of books. Examine with care the texts of verses discovered (by scholars), but don't you depend on anybody's translation blindly. No purpose will be served by licking the feet of scholars like Wilson, Weber, Maxmuller and Cunningham. Nor should you enter the garden cared for by Muir, Bhao Daji, Mair, Mitra and Hunter to undertake the pursuit of a thief. Take up independent research. If you are incapable of that, desist from posing as a teacher."

But Kailash Chandra's attack, was not the last, to be aimed at Bankim. The most virulent attack came from Rabindranath Tagore who was at that time the Secretary of the Adi Brahmo Samaj. While contrasting a certain orthodox Hindu of the old type, who observed all *shastric* rites but was throughly unprincipled in point of true morality, with another Hindu whose deficiency in *shastric* observances was made up by the excellence of his morals, Bankim had written in the article "Hindu Dharma," "This man never tells a lie, but if he does tell one, he does so when the good of humanity makes a lie imperatively necessary, according to a saying of Krishna's in the *Mahabharata*,--that is to say, when lie becomes the truth."

It is obvious that Bankim's sentence was ambiguous enough to make one uncomfortable as to his notion of truth.

Tagore made it the plea for an attack on Bankim's exposition of religion : "Our greatest writer has publicly, shamelessly, fearlessly placed truth and falsehood on the same pedestal. When everyone is quarrelling about the form of worship—idolatrous or otherwise—the basis of religion is being attacked unobserved. No one is coming forward to protect religion and society from that attack. Had cowardice and falsehood not got mingled in the blood of our veins, could our chief writer dare pronounce a single word against truth with such arrogance by taking his stand in the middle of the street ?"

With the publication of Tagore's lecture Bankim broke his silence.

(B) BANKIM'S REJOINDER

It was characteristic of Bankim that, amidst this fury of assault on his character and his religious views, for which he had not given the slightest of provocations, he held his peace with impenetrable dignity. But when Tagore, who, as a valued friend and a younger contemporary, had paid him a great many visits since the publication of his *Prachar* article without ever breathing a word of uneasiness on the score of his (Bankim's) conception of truth, suddenly came out in the open to attack him as a "destroyer of the basis of religion", he decided on a reply. His reply was a mixture of wounded pride, unstinted affection, and highminded solicitude for the avoidance of sectarian frenzy. Also it breathed unutterable scorn for such calumniators as Kailash Chandra Sinha, and supremely polished sarcasm for such fanatics as Rajnarayan.

The reply itself—or rather the operative part of it could thus be summed up. Bankim thanked Dwijendranath for the kindness and sobriety displayed in his criticism but pointed out that had Dwijendranath waited for the full development of his (Bankim's) thought, he (Dwijendranath) would have seen that he (Bankim) was far from being an atheist To Rabindranath he said that his reference to the saying of Krishna involved an instance where truth would lead to murder and thus his acceptance of the utilitarian test (namely, the good of humanity) of truth did not really amount to placing truth and falsehood on the same pedestal, as Rabindranath had implied.

At this point it is worthwhile quoting Bankim's general address to the Adi Brahmo Samaj, which he inserted at the close of his reply. It brings out with unmistakable clarity his attitude to sectarian frenzy in religious discussions. It ran : "I cherish a special regard for the Adi Brahmo Samaj. I am aware that this society has done quite a lot for the betterment of religion in our country and that it is doing so still. I cherish (no little) hope that, from the society, of which Babu Devendranath Tagore, Babu Rajnarain Bose and Babu Dwijendranath Tagore are the leaders, we shall learn many (useful) lessons. But we can hardly hope to learn them through quarrels and altercations. In particular, I believe that the Adi Brahmo Samaj writers have been, and are still being, instrumental in the development of Bengali literature—a literature, for the cause of which we have dedicated our lives. Certainly I am but a small man, and I quite recognise that not anything that the Adi Brahmo Samaj writers would count of any consequence has been, or can be, achieved by me. But no man's sincere effort goes utterly futile. However small the result, quarrels and wranglings can only lessen its output. Even small men achieve great things by helping one another. I say then : Let the Adi Brahmo Samaj writers cease to indulge in such quarrels. For myself, I stop here finally and permanently. They will no doubt do as their own conscience advises them."

It is only necessary to add that the Adi Brahmo Samaj writers' response to Bankim's plea was both honourable and dignified. In particular Rabindranath's later reference to this incident was one of gratefully recollecting the elder writers' forbearance and forgiveness once the controversy was over.

The only discordant voice was perhaps that of Kailash Chandra Sinha, who increasingly indulged in scurrility. But Kailash Chandra was of course a man of little consequence in the field of religion or letters. He was a non-entity.

(C) THE EXTENT OF WESTERN INFLUENCE ON BANKIM

This is the place to attempt an assessment of the extent of Western influence on Bankim's religious thought. We have just seen how Rajnarain reviled Bankim with the epithet "an infamous follower of Comte". But Rajnarain was perhaps only the first to insinuate, by using such language, that Bankim's Hinduism was not Hindu enough to deserve respectful recognition by "true Hindus." The fact of the matter was that Rajnarain had a personal axe to grind : in his view, "true Hinduism" was the doctrine followed by the 'Brahmos led by Devendranath.' Later detractors of Bankim, with far less excuse than Rajnarain, have repeated the allegation. Some of them have said that he was a follower of John Stuart Mill, others that his master was not Mill but the now-forgotten British essayist Seeley, some have gone to the length of seeking the seeds of his humanism in the writings of Keshub Chandra Sen. What, however, such detractors of Bankim have attempted to establish is not the falsehood of his Hinduism – in fact it is his very Hinduism which they find the most objectionable feature in Bankim's thought. Their criticism implies that he was not westernised enough to shed the last vestige of his Hindu ancestry. It aims at showing that he was not an original thinker, but a mere follower of his European masters.

We have already seen(in Chapter-IV) how Bankim's conception of humanism came close to the Greek model. But in chapter-IV, we did not discuss Bankim's debt to utilitarianism. Tagore's criticism of the utilitarian test of truth made Bankim clarify his stand with regard to that doctrine; he indicated very clearly the place of utilitarianism in his exposition of religion. But first of all we need to say something about Auguste Comte's influence on his religious thought.

(i) *Positivism and Bankim*

Comte was possibly the first philosopher to use the expression, Religion of Humanity, to describe an atheistic doctrine in which the abstraction named Humanity was to be worshipped in place of super-sensible 'external God' worshipped by the followers of Christ. But Humanity is of course not a personal Being and we have seen that the whole point of Bankim's religion was that the God envisaged by Hindus was emphatically a personal Being "who pervaded all creation" and thereby avoided the objection raised against the "External God" of Monotheism. We have designated Bankim's theology as Personal Pantheism, which is the notion of Personal God combined with what may be called Pure Pantheism. Neither of these features is to be found in Comte. The distinction between positivism and pantheism is clearly indicated by Bankim himself. Let us quote his words in full : "2) "A second answer (to the problem of religion) is that of Auguste Comte and his disciples. We know that the Universe exists, and that it is governed by laws. Beyond these laws we know nothing and can know nothing ; laws may be self-existent for aught we know. We do not know that they are otherwise......This alone, strictly speaking, is atheism.

3) The third answer seeks to reconcile the other two. It grants that there may be a first cause, and it admits Nature and her laws, if not exactly to be self-existent, but what very nearly amounts to the same thing. Granted, there is a first cause, but why should we seek it beyond Nature ? Is it impossible that the cause of the Universe should be in itself ? God, it says, is in nature ; and all phenomena his manifestations. This is Pantheism."[6]

These extracts clearly show that 'positivism' has little, if any, connection with Bankim's religious views.[7] What then was Comte's influence on Bankim's religious exposition ? What was it that roused Rajnarain's ire ? If we analyse Comte's definition of religion which Bankim quoted with approval in the 'Navajivan' article, we see it is a similarity of approach to religious questions, which characterise both these thinkers. The definition in question is this : "Religion, in itself, expresses the state of perfect *unity* which is the distinctive mark of man's existence both as an individual and in society, when all the constituent parts of his nature moral and physical, are made habitually to converge towards one common purpose."

The point of this definition is that it is both rationalistic and humanistic. An approach to religion may be called theological when it starts with the question of the existence of God. It may be called scriptural when it starts with an exposition of revealed truths. Bankim's approach was neither. He, like Comte, started with the search for the rational unity of man's existence "as an individual and in society." This is clear from his definition of 'happiness' which includes "individual pleasure" as also "service of humanity." Again, like Comte, he also started with the 'constituent parts of man's nature, moral and physical, but sought their 'convergence' not in an abstract "Humanity" (as Comte did) but in a "Personal, Pantheistic God." Also his notion of the "convergence" of man's "physical and moral nature' was hardly a Comtean notion, and his doctrine of "the fullest development of human powers in a state of balance" was essentially a Greek doctrine.

It is certainly true that since the Italian Renaissance, educational thought in Europe has been largely moulded by the idea of 'culture' which is the result of developing human powers in a state of balance. The 19th century "doctrine of culture" (subscribed to by such thinkers as Matthew Arnold. and Seely,) sought to replace Religion by such 'culture', Bankim mentioned both Arnold and Seely as he mentioned Comte. But what his detractors have failed to notice is that his indebtedness to all these thinkers in his approach to the religious question was of the same order as their indebtedness to the Greeks, and that even to the Greeks his indebtedness did not extend to anything more than the notion of "developing the faculties" and the notion of 'balance'. Neither in his classification of the "human faculties" nor in his conception of their development did he follow any western thinker, ancient or modern. To show this, we need only consider his description of the "active faculties", the chief amongst which, in his opinion, was *Bhakti*,— a faculty, which has never been seriously discussed by any western thinker even in the purely human form of "Bhakti to one's parents." What is of far more importance in this connection is that humanism with Bankim was only an approach to religion. It was not, as in any western thinker before him (and, for that matter, in any western thinker to this day) a self-supporting doctrine. The balance of the faculties in their fullest development was sought by Bankim in Bhakti towards a Personal Being who pervaded all creation. This was the essence of his religious views,[8] and for this he was indebted to no western thinker.

(ii)   *Utilitarianism*

It is thus reasonable to say that Bankim's debt to Comte and Positivism was minimal. The same cannot be said of the doctrine of Utilitarianism, which he actually used in *Dharmatattwa* to supply a gap in Hindu thought. We have already seen how, in the controversy with Tagore, he used the utilitarian test for truth where truth led to murder. This train of thought he developed in his essay on Krishna, where, he showed that Krishna's definition of religion as that which 'contributed to the good of humanity' 'that which held the society' led to the application of the test of utility in all cases of special action.[9] In *Dharmatattwa* he supported the sort of social legislation that required the punishment of a "thief who was in distress" and spoke against an uncritical application of the doctrine of love for all creation, which would let the thief off. This legislation was of course based on the principle of the "greatest good of the greatest number."[10] According to Bankim's method this principle was required to balance the faculty of love and obviated an uncritical expression of that faculty in complete disregard of the good of society and self. It was part of Bhakti, because, the "preservation of God's creation" by preserving self and society, required its application. The utilitarian test was thus a part of Religion, though a very small part, calculated to discriminate in certain cases, what course of action was right under the circumstances. Bankim specified the influence of utilitarianism on his conception of religion in these words : "Utilitarians make the mistake of supposing that the whole field of religion is included within their doctrine. Actually, it occupies only a very small part of that field. The place I assign to it covers no more than the part of a corner in the whole field spanned by my discourse"—This is the best commentary on the role of utilitarianism in the shapping of Bankim's religious thought.

NOTES AND REFERENCES

1. Basu, Sankari Prasad (edited) *Vivekananda In Indian Newspapers (1893-1902)* : p 30-1, 274-55 *(The Indian Mirror)*, 355-6 *(The Indian Nation)*.

2. *Vangadarsan* : Chaitra, 1279 B. S. (Prapta Granther Samkhipta Samalochana).

3. The definition is discussed in the following section.

4. *"Hindu Dharma"* *(Prachar)*

5. "A writer of the *Prachar*, a fellow-journal of the '*Navajiban*', wrote, what helps the true progress of man, his physical, mental, social and an all round development, is religion. We endorse it with all our heart." Quoted in *Bankim Jibani* ; Sachis Chandra Chattopadhyay.

6. *Bankim Rachanavali : Letters on Hinduism* : Samsad : p 267

7. R. S. Sharma (Edited) : *Indian Society : Historical Probings in memory of D. D Kosambi.* Essay by Sabyasachi Bhattacharya : Positivism in 19th c. Bengal. This essay does not indicate Bankim's points of difference with Positivism in his religious views.

8. *Supra,* Chapter-*IV.*

9. *Krishna-Charitra* : Section VI, Chapter VI.

10. *Dharmatattwa* : Chapter XXII.

ic. His assertion that he succeeded in turning all the
human powers to God and that this was also how their

CHAPTER VI

SPIRITUAL EXPERIENCE AND THE NEW SYNTHESIS

IN THIS chapter, we intend to take up the question of a
significant ramification of a leading idea of New Hindu Movement i.e. the idea of personal illumination. The life and activities of Swami Vivekananda illustrate how this ramification
occurred.

The search for personal illumination was seen in its
pure form in the lives of Keshub Chandra Sen and Bijoy
Krishna Goswami. Bankim's exposition of Hinduism does
not seem to have concerned itself with this factor—certainly
not with the sort of religious ecstasy by which Keshub
Chandra Sen set so much store. But it would be far from
true to say that Bankim's exposition was only an exercise in
intellectualism. His rationalist structure was certainly a triumph of the intellect, but not in the sense of a rigorous logical argumentation, in which every second step is made meticulously to follow from the first. There were serious gaps
and unwarranted jump in his systematic exposition. The
introduction of God in the middle of a humanistic discourse
was logically unsatisfactory, even allowing for the fact that
God in Bankim's conception was not the external God of
monotheists, but an all-pervading Personal Being who represented the limit of human possibilities. But if Bankim
failed to create a logical structure of cast-iron solidity he rescued his work from degenerating into lifeless intellectualism
by punctuating it with universal insights that had also the
ring of the personal in it,—thereby indicating that he was a
true son of his age. He too was a spiritual seeker and no
mere doctrinaire. His perception that the classical and the
Renaissance conception of humanism emphasizing the fullest
development of one's powers but seeking their harmony
within the limits of one's own self could not make for the
sort of happiness, that was the happiness of a "liberated
soul" (*Jivanmukta*) was not a perception deriving from mere

logic. His assertion that Bhakti consisted in turning all the human powers to God and that this was also how their true harmony was achieved was a major religious discovery, one that was inexplicable except against the background of a life-time's spiritual effort. Actually Bankim, even while giving a rationalist exposition of religion was indicating a way of personal illumination although it was not the sort of illumination achieved through religious ecstasy. He himself was perfectly conscious of the greatness of his discovery, and in one of the many autobiographical passages of his diologue the Guru addresses the disciple thus : "When all the powers are directed towards God, that condition is Bhakti.—This is so hard a saying that I have little hope of your divining its essence by hearing it uttered on a single occasion. I daresay you will face many doubts and experience much confusion in arriving at its meaning. You will probably find many loopholes in it. In the end you may even come to regard it as meaningless prattle. But don't you get discouraged. Turn it over in your mind by taking thought over days, months, years. Attempt to apply it in action. Slowly its meaning will be revealed to you like fire bursting into flames by continuous addition of firewood. If that happens regard it as your life's fulfilment. Of all the truths learnt by man none is profounder. If a man employs his whole life to the learning of proper lessons and in the end reaches this truth, know that his life has attained fulfilment."[1]

Proceeding in a nobler strain, the Guru—who is now seen to be Bankim himself with little attempt at disguise— says : "Even when I was in a state of extreme youthfulness I used to be struck with the thought : what shall I do with this life ? What indeed has to be done with it ? Through the whole course of my life I have sought an answer to this question ; and the search for the answer has almost brought me to the end of my days. I received many answers current amongst men and went through much suffering to ascertain their truth. I read a great deal, I toiled in authorship, I conversed with many people, I did my stint in the way of action. I spared no pains to reach my life's fulfilment. At long last I came to this truth : when a man directs all the powers he was born with to God, that is Bhakti, and without Bhakti there is no virtue in man. This is the answer I have received. This is the true answer, all answers are false."[2]

A sensitive reader, when going through this beautiful passage, will at once realise that Bankim was here referring to a sort of personal illumination, even though it was a very different sort of personal illumination from the one preached by Keshub and his spiritual brethren.   The religious illumination sought by Bankim was a very human affair indeed. It was reached through a life of human suffering and human action from which the motive of self-directedness was removed through infinite pain and the action and the suffering and the pain were all directed to God.   There is poetry in such a passage, but emphatically it is not the poetry of mystical communion with God.   The illumination sought by Swami Vivekananda, which it will be our turn to discuss now, cannot be understood apart from a reference to the sort of illumination sought by Bankim.   Vivekananda's was indeed a search for mystical communion with God—but with a difference.

(A) THE INNER LIFE OF VIVEKANANDA

Vivekananda's life has been treated in so many books by so many authors that it might appear futile to attempt a re-examination of his mission by way of discovering in it a significance that has not been taken due care of by earlier authors.   But it is clear that hardly a single author has yet attempted an analysis of that mission apart from describing it as a powerful restatement of Hinduism.   But it was certainly not the sort of Hinduism preached by Sasadhar Tarkachudamoni and the orthodox School.   An understanding of the distinctive features of Vivekananda's religion has been rendered difficult by the fact that the Swami often appears to

15

preach not a single system of 'Philosophic Hinduism'—but the whole body of doctrines ranging from Vedantic Monism to Puranic Polytheism. All this renders it necessary that we should look for some clue which connects the Swami directly with his historical environment, makes him something more than a mere champion of old Hinduism and explains his grip on the imagination of the English-educated generation of the nineties of the 19th century and the first decade of the 20th. This clue is furnished by the ramification of the idea of personal illumination. Unlike any other seeker before him, Vivekananda invested this search for personal illumination with a new meaning, rendering, in the process, the classic pursuit of a recluse into something very different, into something that never betokened the sort of peace and serenity sought by men of contemplation, but rather the restlessness of men of prodigious energy who have descried in the distant horizon an abode of bliss that passeth all understanding ; but who having once tasted that bliss in a transitory moment of trance have then lost it only to be left with a sense of unbearable desolation nerving them to action, evermore and to a search that knows no end. Vivekananda's new discovery in religion consisted exactly in this : He made the search for mystical communion with God no longer a matter of sundry spiritual practices gone through in seclusion untrammelled by extraneous disturbances but a prototype of all human adventures aiming at human ends and involving human suffering to the uttermost limit as well as human ecstasy of the loftiest kind. A narrative of this adventure in Vivekananda's own life must precede an elaboration of the doctrines by which he rounded off the thoughts propounded by Bankim and included them in a new synthesis by way of a restatement of the philosophy of Vedanta as preached by Sankaracharya.

Such a narrative must start from a point which antedates the events described in the previous Chapter by several years. Bankim's controversy with the Brahmos occurred in 1884 and his rationalistic exposition of religion was completed only in 1888. But Vivekananda's initiation into religious life occurred much earlier, and its occurrence was wholly independent of Bankim's exposition. We shall see in due course that in point both of doctrine as well as its social application Vivekananda's religious teaching approximated to that of Bankim closely enough to render the historical role played by both in the national life of Bengal in the succeeding decades a role of almost identical significance. But this must not blind us to the fact that the Sannyasin reached his destination through a course that was very different from that pursued by the writer. The latter's was an achievement of the intellect—the former's of experience. How and when did that experience start ?

According to the biographers[2], the years 1880-81 were, in the life of young Narendranath, years of acute spiritual unrest. This unrest did not differ in kind from the intense craving for communion with God, which we have already witnessed in the lives of Keshub Chandra Sen and Vijoy Krishna Goswami. But there was certainly a difference in quality ; for Narendranath differed from his older contemporaries by being a man of a very different stamp in certain respects. In the first place 'Naren' was extremely youthful— he was only 17 in 1880 ; in the second place neither by temperament nor by constitution was he cut out to be a mystic. He had a most powerful physique and there was not a trace of the introvert in him—indeed he was a Bohemian very much given to fun and frolic, whiling away his leisure in interminable gaiety sometimes being led to very questionable company by thoughtless pursuit of pleasure. A story is told of his being wheedled into the aquaintance of a rich and beautiful lady from whose amorous approaches he extricated himself only with some difficulty. He himself was not immune from the imperious demands of his superpowerful body, and on one occasion he extinguished an uncontrollable bout of sexual passion by applying a burning coal to his genitals. The act was characteristic, indicating not only a neglect of the usually prescribed course like fasting and abstention from sexually stimulating articles of food by way of chastising the demands of recalcitrant flesh, but also a fierce will power that would stick at nothing to prevent the body, (which in the eyes of the later Vivekananda was only a cloak that entangled the soul within) from running away with its impulses. Speaking about fasting and similar observances, it is interesting that, unlike Mahatma Gandhi, the Swami never preached their necessity although he was absolutely uncompromising in his demand of a spotless celibacy from every prospective religious seeker. This was perhaps the only restraint— admittedly a very powerful one—apart from a childish fondness for the idolatrous lore of orthodox Hinduism inculcated by his mother, that characterised the otherwise easy-going Bohemian life of Naren. He was in great request in all sorts of social circles formed by college boys in Calcutta. He was extremely musical, and his powerful voice resounded the hall when he joined a soiree, and held the audience spellbound by the generous amenity of its cadence. Whatever else he was, young Naren was hardly the stuff of which mystics are made.

Far from betraying any desire for religious ecstasy Naren was gradually drifting away from his ancestral religion, and, when in 1880 or thereabouts, he joined the Brahmo Samaj he joined that section of it which had grown as a protest against Keshub Chandra Sen's predilection for mystical contemplation. One of his biographers expressly states that "he did not take kindly to the ecstatic spells of the New Dispensationists nor to their maudlin extravagances in acclaiming Keshub as a sort of Messiah."[3] Whether this opinion is true or not, there is evidence that Naren's joining the Sadharan Brahmo Samaj was due more to his enthusiasm for social reforms than to any deep-seated religious craving.[4] Apart from his austerities directed to observing the strictest celibacy —a practice that was of course abhorrent to the Sadharan

Brahmo Samaj—there was nothing in young Naren to beto- ken the religious enthusiast.   He was actually been portray- ed as an agnostic,—as a disciple of Mill and Spencer.   Even his passion for strict celibacy was probably an exercise in will-power rather than a preparation for a religious life.

Naren's spiritual unrest during the 1880s has to be seen against the background of these facts.   We need not go into the details of what transpired between him and his *Guru* during the years 1881-86.   Every reader of his biography knows how the skeptical Naren was gradually won over to the cult of *Advaita ;* how he was led to shed his disbelief in Kali, the Divine Mother ; how on one or two occasions Ramakrishna induced in his favourite disciple the mystical trance for which he was famous, despite the latter's persistent efforts to resist what he began by suspecting as a sort of hyp- notic spell ; and, last, but not the least, how Ramakrishna in his dying hours, as if in answer to his disciple's innermost thought, confounded him by declaring that he was an Avatar —the same person, in fact, as in old days used to call himself Rama and Krishna.   These are well-known facts attested to by no less a person than Vivekananda himself on many occa- sions.[5] Every biographer of Vivekananda has mentioned them, and the conclusion they have invariably reached is this : Naren started by being an unbeliever and ended by becoming the staunchest of believers as a result of the mystical experi- ences he underwent through the guidance of Ramakrishna.[6] The conclusion is no doubt true but we should be on our guard against putting it so baldly before examining the back- lash of his skeptical intellect on those mystical experience through the remaining years of his life. We shall see that the rest of his life was a struggle to achieve a human, a social transformation of the mystical experiences induced in him by Ramakrishna.

There is a good deal of evidence that Naren, who up- on his master's death, launched on a career of almost super- human toil and suffering in the cause of religon, steadily wore himself out to death doggedly pursuing the aim of mystical experiences vouchsafed to him by Ramakrishna. Mahendranath Gupta, the chronicler of Ramakrishna's dialogues has recorded a conversation which took place during the middle of 1887, barely nine months after the Saint's death. In this Naren is represented as being in a state of extreme unhappiness and despair at his failure to see God whose very existence appeared doubtful to him. Evidently his intellect doubted the evidence of the mystical experiences till he had mastered his Guru's art of entering into *Samadhi*, as many times as he chose. Two years later we find him writing to Pramada Das Mitra of Benaras to the effect that though his faith in the guiding hand of Providence was unshakable and though he was in possession of the ideal scriptures and the blessing of the ideal amongst men—meaning of course his master—he had failed to do anything by himself. A year later, during February and March, 1890, we find him seeking the discipleship of Pahari Baba of Ghazipore in the hope that the latter would teach him what his master had not—apparently an unfailing system for recapturing the mystical experiences in a permanent and lasting manner. The attempt failed and Naren, now became the Swami Vivekananda of the Ramakrishna Order, set out in search of a Himalayan retreat to attain his goal by uninterrupted meditation. The meditation was no sooner begun than broken by the arrival of terrible news. One of his sisters, a victim of an unhappy marriage, had committed suicide. Vivekananda was heart-broken. He travelled over the length and breadth of India and for two whole years knew hardly any rest. He visited princes, lords, merchants and was often a guest with the poorest of the poor. He saw India's abject poverty and was fascinated by the deep piety of her poorest children. It was an experience he never forgot and in his later years he was never tired of pointing out the contrast between the poor in the West and the poor in India. In the West, he thought, poverty meant vice and all manner of moral degeneration. But in India the poorest of her children were the repositories of her spiritual greatness. This was the Swamiji's great discovery and it was realistic enough to unfold its full significance to him only after the terrible helplessness of those of his poor brethren and the thousands of Indian women ('the emblems of the Divine Mother') like his own sister had been revealed to him as a sort of unique experience as powerful as the one induced in him by the touch of his master. At any rate, this new experience inspired the Swami to give to his master's teaching an interpretation that changed the whole course of his life.

Before taking up the interpretation, we must discuss this sudden change in the course of Vivekananda's life. The change was actually one from the life of a despairing recluse seeking a Himalayan retreat for meditation aimed at personal illumination to that of a warrior preacher proclaiming in a voice of thunder, the timeless truths of Hinduism to raise a whole unbelieving world to the level of Vedanta and asking this same unbelieving world to raise, in its turn, the masses of India from their state of extreme wretchedness by lending a helping hand. The biographers are silent as to the impact of the news of his sister's death on Vivekananda. It was in fact tremendous. "I went years ago to the Himalayas, never to come back", he wrote from America many years after. "The news (of my sister's death) reached me there and that weak heart flung me off from that prospect of peace ! Peace have I sought, but the heart, that seat of Bhakti, would not allow me to find it". Thus he wrote in 1899[7]. It has only to be added that in Vivekananda's eyes the terribleness of his sister's fate was multiplied a hundred fold by illustrating, as it were, the fate of myriads of Indian women whose lot was similar if not identical. The drama was heightened by including in the performance and as part of the same personal history the frightful condition of the Indian masses—in Vivekananda's reckoning so many "Children of Bliss". "It is the weak heart that has driven me out of India to seek some help for those I love, and here I am!" wrote in the same letter. To Nivedita, he said,

"Never forget the word The women and the people". Such was the background to the transformation of the recluse to the warrior.

Let us try to grasp the nature of this transformation a bit more closely. Vivekananda's mission in the West was, of course, to preach the timeless truths of Hinduism there. But it is clear from his letters that he intended his gift of Hindu scriptural truths to be reciprocated by the American gift of men and money to place the poor in India securely on their feet. "Just as in our country social virtue is singularly lacking, so here (in America) there is little spirituality. I am giving them spirituality, they are giving me money......This is why I have come to America—to earn money by my own effort and devote the rest of my life (in India) to realise this one aim (i. e., to raise the masses of India)." This was how Vivekananda expressed himself in one letter, conveying unmistakenably, the impression of a tradesmanship in religion. Actually such letters were so numerous, and, on occasion, his condemnation of the religious recluse was so violent that he was apt to be mistaken for a mere secular spokesman of "the woman and the people". "Who cares for Bhakti and Mukti ?"—he thundered on one occasion. "Who cares what the scriptures say ? I will go to hell cheerfully a thousand times, if I can rouse my countrymen, immersed in Tamas (slauth, ignorance and timidity), and make them stand on their own feet and be Men......I am not a follower of Ramakrishna or any one, I am a follower of him only who carries out my plans." Such was the voice of Vivekananda after his dream of personal illumination in Himalayan retreat was shattered by an experience of the condition of India's 'woman and people'.

But such utterances have to be placed beside the ones that follow in order to bring out the relation between Vivekananda, the fighter for 'the woman and the people' and Vivekananda—the seeker for personal illumination. "I don't want to work", he writes to Nivedita on his second (money-

earning) mission to America : "I want to be quiet, and rest.
......But the fate or Karma, I think, derives me on—work,
work. We are like cattle driven to the slaughter house—
hastily nibbling a bite of grass on the road-side as they are
driven along under the whip",[8]—"After all, Joe", he writes
to Miss Macleod a few days later, "I am only the boy who
used to listen with rapt wonderment to the wonderful words
of Ramakrishna under the Banyan tree at Dakshineswar. That
is my true nature ; works and activities, doing good and so
forth are all suprimpositions.......The sweetest moment of my
life have been when I was drifting......Behind my work was
ambition, behind my love was personality, behind my purity
was fear, behind my guidance the thirst for power ! Now,
they are vanishing, and I drift".[9] "My nature"—(this to
Mary Hale) "is the retirement of a Scholar. I never get it."[10]
Again,—"I have worked for this world, Mary, all my life,
and it does not give me a piece of bread without taking a
pound of flesh......If ever a man found the vanity of things, I
have it now. This is the world hideous, beastly corpse. Who
thinks of helping it—is a fool."[11]

What is clear from a comparison of such utterances is
this : the transformation of Vivekananda from the religious
recluse of the Himalayan retreat to that of warrior for the
woman and people was achieved at a terrible price which was
ultimately to kill him. A warrior whose vocation was determined by the "weakness of his heart", that is to say, by his
sensibility taking fire from the condition of "the woman and
the people", while his whole soul demanded a solution to the
riddle of personal illumination attained momentarily and
then lost, must have a tremendous struggle going within himself and giving him no rest. How intense the struggle was in
the case of Vivekananda, can be judged from the fact that
during the nine years from the date of his Chicago address
till his death, he worked like one possessed, flinging himself
across the world as if in a whirlwind talking, lecturing, bringing people round to his point of view, sometimes tearing
16

them asunder by a mighty force from their settled avocations and condemning them to a whole life-time of toil and suffering, sometimes killing them outright by sheer exhaustion ; injecting super-human vigour into the faint-hearted, infusing a part of his superabundant energy into the lazy and the lack-a-daisical,—in a word, acting like one in a terrible fit of madness. He was wearing himself out, slowly, steadily and irrevocably. An American admirer, watching him in the course of a lecture in 1896 noted : "Never had I seen the Master look as he looked that night. There was something in his beauty not of earth. It was as if the spirit had almost burst the bonds of flesh and it was then that I saw a forseshadowing of the end. He was much exhausted from years of overwork, and it was even then to be seen that he was not long for this world. I tried to close my eyes to it, but in my heart I knew the truth. He had needed rest but felt that he must go on."[12]

Another, describing th effect of the Swami's presence on people about him wrote in the same year. "He could rivet attention on himself : and when he spoke in all seriousness and intensity—though it seems well nigh incredible—there were some among his hearers who were literally exhausted..... In one case I know of a man who was forced to rest in bed for three days on the result of a nervous shock received by a discussion with the Swami".[13]

These descriptions bring out two aspects of the struggle within Vivekananda—one, the utter exhaustion of his body brought about by a quantity of work no human flesh would endure, and the other his superhuman will-power growing steadily even as his body was going to pieces. In other words, it was Naren over again in the practice of chastising the demands of recalcitrant flesh to make the spirit shine forth in all its splendour. He was striving in his person to render the fight for the cause of "the woman and the people" an act of terrible renunciation. Actually he was striving to render that fight a substitute for meditation in the Himalayan retreat.

The interesting thing about Vivekananda was this. Such a struggle, instead of making him fearfully abnormal attracted to him men and women of all sorts whose love for him was tinged with infinite tenderness. "We saw him leave us", wrote another admirer, "with the fear that clutches the heart when a beloved, gifted, passionate child fares forth, unconscious, in an untried world."[14] Such words written about the lion-hearted Vivekananda strike us with wonder. But it is perfectly obvious that his friends' love for him was not merely the love one feels for great religious teacher. In the first place his lion's heart itself found expression in a sort of courage which was in some sense very exceptional and by that very reason calculated to inspire people with love rather than mere veneration. Unlike most men of religion he exemplified a courage which was not of the stoical, forbearing kind, but rather of an exceedingly youthful and masculine one. Nivedita has narrated an incident in England in which Vivekananda, while travelling across some fields in the company of two English friends—one of them a lady—was assailed by a mad bull which came tearing towards them. The Englishman ran away, but the lady sank to the ground quite exhausted by her attempt at running. The Swami at once planted himself between the bull and the lady and escaped sure death only by the bull's turning away at the last moment. Such incidents were by no means exceptional, and the Swami easily won the hearts of people he came across by such demonstrations. But these do not explain the tenderness with which he was treated by most of his admirers. His letters bear ample testimony to such tenderness. "Mr. and Mrs. Sovier", writes the Swami himself, of two of his English friends, "have clad me when I was cold, nursed me better than my mother would have, borne with me in my weakness, my trials ; and they have nothing but blessings for me." The biographers assure us that these elderly people, while looking upon the Swami as their master in their search for religion, at the same time, treated him as their son. Similarly, of his American friends Mrs Bull and

Miss Josephine Macleod, Vivekananda writes thus : "Mrs. Bull and Miss Macleod have been to our country, moved and lived with us as no foreigner ever did, roughing it, and they do not ever curse me for my luxuries either ; they will be only too good to have me eat well and smoke dollar cigars if I wish." There is only one explanation for such love and tenderness : these were inspired by the very recklessness of Vivekananda's struggle and his terrible renunciation for the cause of "the woman and the people." This is brought out more clearly by the writer from whose description of Vive ka- nanda as a "beloved child faring forth in an untried world" we have just quoted. This writer precedes this description by actually comparing Vivekananda's religious mission with his project of raising of the masses of India by American help, and he leaves us in no doubt that it is the latter mission that, in his mind, gives to the Swami's character a tragic in- tensity, which is unthinkable in a man with purely religious mission. To quote the writer's exact words : "He spoke of holy men who at a single glance converted hardened sin- ners and detected men's innermost thoughts… ..But these things were trifles ; always his thoughts turned back to his people. He lived to raise them up and make them better and had come this long way in the hope of gaining help to teach them to be practically more efficient. We hardly knew what he wanted ; money if money would do it ; tools, advice, new ideas. And for this he was willing to die to morrow."[15]

It is unnecessary to labour this point any further. What we are trying to establish is this : In Vivekananda the spiritual unrest of the 1870s, of which the greatest symptom was a desire for personal illumination through religion, reach- ed its fulfilment in a manner which was as unexpected as it was captivating in its intensity. The illumination sought by Keshub Chandra Sen, Bijoy Krishna Goswami and Rama- krishna Paramahansa was through mystical communion with God, –a method, of which Ramakrishna was the greatest exemplar. Vivekananda was Ramakrishna's disciple, and

it was he who preached to the world his Master's doctrine that
'direct experience' of God—was the alpha and omega of religion. Religious practice is nothing if it does not lead to direct
experience—such was the substance of his preaching. Yet
in his own life it was not the trances of Ramakrishna that
he sought, not at least after his failure to achieve them in a
Himalayan retreat. He socialised, as it were, the doctrine of
personal illumination by transforming the gospel of salvation
for one's ownself to one of dedicated humanitarianism. This
is not to say that he superseded the one for the other—quite
the contrary. In the watchword for all future monks of his
master's order he united the two. 'Atmano moksharthan
Jagaddhitaya Cha'—for one's salvation and for the service of
all—this was the watchword of the Order. But no watch-
word is ever fool proof : just as the search for one's own salvation may be degenerate into a selfish longing for the Himalayan retreat, so the proposed service for all may degenerate
into secular altruism ; also for all we know the unity may
be illusory, Vivekananda's life was a struggle to achieve this
unity ; to serve humanity by an act of terrible renunciation
and to render persona illumination a flashlight into "the sum
total of all souls", which,—as he put it—was, "the only God
I believe in, and above all my God the wicked, my God the
miserable, my God the poor of all races." It was how he
resolved the spiritual unrest that started during the 1870's.
To say this is not to belittle the achievement of Keshub, Bijoy
and Ramakrishna, but to point out that, whereas these three
pre-eminently embodied the truth that religious thirst when
arising from the depths of the soul, is not to be quenched by
programmes of social reform,—Vivekananda prevented that
thirst from getting lost in a quagmire of subjectivism by
giving it a social meaning, but at the same making it retain
all its intensity. This was the significance of his inner life.

(B)   RAMAKRISHNA AND VIVEKANANDA

Before taking up Vivekananda's teachings in their phi-

losophic formulation we must understand in which manner
they followed from the teachings of his master. From the 'Dialogues'[16] ('Kathamrita) we know that the most characteristic
teachings of Ramakrishna were two in number : The first was
his overriding emphasis on religion as a matter of personal
illumination rather than of social reform and belief in certain
doctrines; and the second was his doctrine of Universalism—
his assertion that all religions led to God. It should be clearly
understood, however, that it was not these teachings but rather the form in which Vivekananda put them, and,—more
than that,—the dramatisation of Hindu greatness in the person of the Swami that took the world by storm. If it be true
that without Ramakrishna there would have been no Vivekananda, it is no less true that, without Vivekananda, Ramakrishna's teachings would have remained confined to a coterie
of mystics, at best giving rise to a cult of Ramakrishna rather
than to restatement of Hinduism, which in Vivekananda's
eyes, was the essence of Ramakrishna's teachings. It would
not be an unfair assessment of Ramakrishna's contribution to
the religious scene of 19th century Bengal to say that this contribution was essentially in the nature of a personal influence
rather than of ideas that were of any great historical importance. The ideas that proved to be of the greatest historical
consequence were due to Vivekananda in the sense that he
formulated his master's teachings in a certain manner which
was by no means the only manner in which those teachings
could be interpreted. We have already seen that Ramakrishna's emphasis on religion as a matter of personal illumination
rather than of social reform and belief in certain doctrines
was interpreted by Keshub Chandra Sen and Bijoy Krishna
Goswami in a manner which had little, if anything, to do with
service to humanity. In Vivekananda's interpretation the
relation between the two was central. Again Ramakrishna's
doctrine of Universalism, namely his belief that all religions
led to God, could easily lead to the sort of eclecticism that
gave rise to Keshub's New Dispensation which was a conglo-

meration of beliefs and practices deriving from diverse religious sources;—in Vivekananda's formulation of this doctrine,
the Universalism was a way of expressing that fact that all
religions were an approach to Advaitism. It is of course arguable that Keshub and Bijoy, since they never professed to
be disciples of Ramakrishna, were hardly in a position to interpret the latter's teachings correctly. But there is a good
deal of evidence to show that even amongst the direct disciples of Ramakrishna there was some skepticism regarding
Vivekananda's teaching of service to humanity as in any way
connected to Ramakrishna's teaching of personal illumination
as the essence of religion. To bring out the relative contribution of Ramakrishna and Vivekananda in the religious debate
of the 19th century, an examination of this evidence is essential.

The writer of "The Dialogue of the Swami with a Disciple", has narrated an incident[17] in which Swami Jogananda,
a direct disciple of Ramakrishna is shown to be finding fault
with the project of founding a Mission in the name of Ramakrishna for humanitarian and educational work, on the ground
that Vivekananda was acting under foreign influence and that
Ramakrishna's "method of doing things was different".
Vivekananda replied to the effect that Ramakrishna, who was
the embodiment of infinite ideas, could not be confined within the limits his disciples would prescribe for him. It is obvious that such a reply was tantamount to evading the issue
raised by Jogananda, and it clearly indicates Vivekanand's
propensity to look upon his master's teachings as extremely
flexible, admitting of a variety of interpretations not directly
indicated in the form in which Ramakrishna had expressed
them.

Another incident was more serious. According to the
standard biography : "One of the Swami's Gurubhai's was (on
a certain occasion) taking him to task for not preaching the
ideas of Shri Ramakrishna and challenging him to prove how
his plans could be reconciled with their Master's teachings.

For Shri Ramakrishna insisted, above all, on Bhakti and practice of Sadhanas for the realisation of God, while the Swami
constantly urged them to go about working, preaching and
serving the poor and the diseased—the very things which forced
the mind outward, which was the greatest impediment to
the life of Sadhana. Then again, the Swami's ideas of starting
Maths and Homes of service for the public good, his ideas of
organisation and of patriotism which were undoubtedly western in conception, his efforts to create a new type of Sannyasin with a broader ideal of renunciation, and others of a similar nature were incompatible with Shri Ramakrishna's ideal
of renunciation and would surely have been repudiated by
him".

This passage is extremely revealing, bringing out, in
the most unmistakable manner, the difference between Vivekananda's interpretation of his master's teachings and that of
some of his brethren. No less revealing is the fact that, here
again, Vivekananda did not attempt to bring his brother-
monk round to his point of view by argument and reasoning.
He ridiculed the poor man for his obsession with personal
salvation and reduced him to silence by a passionate outburst. As the writer of the standard biography put it :
"Growing more and more serious he thundered on :
You think you understand Ramakrishna better than
myself ! ......your Bhakti is sentimental nonsense and makes
one impotent, you want to preach Ramakrishna as you have
understood him which is mighty little."[18]

The biographers tell us that this outburst thoroughly
scared the brother-monks who were henceforth extremely
careful to avoid a repetition of such outbursts by questioning
Vivekananda's interpretation of their master's teachings.

An American disciple of the Ramakrishna Order has
recorded another brother-monk of Vivekananda as saying :
"If we had dreamed of the labours that lay before us, we
would not have spent our strength in severe austerities or tax-
ed our bodies by privations and long wanderings. All that

was asked of us, we thought was a simple life of renunciation obeying in humble spirit what our Master had taught
us."—Clearly, in his thinking, Vivekananda's teaching was
something different.

Such evidence could easily be multiplied. The three
incidents described above make it abundantly clear that Vivekananda's interpretation of his master's teachings differed
substantially from that of the generality of his brother-monks
who were apt to look upon their master as a teacher of personal salvation—and indeed such is the impression derived
from a careful reading of the dialogues of Ramakrishna recorded by Mahendranath Gupta. It is true that Vivekananda's biographers try to explain away the dissimilarity between
the teachings of the master and his foremost disciple by nar-
rating an incident in which Naren's appeal for personal salvation was pooh-poohed by Ramakrishna on the plea that
he expected greater things from his favourite. But this incident hardly explains the very different forms in which the
teachings of Ramakrishna and Vivekananda were respectively
expressed.

The only explanation which suggests itself is this.
Ramakrishna's influence on Vivekananda was personal rather
than intellectual. Intellectually Vivekananda was a child of
the age to which he belonged : his interest in religion was
more social than personal. He was fully alive to the challenge thrown to Hinduism by Christianity and,—in a far more
formidable way—by the western Enlightenment. He faced
the challenge, not defensively, as even Bankim, in the ultimate analysis, faced it,—but aggressively, in the manner of a
conquering hero, throwing the whole weight of his superpowerful body against a hostile world. This is the reason
why his message strikes us as something quite different from
his master's, who, of course knew nothing of that challenge,
and never cared to formulate an answer to it. But Ramakrishna's influence on Vivekananda even if personal, (rather
than intellectual) was tremendous. To Vivekananda no lan-

17

guage was too extravagant when it applied to his master. He was 'Avatara Varistha'—the greatest among Incarnations ; he was greater than Buddha and Krishna and Christ ; he could create a hundred thousand Vivekanandas if he chose. Such language is explicable only on the hypothesis that it was Ramakrishna from whom Vivekananda learnt the lesson of renunciation and the art of that divine intoxication, in which, a man, spurning even the faintest semblance of a desire for gold and the love of the sexes, sailed out, fearless, in search of something which, while it inevitably killed the body, liberated the soul and made it shine forth in a trans-cendent brightness. Such a hypothesis explains the dissi-milarity of Vivekananda's message from that of his master in a much more satisfactory way than any heroic effort to fit the Swami's words into the procrustean bed presented by the dialogues of Ramakrishna. To see this more clearly let us now take up the message itself.

(C) VIVEKANANDA'S MESSAGE

Intellectually, Vivekananda's kinship was nearest with Bankim, and it is by studying the close resemblance of the former's thoughts on the Activism of Vedanta and his doctrines of Impersonal Pantheism with the latter's pronouncements on the Activism of the *Gita* and Personal Pantheism, that we reach the heart of Vivekananda's message. As we explained in Chapter-IV, Bankim's interpretation of the doctrine of Action as preached in the Gita consisted in breaking away from all the classical commentators who argued that, by Ac-tion, the Gita had meant worship of the ritualistic type pres-cribed in the scriptures. According to Bankim, it was not Vedic sacrifices or worahip of the ritualistic type that was enjoined in the Gita, but rather that true worship which consisted in acting for God who pervaded all humanity. As Vivekananda put it : "Let all other vain gods disappear for the time from our minds. This is the only god that is awake, our own race—'everywhere his hands, everywhere his feet, everywhere his ears, he covers everything'. All other gods are sleeping. What vain gods shall we go after and yet cannot worship the god that we see all round us, the Virat ? When we have worshipped this, we shall be able to worship all other gods. Worship is the exact equivalent of the Sanskrit word, and no other English word will do. There are all other gods,—men and animals : and the first gods we have to worship are our countrymen."[19]

The important point here is to note that the God of Humanity preached in such an extract was with Vivekananda, as with Bankim before him, not an allegorical god, constructed with the object of dramatising his notion of serving "the woman and the people", but it was actually the very essence of Vedanta as he preached it. We have seen that Bankim's humanistic approach to religion necessitated a conception of God whose worship was to lead to the fullest development of all human faculties in a perfect condition of harmony amongst one another, and in particular to the fullest development of the faculty of love so as to embrace all humanity. In Vivekananda's words : "Where is the eternal sanction (of ethics) to be found except in the only Infinite Reality that exists in you and in me and in all, in the self, in the soul ? The infinite oneness of the soul is the eternal sanction of all morality, that you and I are not only brothers—every literature voicing man's struggle towards freedom has preached that for you—but that you and I are really one. This is the dictate of Indian philosophy. This oneness is the rationale of all ethics and spirituality."[20] (The Mission of the Vedanta).

Here we come to the central doctrine preached by Vivekananda. The oneness of all creation is a metaphysical doctrine preached by the so-called Vedanta philosophy. But Vivekananda extracted the religious core of this doctrine out of the metaphysical cobwebs under which it had lain hidden for centuries, and converted what had been a life-denying pessimistic creed held by a handful of mystics into the cornerstone of the religion of the Hindus.

In its classical form, the religion of Vedanta, as distinct from its philosophy, was a creed with an extremely dogmatic and narrow-minded conception of Personal salvation. It was essentially monastic and mystical : meditation and Yogic practices were supposed to be the only system of practical piety connected with it. Vivekananda was the first to make the ethics of love for all fellow beings a necessary component of this creed, and, by the introduction of that component, he made it available to people of all walks of life and destroyed, by one stroke, the monopoly so long enjoyed over it by mystics. What he said in effect was this : The unity of all creation, if it was to be a true unity, could not possibly be the result of some mystical experience alone,—for that would be a denial of its universality—but had to form a part of the normal human experience of everyone. The way this could be done was through love. As he put it: " Love for God and compassion for all creation,—this is what Chaitanya preached and this is no doubt admirable. It is admirable from the standpoint of dualist who believes in a Personal God separate from creation. But for us, who are Monists, this notion of separateness of God and Man is a notion that is apt to subject us to bondage. Our principle is, therefore, love, not compassion. According to our faith, the notion of compassion as applied to creation is a presumption".

This passage is extremely important as it brings out in a most logical manner, Vivekananda's original contribution to Vedantism. Classical Vedanta sought the unity of God and His creation in mystical experience. But Vivekananda pointed out that even if we apply this notion of unity to our normal human experience, we have a way of achieving that unity and that is through the sort of love that does not desire any return. This is how Vivekananda made Vedantic Monism a creed of universal applicability by relating it to our normal human experience.

Thus far Vivekananda's views are identical with Bankim's, and the sort of reasoning Vivekananda applied to the pantheistic notion of an all-pervading God to extract from it the ethics of service and love, could as well be done on the basis of a God who was pantheistic and personal and not on the basis of Impersonal Pantheism. For it is clear that Vivekananda's reasoning as well as Bankim's was based on the notion of pantheism alone and not on the personality or impersonality of that pantheism. It is, therefore, important to examine the divergence of Vivekananda's views on that point.

(D) PANTHEISM—PERSONAL AND IMPERSONAL

As we saw in Chapter IV, the most impotant article in Bankim's humanistic approach to religion was his insistence on Bhakti to God as the essential factor in the fullest development of human powers in a perfect condition of harmony. His God, too, was, of course, a humanistic God in the sense of being a God who was the limit of human possibilities, and His all-pervadingness was required to make an individual's faculty of love all-embracing. These criteria of a God-head were satisfied by the Hindu conception of a Personal God who pervaded all creation. But Bankim left unanswered the question of the existence of such a God apart from remarking that, in his belief, the existence of such a Personal God "becomes self-evident to one who has developed his faculties and has rendered his heart pure". It was thus very much a matter of belief and the question was not really answerable on the plane of intellect but was relegated to that of religious practice.

Vivekananda, following the clue supplied by classical Vedanta philosophy, suggested that religion did not really require the existence of a personal God but that the hypothesis of the divinity of the soul was enough to constitute a truly rational religion. This hypothesis was of course implicit in the supposition of a divine unity subsisting in all creation, and Vivekananda proceeded to show how this could form the basis of a religion.

Again following the lead supplied by classical Vedanta, Vivekananda asserted that religion consisted in realising the divinity of the soul.   This divinity was demonstrable in the sense that it could be actually realised and bliss was attainable ; the soul that was in bondage could really become free. Absolute purity of body and heart, total renunciation of lust and gold and burning love for all fellow-beings liberated the soul while still in body.

(E)   THE NEW SYNTHESIS

Yet it will not be true to say that Vivekananda's Neo-Vedantism—as it has been called—excluded the sort of Personal Pantheism preached by Bankim.   Bankim's was an attempt at reforming the doctrine of Bhakti, which in orthodox Hinduism is inculcated by the cults of Rama or Krishna by discovering their 'Kernel' after separating their 'husk'. The ethical 'Kernel' discovered by him consisted in the doctrine of 'work aimed at God' and 'love for all fellow-beings' which was a direct corollary of the metaphysical doctrine of pantheism.   The religious Kernel was Bhakti towards a Personal God who was the limit of human possibilities.   Vivekananda followed Bankim as regards the ethical Kernel closely enough to give the impression of an identity of views in this matter. As regards the religious Kernel of Hinduism, Vivekananda's views were of course different, but it is far from true to say that Vivekananda repudiated the doctrine of Bankim towards a Personal Cod ; actually he applied Ramakrishna's dictum that every religion was a way to God to the whole body of sects and creeds which went by the name of Hinduism, and attempted to achieve a new unity and new synthesis.   In this as in his Neo-Vedantism Vivekananda was a true reformer.

Ramakrishna had asserted that all religions were equally true. This was of course in the nature of a paradox, because if monotheism was true pantheism could hardly be so without landing us in a palpable contradiction. Vivekananda resolved the pardox by asserting that, as regards dogma, only Vedantic Monism could possibly be true because it presupposed only the divinity of the soul, —the notion of a Personal God, monotheistic or otherwise, being essentially in the nature of an untestable hypothesis. But as regards a system of ethical and religious culture, and also as regards a 'relative' view of an 'absolute' truth— all religions could unhesitatingly be declared true. Each of them prescribed systems of religious and ethical culture that purified the heart ; each of them emphasized a certain aspect of the divinity which could not help being included within the total view that was, of necessity, indescribable, because every human description of Divinity was in the nature of things, incomplete.

With such a view of religious truth, Vivekananda was of course the sternest critic of certain religious sects who were slack in their ethics, while he had nothing but unqualified approbation for their conception of Divinity. He vigorously condemned the followers of the so-called *Vamachara Tantras*, with whom religious culture had degenerated to the level of sexual orgies, and pronounced thee xisting Vaishnavic cult of Radha and Krishna, glorifying the illicit union of the two, as veritable poison. The wheel thus came full circle on the religious stage of Bengal since the days of Rammohan who had started his reforms by denouncing the Vaishnavism of Chaitanya, but on how different an outlook !

(F) HINDUISM BECOMES A MISSIONARY RELIGION

How different that outlook was can be judged from the fact that, within the distance that separated Rammohan from Vivekananda, the conception of the relative position as between the religion of the Hindus and the other great religions of the world had undergone a sea-change. Whereas Rammohan had felt it necessary to seek in the Upanishads the seeds of a Monotheist which would closely resemble the sort of monotheism held by the Unitarian sect among Christians and to supplement Hindu ethical speculations by publishing a compendium of precepts of Jesus for the benefit of the Hindus, Vivekananda would be satisfied with nothing short of a flooding of the Western world by Hindu ideas.[21] According to Vivekananda : Hinduism was the "mother of religions"—the others were its "patchy imitations". Just as the rationale of all ethics was furnished only by the notion of a God who pervaded all creation, which was characteristically a Hindu notion, in the same manner, it was Hinduism alone that taught the realisation of the Divinity within us while still in the body, and prescribed a system of religious culture to that end. These were the ideas, which, together with Hindu Universalism, worded by Ramakrishna in his celebrated formula, 'Jato Mat, Tato path', and re-explained by Vivekananda in the manner we indicated just now, could justly claim a hearing before a parliament of all world religions, the rest among which had nothing to match these ideas in breadth of vision and spiritual loftiness. With these ideas Vivekananda dreamed of conquering the world, and if he succeeded in making only a very modest beginning, he certainly imbued Hinduism with a spirit of unprecedented aggressiveness. Hitherto Hinduism was apologetic and thought nothing of borrowing, from other religions, ideas that were supposed essential for its own recovery. With the arrival of Vivekananda a point was reached where, in the traffic of ideas started by Rammohan as between Hinduism and other world-religions, the former's place was no longer on the receiving end of the line but on the donor's.

(G) NEW HINDUISM

We are now in a position to sum up the doctrinal results achieved by the efforts of Bankim and Vivekananda, within the years—1882—1902—results which at long last brought the religious debate of the 19th century to a decisive issue. First of all we should enumerate the doctrinal results one by one.

1. The first result was philosophical. An analysis of the humanistic position regarding the search for happiness was shown to necessitate a turning of the human faculties to God in order to lead them to their fullest development in a perfect condition of harmony. This result was

due to Bankim alone, who showed that this humanistic approach to religion led to the teachings of the *Gita*.

2. The second result was theological. It centred round the conflicting claims of Monotheism and Pantheism to superiority as regards theological truth. The superiority of Pantheism was asserted by both Bankim and Vivekananda,—Bankim basing his argument on grounds of reason which militated against the conception of an essentially external God ruling the universe from a seat in heaven. Vivekananda called the conception tribal, and pointed to its historical evolution in Judaeo-Christian religions, which was a way of constant strife amongst Jewish and Babylonian tribes. He pointed out that, Monotheism was, historically, the result of a triumph of the tribal God Moloch Yahveh, over other tribal gods and that even in subsequent history its triumph over other races was achieved by blood-shed and persecution.

As regards Pantheism, both Bankim and Vivekananda showed that it was, amongst Hindus, a true religious conception and not an abstract truth of metaphysics. With the Hindus it was connected with the conception of a Personal God of love and of the Divinity of the soul. Both of these conceptions showed ways of spiritual fulfilment,—the latter, in particular, teaching a lesson in spirituality which aimed at realising the Divinity of the soul while still in the body. No other religion taught ways of salvation which were not essentially conjectural and unreasonable in the flesh.

3. The third result was ethical and was a direct corollary of the theology of Pantheism. If God pervaded all creation, love towards him would be a mockery if it did not include love for all fellow-beings. Both Bankim and Vivekananda regarded the theology of Pantheism as providing the rationale of all ethics. Both of them pointed out that it was the peculiar glory of Hinduism that it alone, of all world-religions, did this. It was true that other re-

18

ligions preached love of humanity as much as Hinduism
did, but the worship of the external God of their conception had no necessary connection with love of humanity. It was therefore an extraneous result,—requiring a
special commandment or special revelation to make the
love effectual. It was in Hinduism alone that love of God
and love of humanity were indissolubly linked.

4. The fourth result was the synthetic, Vedantic approach
to the multiplicity of sects in Hinduism and more generally to the whole body of religions existing in the world.
This approach was already foreshadowed in Bankim's
Commentary on the Gita. "I am available to all wor-
shippers irrespective of their mode of worship"[22] ;
"They also who worship other gods are actually worshipping me even though their mode of worship might not
be according to the proper form"[23]—these verses were
explained by Bankim as voicing the gospel of religious
toleration. Vivekananda, following Ramakrishna, developed the notion further. He declared all religions true,
insofar as they were different modes of spirituality,—
in other words, different modes of realising God,—even
though, as regards dogma, only the Vedantic theory was
possibly true because in Vedanta alone the practice followed directly from the dogma. As Vivekananda preached this doctrine of synthesis, it was no longer a message
of uncritical toleration of every obscure sect that traded
in religion. It was a powerful critical apparatus to examine every species of spiritual practice by the results
it aimed at. If it brought one nearer to God, it was all
right irrespective of the dogma it preached—this was
Vivekananda's teaching.

We should only add that with the development of
these four doctrines was begun a new era in Hinduism which
should be characterized as 'New Hinduism' rather than orthodox Hinduism. The newness of the doctrines comes out most
clearly in their relation to the New Learning of the West. It

is true that it was Bankim alone who addressed himself to a
systematic examination of the religion of the Hindus in the
light of the New Learning.   But Vivekananda's preaching of
the ethical core of Hinduism was inspired by that learning no
less than Bankim's was. Ramakrishna's message could as well
be interpreted as a species of mysticism without deriving any
activist meaning from it. That interpretation would have certainly failed to meet the challenge thrown by Brahmoism and
Christianity, the essence of whose criticism consisted in pointing out that Hinduism in its mystical flights was supra-ethi-
cal, and in its popular idolatrous forms, asocial.[24]   Both
Bankim and Vivekananda addressed themselves to answering
that criticism by discovering the ethical core of Hinduism,
which was the ethics of love and service.   Again, the examination of the doctrines of monotheism and pantheism and of
their relation to ethics was conducted on a strictly rational
plane, and the superiority of Pantheism was established critically without any appeal to orthodox sentiments.   In Vivekananda's synthetic approach to the multiplicity of religious
sects in Hinduism was indicated a powerful force of unity
without any concession to the infamous practices which,
amongst a great many sects, flourished under the guise of religion.

In the light of these facts the charge of 'revivalism' that
has sometimes been levelled against the new movement by a
number of interested parties is open to question. If by 'revivalism' is implied a term of derogation, if it be said – as some
latter-day apologists of the Brahmo faith have said, or rather, implied—that Bankim and Vivekananda sought to revive
the whole spectrum of beliefs and practices associated with
Hinduism which eventually undid the glorious achievements
of Brahmoism, then that charge, insofar as it is confined to
religion properly so-called is evidently baseless.   The qualifi-
cation is important, because the charge of 'revivalism' cannot
be adequately answered before discussing the New Hindu
attitude to social reform as also the New Hindu efforts in the

direction of reinterpreting some of the achievements of the ancient Indian Civilisation.

NOTES AND REFERENCES

1. *Dharmatatta* : Chapter XI.
2. *Dharmatattwa* : Chapter XI.
2. Nikhilananda, *Swami Vivekananda : a Biography*, New York, 1953. Basu, Pramatha Nath : *Swami Vivekananda* : 4 vols. Eastern and Western Disciples : *Life of Swami Vivekananda* : Advaita Ashram, Calcutta, 1912.
3. Satyendranath Majumdar : *Vivekananda Charit*.
4. Eastern and Western Disciples : *The life of Swami Vivekananda* : Advaita Ashram, Calcutta, 1955 pp. 27-28.
5. The earliest reference to the mystical experience of Naren is Katha-mrita probably in Mahendranath Gupta's *Shri Shri Ramakrishna Kathamrita*, Part-II, Appendix ; Part-III, Appendix. Naren himself refers to his experiences in Conversation with Mahendranath (Shri 'M'). The conversations are dated March, April, May, 1887—less than a year after Ramakrishna's death (August, 1886).
6. *Prabuddha Bharat*, April, 1907 : Dr Brojendra Nath Seal's reminiscences of Vivekananda : An early stage of Vivekananda's mental development.
7. Letter to Mrs Bull, dated December 12, 1899 : *The Complete Works of Vivekananda*, Mayavati Memorial Edition, ·Vol. VI, p. 420.
8. Letter to Nivedita, San Francisco, dated March 4, 1900. *Ibid.* pp. 428-29.
9. Letter to Miss Macleod, Alameda, California, 18th April, 1900. *Ibid.*, pp. 431.
10. Letter to Miss Mary Hale, 22nd March, 1900, San Francisco, *Complete works*, vol, VIII. pp. 503.
11. Letter to Miss Mary Hale, 17th June, 1900, Los Angeles : *Ibid.*, pp. 524-25.
12. Eastern and Western Disciples : *The life of Swami Vivekananda*, Advaita Ashram, Calcutta, 1955, p. 388.
13. *Ibid.*, pp. 400.
14. *Ibid.*, pp. 412.
15. *Ibid.*, pp. 411.
16. *Sri Sri Ramakrishna-Kathamrita* by Sri 'M' (5 vols).

17. *Swami-Shishva Sambad* : Swamijir Bani o Rachana : Centenary volume No. IX, Udbodhan Karyalaya, Calcutta, p. 62.
18. Eastern and Western Disciples : *The Life of Swami Vivekananda* p. 507.
19. *'The Future of India'*, *Complete works of Swami Vivekananda,* vol. III.
20. Vivekananda : *The Mission of the Vedanta* cf. Bankim.
21. "This is the great ideal before us, and everyone must be ready for it—the conquest of the whole world by India—nothing less than that." *(The Work Before us : Complete Works,* vol. III).
22. *The Bhagavadgita* Chapter IV, 11.
23. *The Bhagavadgita*, Chapter IX, 23.
24. Vide Rammohan's criticism of Hindu Idolatory quoted in Chapter I.

CHAPTER- VII

REFORM AND REGENERATION

FROM WHAT has been said in the preceding chapters it is clear that the New Hindu Movement was a reform movement and the operative word in this connection was 'activism', which was of the essence of Bankim's exposition of the *Gita* and Vivekananda's Non-Vedantism. The ethics of 'love for all creation' called for a programme of humanitarian service in the broadest sense—educational as well as political,—not to mention such works of charity as are included within programmes of relief aimed at the distressed and the poor. Before discussing these programmes, which, it must be admitted, were never carried out in their entirety, we intend to take up the question of the New Hindu attitude to 'reform' in general and 'social reform' in particular.

(A) SOCIAL REFORM AND BANKIM

It cannot be denied that Bankim opposed a certain species of social reform, sometimes with great vehemence. He opposed the agitation against polygamy launched by Vidyasagar, and was probably instrumental in preventing legislation against that practice. He poured ridicule[1] on the school of reformers headed by B. Malabari whose 'Notes' published in 1884, had created a sensation and led to the promulgation of the Age of Consent Act in 1891. Thus Bankim, to all appearances, was as regards social question, as much an obscurantist as Sasadhar Tarkachudamani whose fulminations against that Act were meant to imply that the Hindu religion was endangered by a piece of legislation which aimed at protecting Hindu wives from enforced sexual intercourse before the age of twelve. These are serious allegations, and if these are found to be true, it is legitimate to infer that the New Hindu Movement was a socially retrograde movement.

To answer this question, we must examine Bankim's criticism of Vidyasagar's social reform movement a bit more

closely. Vidyasagar's publication in 1873 of "An Examination of the Question whether Polygamy should be Abolished"[2] was the occasion of a *Vangadarsan* article, written by
Bankim himself, which purported to show that Vidyasagar's
style of social reform was wrong in principle and useless in
practice. Vidyasagar was trying to mount an agitation against
polygamy on the plea that the Shastras had not sanctioned
the practice in an unrestricted way ; on the strength of that
Shastric prohibition Vidyasagar was seeking a legislative
measure to abolish it. Bankim pointed out that the Shastras
were hardly a dependable guide in social matters ; actually
they, or rather their social injunctions, were a cause of India's
downfall.[3] Bankim wanted a divorce of social questions from
Shastric discussions, and in consequence, he could not but
oppose Vidyasagar's manner of social reform which was going to perpetuate India's dependence on Shastras.

It is clear that far from being the stand of an obscurantist like Sasadhar Tarkachudamani, such a stand on social
questions was far ahead of Vidyasagar's own, which was
strangely inhibited in its reforming postures by an uncritical
acceptance of Shastric injunctions. The whole point of Bankim's attack was to do away with this source of inhibition.

But did Bankim actually plead for inhibited social reform ? Apart from attacking the source of inhibition that
prevented a rational treatment of social questions, did he do
anything in the way of active social reform ? Vidyasagar's
manner of social reform might be objectionable ; but there
was such a thing as 'rational philanthrophy', just as there
was the gospel of 'utilitarianism', the holders of both the
doctrines insisting on reform in antiquated social customs.
Did Bankim, who, in political matters as also on certain
points of religion was a disciple of J. S. Mill, and thoroughly acquainted with doctrine of utility, appeal to that doctrine in the cause of social reform ? Did he not rather attack
the social reformers as a set of sensation-mongers[4] ? Did he
not rather suppress his work on "Equality" in mature years,

and thereby, give sufficient ground for the later critics' complaint that he died a social reactionary,—a Hindu chauvinist, a religious fanatic ?

To answer such criticism we need only compare Bankim's reaction to the Age of Consent Act of 1891 with that of Sasadhar and Vidyasagar. But first of all, we must say something about the agitation that led to that Act. We know that this Act had its origin in the sensational publicity given to such consequences of child-marriage as were witnessed in the death of ten year old Phulmoni owing to her thirty-five year old husband's attempt at forcible sexual intercourse with her. The husband whose name was Hari Maiti was acquitted by a court on the ground that the law of rape did not apply to the spouse of a girl who had reached her tenth birthday. The case was tried in 1890, that is to say, only a year before the consent Act was passed. But it is not improbable that the judge's verdict, which might have facilitated the promulgation of the Act, was itself influenced by the propaganda started by B. M. Malabari against infantile marriage and perpetual widowhood prevalent in Hindu society. Malabari, whose "Notes" published in 1884, had created such a sensation, was a Parsi reformer. His "Notes" were directed against the evils of Hindu society, particularly against perpetual widowhood and child marriage. Malabari was a journalist, and his reforming zeal coupled with his journalistic career, had created a work in which sober judgment was clouded by a wholly admirable, if a little histrionic, solicitude for widows and child-wives, in Hindu society. The "Notes" were a product of sentimentality rather than sober social criticism. Regarding widows he said : "(The sights of mistreated widows) burnt themselves into my brains. It is not only that I know the miseries of widowhood, not merely that I feel them, fell for and with the widow ; I am the widow for the moment."[5]

It is quite understandable to what lengths of exaggeration the author of so fantastic a statement[6] would go in discussing the fate of child-wives, which was worse than that of the widow by reason of the threat of enforced sexual intercourse hanging over her head from the very day of her marriage. Malabari asserted quite seriously that the majority of child-marrying Hindus were inveterate child molestors.[7] Malabari was not content to publish a work embodying these opinions and leave the matter at that. He organised extensive tours throughout the length and breadth of India and rent the Welkin by furious public demonstration of his solicitude for widows and child-wives. Quite a few members of Hindu society were rash enough to challenge the reformers' opinions. The Government itself was infected with Malabari's enthusiasm, but in face of stiff Hindu opposition Sir Auckland Colvin, the then Finance Minister of India, had nothing more to offer to the reformers than a modest counsel of patience : "You and I and the widow and the five year old bride must possess ourselves in patience until a humbler and truer conception of its needs and duties breaks in upon the native mind." Malabari was not to be put off by such vague assurance. He started for England. He met Max Muller and many other gentlemen sincerely interested in India's well-being. He organised meetings and impressed upon the high-minded British public the desperate state of Indian girls in the hands of their child-molesting husbands. In India, too, the course of events began to move rapidly. Malabari's campaign had started in 1884. In 1890, was tried the case of Hari Maiti, and the child-molester was acquitted on grounds already noted. Malabari's disciple Dayaram Gidumal proposed the Age of Consent Bill as the least that could immediately be done to save the lives of ten or eleven year old child-wives. The Bill was passed in 1891.

It is against this background that we must compare Bankim's attitude towards the Act with that of Vidyasagar and Sasadhar. Neither Vidyasagar nor Sasadhar supported the Act, as we saw in Chapter-I, the latter actually raised a hue and cry against it. Vidyasagar who had been instrumen-

tal in giving shape to the original version of the Act (pro-
mulgated in 1860, and stipulating that sexual intercourse with
a girl below the age of ten be an act of rape) wanted to re-
phrase the new version in a manner that would make it virtually inoperative. He sought to delete the mention of any
specific age-limit for consummation of marriage and insert
instead the phrase 'the time of the first menses.' The meaning of this objection was clear—the Shastras made sexual
intercourse compulsory at the time of the 'first menses' and
preached damnation for parents who did not marry their
daughters before that time. Also Indian girls often attained
that condition before the age of twelve. Thus Vidyasagar by
his obedience to the Shastras was inadvertantly led to the
countenancing of child marriage in Hindu society and, what
was worse, to the countenancing of sexual intercourse with a
girl of eleven, if and when she attained puberty at that age.
Vidyasagar believed that "as the majority of girls do not exhibit that symptom before they are thirteen, fourteen or fif-
teen, the measure I suggest would give larger more real and
more extensive protection than the Bill."[8] But there is no
getting round the fact that his devotion to the Shastras precluded his adopting any truly rational measure against the
evil of child-marriage ; his own amendment to the Consent
Bill only put his seal of approval to the custom.

Very dissimilar was Bankim's reaction to the Act. To
understand why Bankim maintained absolute silence about
the Act itself, but attacked Malabari with such ferocity after
the Act was passed, we must remember two things. Bankim
knew that Sasadhar's opposition against the Act was obscurantist in the extreme. But neither could he countenance
Vidyasagar's manner of reform. He was acutely conscious
of the danger involved in the sort of reform which while trying to get rid of wicked social customs, appealed to Shastric
injunctions, which in this particular case were worse than the
custom itself.[9] At the same time he was perfectly aware of
the disastrous consequences of toeing the line of 'liberal' re-

formers like Malabari whose attacks against Hindu social customs ended in an Act which had the effect of representing all Hindus as rapists and child-molesters. The controversy about the Age of Consent Bill was obscure in the extreme. Mr Heimsath has quoted Tilak's summing up of the controversy in these words :

"We have been mischievously and shamelessly represented as a nation of savages and the Sudharaks (reformers) have shamelessly testified to it. Let these Sudharaks therefore form a separate nationality. We wought no longer to allow to be amongst us those of our fellow-countrymen who are really our enemies but who pose as our friends."[10]

Bankim's language, aiming not at the Act but at its father, was similar :

"The other day, a Parsi named Malabari, in his eagerness to attain the sort of fame or notoreity (open to the class of people who aim at revolution of society by appeal to Shastras or by enacting legislation) raised a terrible hue and cry."[11]

The meaning of this is clear enough : Bankim's attack was directed not so much at the reform itself as at reformers of the school of Malabari, who scarcely shrank from painting the society, for the good of which they were agitating in the blackest colour possible. Also it was directed at the manner of reform that would call in its aid Shastras which themselves treated social customs as something static with laws prescribed at the dawn of creation and some of them positively scandalous. The sort of social reforms desired by Bankim would, therefore, have to proceed on a line different from that pursued by the School of Vidyasagar as well as the School of Malabari.

(B) VIVEKANANDA AND SOCIAL REFORM

Vivekananda's attack on social reformers occurred in 1897—just five years after Bankim's attack on Malabari. It was occasioned by an act typical of the social reformers.

Vivekananda's triumphant preaching of Hinduism in America
and his complete silence about such questions as widow-
marriage had led these reformers to spread calumny against
him. When he returned to India in 1897, they suddenly began
to clamour that being a Sudra by birth, he had no right to
pose as a Sannyasin, as the garb of a Sannyasin was allowed to
Brahmins alone.[12]   In their anxiety to lower Vivekananda's
credibility in the eyes of the orthodox, the reformers were only
making themselves ridiculous, for of all people they were certainly the last from whom an aspersion against Vivekananda's
caste status could be expected.   Social reformers fastidious
about the Brahminhood of a Sannyasin could hardly be said
to be true to their own creed.   But in this case the reformers
had their own reason for this apparently self-defeating move.
They were trying to intimidate Vivekananda into joining their
own set, so that the great prestige of Vivekananda's name
could be harnessed to the cause of reform.[13] The Swami's
answer when it came, was one of the masterpieces of his ora-
torial career.   In a Madras hall crowded to capacity, he un-
folded what he called his 'plan of campaign'.   It is not necessary for our purpose to give here a summary of the whole
speech which was one of the noblest he ever uttered, but his
attitude to the social reform movement was revealed in it with
the best possible clarity.   He roundly called the reform societies "condemning societies" and asked :

      "What good has been done (by a hundred years of re-
form movement) except the creation of a most vituperative, a
most condemnatory literature ? ...... They have criticised,
condemned, abused the orthodox, until the orthodox have
caught their tone and paid them back in their own coin ; and
the result is the creation of a literature in every vernacular
which is the shame of the race, the shame of the country. Is
this reform ? Is this leading the nation to glory ?"[14]

      It is reasonable to suppose that Vivekananda, in this
extract was referring to the obscene controversy surrounding
the Age of Consent Bill, as much as to the 'literature' created

against his own character. This seems all the more probable because the reference to the orthodox community paying back the reformers in their own coin cannot be understood except in that context. Whether this supposition be true or not, Vivekananda's attitude to social reformers in general is identical with Bankim's attitude to the reformers of the school of Malabari.[15] Both of them condemned the contemporary social reform movement on the same ground : that movement was striking at the very root of the society they were trying to reform.

(C) REFORM AND REGENERATION

This is the background against which we must examine the reform programmes of Bankim and Vivekananda. Neither of them was interested in the social reform programmes of the day not because they wished to preserve the existing Hindu society with all its abuses and evils—as Sasadhar Tarkachudamani and other leaders of orthodoxy did—but because in their eyes the reformers were putting the cart before the horse. The ideal social leader, according to Bankim, was Krishna who did nothing to eradicate so evil a custom as "marriage by abduction"[16], but actually made use of it in marrying his sister Subhadra to Arjuna. Instead of taking up the work of social reform, Krishna dedicated his whole life to the cause of spreading true religion and founding a "Commonwealth of Righteousness." In Bankim's words : "What Krishna aimed at was the moral and political regeneration of the land : propagation of religion and the founding of a kingdom of righteousness. If and when these ends are achieved, reform of society follows automatically ; if not, social reformation remains an impossibility. Krishna, the ideal man knew this. He knew that in horticulture as in social reformation watering a (dead) branch is not the best way to secure the most plentiful fruitage..... This was why the ideal man did not strive to become a Malabari."[17]

Here is a new approach to social question—the app-

roach of "regeneration" as contrasted to that of 'reform'.
Vivekananda's attitude was similar. In the Madras address
already referred to he called the reformer's method the method
of 'destruction' his own being the method of 'growth.'[18] Bankim clarified the approach further in a letter to Kumar Benoy
Krishna Deb of the Sovabazar Raj family, in which he supported the sea-voyage movement sponsored by the latter, but
did so from an angle which was quite different from the latter's orthodox approach. Binoy Krishna Deb had started the
movement in the manner of Vidyasagar and was looking for
Shastric support in favour of sea-voyage amongst Hindus.[19]
Bankim's letter[20] was in response to his (Benoy Krishna
Deb's) request asking him to expound what in his opinion
was the true Hindu attitude to sea-voyage. Bankim argued
that Shastric injunctions were quite irrelevant to the matter
and that both the Shastric approach to reform as well as reform by means of legislative measures were equally futile.
According to him, "In the absence of a moral and religious
regeneration of the land, no deep-rooted change could be
effected in social customs by merely appealing to certain
Shastras." Society, in his opinion, was moved by tradition
(Deshachar) and not by Shastras, and tradition, however
evil, "could not be changed except by changes in religion
and morality." He examined the sea voyage question from
that angle and showed that sea-voyage being conducive to
social well-being was countenanced by the "eternal principle
of religion" (Sanatan Dharma) as expounded by Krishna.
Shastras in his mind, were subservient to those eternal principles, and "religious and moral regeneration of the land
was nothing but a re-assertion of those eternal principles."

Vivekananda's language was almost identical : "Every
(social) improvement in India requires first of all an uphea-
val in religion. Before flooding India with socialistic or political ideas, first deluge the land with spiritual ideas. The first
work that demands our attention is that the most wonderful
truths confined in our Upanishads, in our Scriptures, in our

Puranas must be brought out from the books, brought
from the monasteries, brought out from the forests, brought
out from the possession of selected bodies of people, and scat-
tered broadcast all over the land, so that these truths may
run like fire all over the country from north to south and east
to west, from the Himalayas to Comorin, from Sindh to the
Brahmaputra."[21]

(D) THE NEW HINDU PROGRAMMES OF REGENERATION

It is clear that, with such a view of social regeneration,
New Hindu leaders like Bankim and Vivekananda could
hardly be satisfied with laws of marriage or marriage consummation, by which the reformers of the day set much store. It
is clear they would rather look for reforms of a more fundamental kind—reforms, that is to say, that would make for
changes of a far more positive nature. Vivekananda's slogan
was : "Raising of the Sudras",— and we have already seen in
what tragic intensity his own character expressed the message
in his restless journeys over India and across the seas. That
the message was not a matter of mere tragic emotion, but an
answer to India's greatest need is made clear from an examination of the practical form in which the Swami expressed it.
But, here as elsewhere, he was anticipated by Bankim. It is
relevant here to discuss the latter's thoughts on raising the
Sudras.

In Chapter-II, we referred to Bankim's celebrated essay,
'The Peasants of Bengal' published in the early years of
Vangadarsan. It was an epoch-making essay, though not the
first to bring the plights of the peasantry to public notice. Actually the condition of Bengali peasants was being discussed
since the time of Rammohan. But Bankim's essay was epoch-
making in the sense that it was the first of its kind to relate
the decline of India to the age-old degradation of the Sudras.
Even in this analysis, Bankim was extremely original. He did
not repeat the hackneyed missionery (and Brahmo) charges
against the manifold evils of casteism but attributed the mis-

ery of the Sudras to the strikingly early growth of the Brahmanical intellect—a fact which led to the subservience of the non-intellectual classes from the earliest times. Contrary to popular belief, Bankim showed that this subservience of the non-intellectual classes ultimately led to the decline of the Brahmins themselves and not the other way about. This was tantamount to asking the Brahmins to espouse the cause of the Sudras for their own good—a very different approach to the caste question from that of most reformers who were incessantly preaching the abolition of the Brahmins. Also, according to Bankim, the superstitious excrescences of Hinduism were a result of that decline and not its cause. The Smritis, in particular—those numerous Sudra-baiting Shastras on which the reformers of Vidyasagar's school were basing their reform programmes were also a result of the same decline. Thus, even as early as 1872-73 Bankim had rejected the 'reformers' programmes by looking far ahead of them and bringing to the forefront the raising of the lower classes as the greatest of all social questions in India, and implying that most of the reforms advocated by reformers were included within that one reform which preceded them all and superseded them all.

It was left to Vivekananda to render Bankim's critical insight into the cause of India's decline and his attribution of that decline to the condition of the lower classes in India a supremely powerful social message revealing with the fullest possible clarity the futility of the routine social programmes of the various schools of reformers. "Most of the reforms that have been agitated for during the past century have been ornamental,"[22] he told his Madras audience. "The question of widow marriage would not touch seventy percent of the Indian women, and all such questions only reach the higher castes of Indian people who are educated at the expense of the masses."[23] Vivekananda pointed out that, in the name of reform, the higher castes were "cleaning their own houses." He refused to call it 'reformation' and re-

marked that 'the tyranny of the minority' was the worst
tyranny of the world. He implied that reformers were a
handful of upper-caste busybodies cut off from the main-
stream of national life, but nevertheless trying to ram down
the throat of the 'nation' their own fads and crotchets with
hardly any attempt to understand how the nation really felt
or what she desired.

Vivekananda wanted to create a body of religious workers (a) who would carry education to the masses, education
in this context including both secular as well as spiritual education ; (b) who would serve the poor in all possible ways,
especially by taking up works of relief in times of distress,
and those of nursing the sick and the disabled throughout the
year ; (c) and who would set up a traffic of ideas between
India and the West, by spreading the spiritual truths of
Hinduism in the Western countries, and bringing in return,
knowledge and money required to set the poor of India on
their feet.

It is only necessary to and that Vivekananda founded
the Ramakrishna Mission with these very aims in view. We
intend to stress one aspect of these aims which has not been
taken due note of by historians and the general run of critics.

The aspect in question is this : Educating the poor,
serving the sick and sending Hindu missionaries to preach
spirituality in the West may all be laudable aims in themselves; but one may well ask : why should these things be regarded as intrinsically superior to remarriage of ten year-old
widows or protection of twelve-year-old brides from molestation by their thirtyfive year old spouses ? Put in this crude
manner, superiority of Vivekananda's (and Bankim's) social
programmes is not made immediately evident. It needs to be
emphasised that Vivekananda's efforts were guided by the
aim of spirituality in comparison to which he held every
other consideration as secondary. Giving a widow in marriage was not an act of spirituality even if accompanied by a
hundred verses culled from the Shastras ; at best it was more

20

than opening to her the gate of those worldly pleasures from which most non-widows were not barred.   But serving to the best of one's powers one's "God, the wicked, God the miserable and God the poor of all races", was a spiritual act—it glorified one's existence even in failure.   This was the meaning of Bankim's doctrine of 'regeneration' and Vivekananda's doctrine of 'growth'.   This distinction must be clearly borne in mind when we set out to draw a balance-sheet of the comparative achievements of the 19th century reformers and 19th century New Hindu thinkers.

But even on a critical historical estimate apart from considerations of intrinsic value, we must pronounce the reformers' achievements negligible in comparison to those of such a man as Vivekananda. It is true that Vivekananda never found the band of religious workers who would carry education to the lower classes, and to this day the vast majority of Indians remain as illiterate and down-trodden as they were in Vivekananda's time. Also, the Mission through which he sought to achieve the deliverance of India's millions from poverty and ignorance can hardly be said to have yet come to serious grips with these basic questions of Indian society. But Vivekananda was unquestionably the first great 'populist' leader in modern India with Bankim as his intellectual forerunner, Mahatma Gandhi following closely in their footsteps though with far greater success in his work in the service of the poor.   But Mahatma's programmes of social service closely followed those of Vivekananda, both of them emphasizing the spiritual aspect of service rendered to the poor as distinct from the political or the legislative. No 19th century reformer, not to mention the latter-day leaders in 'populist' politics can be pronounced fit—if we may use a popular phrase—to hold a candle to them.

(E) NEW HINDU PROGRAMMES OF REFORM

Even on the level of reform that could not properly be included within the scope of Bankim's doctrine of 'regeneration' and Vivekananda's doctrine of 'growth', these two thinkers made a current of fresh air blow through the lifeless ritualism of Hindu customs which had been responsible for much of the pernicious rigidity of orthodox caste regulations. Bankim and Vivekananda insisted on separating the question of food from the sphere of religion. The Brahmos themselves from Keshub Chandra Sen onwards, had begun insisting on the shedding of the Brahmonical thread and on intercaste dining—to name only two amongst a host—as compulsory customs attendant on the Brahmo faith. This was of course ridiculous, for, shedding the Brahmonical thread no more contributed to genuine piety than wearing it did. When Bankim refrained from admonishing all Brahmans to shed it, but at the same time denied the Brahmanhood of one "who wore the most resplendent of sacred threads around his neck, but passed his days in malice and ill-behaviour", he initiated a process which marked the end of the age of thread-shedding revolutionalism as well as of the age in which the wearing of the thread was the easiest passport to the gate of spirituality. When he refused the Hindu name to any one "who neither had nor strove to have any knowledge of the spirit that pervaded all creation, who neither perceived nor strove to perceive his identity with all creation, and who neither was nor strove to be non discriminating"[24]; when he held up the non-Brahmin Keshub Chandra Sen as every whit a proper spiritual guide for Brahmins[25] ; when he proposed the low-born Muslim peasant Kachhimuddi Sheikh as in every particular fitted to cook and serve dishes of chicken to Hindu guests in a Durgapuja gathering ("for true Hinduism preached non-discrimination and forbade looking at this man as Hindu, that man as Mussalman, this man as low born and that man as high born"[26]—Bankim silently and without any flourish of revolutionism initiated an era in which caste and food regulation would no longer be regarded as the essence of Hinduism.

The point of these reform schemes of Bankim was this :

Unlike the reformers, Bankim did not propose the elimination of food and caste regulations as indispensable prerequisites for a reformed Hindu society, but sought to eliminate them by appealing to the essence of Hinduism and condemning them only when they came in conflict with that essence. Unlike the reformers Bankim was aware that, just as there were Brahmins who abhorred the food served by a Mussalman as contaminated and left the Mussalman in no doubt about his abhorrence, there were also Brahmans like Bhudev who, while avoiding inter-dining with Mussalmans, yet were the soul of charity in their personal relations with them. The elimination of the said regulations was thus prescribed where these clashed with that spirit of charity. In other words, with Bankim, the schemes of reform were schemes of 'regeneration' and not ends in themselves.

The distinction is important and needs emphasizing because it is often overlooked in discussions about Vivekananda's reform schemes. It is now generally recognised that Vivekananda's attack on what he called the Untouchability of orthodox Hindu society has been perhaps the most potent force in doing away with those invidious caste regulations which have kept Hindu society so divided in past ages and which are by no means extinct as yet. His letters (especially those in Bengali) are veritable arsenals of shame, ridicule and towering indignation directed against food and caste regulations, which, to most Hindus of his time formed the essence of their religion. Unfortunately, this very effectiveness of Vivekananda's tirade has given rise to an impression that he sought the elimination of caste regulations as an end in itself.

Nothing indeed could be further from the truth. The identity of Vivekananda's views in this matter with those of Bankim is evident to anyone who has gone through his letters carefully. Like Bankim, Vivekananda, whenever he refers to the Hindu practice of caste and class discrimination, invariably contrasts that practice with Hindu doctrine of non-discrimination ; and it is clear that he intends no Malabari-type reform in these regulations. Even on so trumpery a matter as interdining amongst Brahmans and Sudras Vivekananda took no rigid line except when the customary restriction seemed to militate against the true spirit of Hinduism. The chronicler of "The Dialogue between the Swami and His Disciple" has narrated an incident where Vivekananda persuades the orthodox disciple to take tea with Nivedita, but elsewhere he is reported to have insisted only on interdining amongst people of the same caste without discriminating as between Brahman of one part of India and another. It is clear that he was not obstinately bent upon making of the concession he was ready to grant in the case of such a woman as Nivedita a law that would bind the whole of Hindu society. He was not in favour of fanatically eradicating from Hindu society so pernicious an evil as 'untouchability' and would scrupulously respect an orthodox Hindu's inhibitions as long as his inhibitions did not lead to caste-hatred or other abominations. Miss Macleod has narrated an incident which is more revealing. Alasinga Perumal was one of Vivekananda's most devoted disciples. He was a Madrasi Brahman brought up in an atmosphere of the most rigid orthodoxy and observing the most stringent of 'untouchability' in his personal life. But Vivekananda never asked him to shed a jot or tittle of his orthodoxy. Miss Macleod who had just arrived from America, was not agreeably impressed by Alasinga Perumal's quaint Vaishnavite marks, spread all over his forehead, and she privately made a remark to that effect to Vivekananda. In her own words :

"Instantly Swami turned and said with great sternness, 'Hands off ! what have you ever done ?' I did not know what I had done then. Of course, I never answered. Tears came to my eyes and I waited, I learnt later that Mr. Alasinga Perumal was a young Brahmin teaching philosophy in a college in Madras earning 100 rupees a month, supporting his father, mother, wife and four children, who had gone from door to door to beg money to send Vivekananda to the

West. Perhaps without him we never would have met Vivekananda."[27] Obviously with Vivekananda, such a man as Alasinga Perumal, with all his superstitious devotion to the most rigid of caste rules, was worth a hundred reformers who interdined with all Mlechchas and had no use for ridiculous Vaishnavite marks.

Even on the plane of reform demanded by the Brahmo Samaj and other reforming bodies of the 19th century, Bankim and Vivekananda were not thus merely parroting contemporary progressive opinion, but infusing the doctrine of reform, with the spirit of regeneration. This is why Vivekananda's attack on 'untouchability' strikes us as so much more convincing than the reformers' fulminations against food and other taboos of orthodox Hindu society.

It would also be relevant here to discuss Bankim's and Vivekananda's attitude to two other reform schemes of contemporary reformers. Bankim supported inter-caste marriage but never agitated for it. Vivekananda was rigidly opposed to the custom of child marriage, but expressly advised his disciples against mounting an agitation to ban the custom. Hostile critics have been quick to raise the outcry of 'revivalism', but they have totally failed to understand why these thinkers did not match profession by expenditious practice.[28]

Bankim says clearly in the commentary on the *Gita* that to look for strictures against inter-caste marriage in the *Gita* is futile, because the whole point of Krishna's discourse is to replace Arjuna's pre-occupation with caste purity or caste religion (Kuladharma) by a truer and loftier conception of religion.[29] Bankim ends the commentary with a 'progressivist' flourish asserting his readiness to prove that "a mixture of castes is wholly beneficial to modern society."[30]

One would miss Bankim's point altogether, if, from this one would jump to the conclusion that Bankim ought to have started a campaign in favour of inter-caste marriage. Actually, Bankim was more interested in removing the religious taboo against mixture of castes than in opening new ways of marriage. Bankim was emphasizing that aspect of Hinduism, which, by denouncing, caste taboos as false religion, sought to be 'regenerative' rather than merely 'reforming'. Bankim was well aware that, beneath the claptrap of progressivism, 'reforming' marriages often concealed a story of infamy and scandal. Thus in some of the widow marriage arranged by Vidyasagar, the bridegrooms were known to have married for money, following it up—not of course, in Vidyasagar's knowledge, far less with his consent—by another marriage contracted with a virgin.[31] Bankim, with his insistence on the regenerative aspect of reform, could hardly undertake reforms of this kind, which in the case of intercaste marriages were likely to lead to grosser scandals. Bankim would rather seek to educate Hindus in the true spirit of Hinduism in regard to caste taboos, and leave the matter to individual conscience.

Very similar was Vivekananda's treatment of the question of child marriage, against which custom his language was a thousand times more intemperate than that of the most obstreperous of reformers. In his letters, he repeatedly advises his brethren to pay no heed to public criticism, because, in his opinion, most Indians "had lost their wits by forcing pregnance on twelve-year-old girls."

Vivekananda could not help thinking that the wedlock thrust on minor Hindu girls was a monstrous injustice, and, against this custom no language struck him as being too harsh. But this was hardly a reforming matter ; it was a matter of education—of preaching to women their Vedantic divinity. Vivekananda's doctrine certainly included the liberal doctrine of 'emancipation of women', but it went far beyond that, for in the Vedantic sense, emancipation was nothing if not going beynd marriage. It was certainly not merely the leaving to women the choice in their marriage or in other pursuits. Vivekananda was far more interested in winning for women their right to celibacy than in promoting the reformers' scheme

of adult marriage. He could well say by slightly changing
a celebrated saying of Christ : In emancipation there is neither marrying nor giving in marriage ; ('in that condition
women no less than men are as angels in heaven').

Neither Bankim nor Vivekananda was thus a reformer
in the then accepted sense of the term, even though their (especially Vivekananda's) preachings promoted the cause of reform much more steadily than the reformers' own efforts did.
They were not refomers because in the first place, they founded no reforming association ; in the second place, their reform schemes were educative rather than legislative, and, in
the third place, they were quite ready to suffer orthodox people to observe all caste rules meticulously but do so in love
and amity towards fellow Hindus, rather than in hatred and
ill-will. Reformers on the other hand made it a matter of
principle to shock orthodox conscience by endless demonstrations of unnecessary heterodoxy.

(E) NEW HINDU ATTITUDE TO THE 'WOMAN QUESTION'

This examination of Bankim's and Vivekananda's attitude to social reform provides a clue to a clearer understanding of their attitude to the so-called 'woman question.' Here,
it must be admitted, Bankim's attitude strikes us as somewhat more orthodox than Vivekananda's. The latter's intense
hostility to child marriage is totally absent from Bankim's
writings. On the contrary, the violence of his language to the
reformers of the school of Malabari,[32] though by no means
indicating hostility to reform as such leaves some room for
suspicion that he did not consider the custom of compulsory
child marriage wholly objectionable. Also his suppression
of the work on 'Equality' in the later years of his life and
republication of the same in a modified from[33] from which
the part dealing with questions of reform in the status of
Hindu woman was carefully excluded, strengthens the suspicion that in matters of reform concerning the rights of woman in Hindu society he had gradually veered round to a
rigidly orthodox stand. The following extract from *Dharma-*

tattwa almost confirms the suspicion.

Disciple : am I to think, then, that the equality of the sexes
sought to be established by Europeans is a sort
of social nuisance ?

Teacher : How is this equality going to be made possible ? Is
it possible for a man to give birth to and suckle a
child ?   On the other hand, is it possible to start
a war with help of an army constitued of women
alone ?[34]

It is evident that, in clear repudiation of his own earlier stand on the equality of the sexes, Bankim is here resorting to a species of argument that is wholly sophistical. For
surely 'biological inequality' is no valid argument against the
desirability of social equality[35]—as Bankim himself had pointed out in the earlier work. There is therefore a grain of
truth in the modern critics' dig against Bankim on the score
of his supposed blindness to the injustice perpetrated by
Hindu society on its women from time immemorial.

The charge, whose validity is discussed in the last section of this Chapter, does not apply to Vivekananda whose
fierce tirade against child-marriage alone is enough to convince one that Vivekananda needed no reformer's prodding to
take arms against the injustice his countrymen had been per-
petrating on their women in the name of religion.

However, with Vivekananda as with Bankim, a change
in the custom of marriage was far from being of the first
consideration as with the social reformers of the time. Both
of them sought to redefine the position of woman in Hindu
society irrespective of any immediate programme of social reform—apart from education—to give effect to that definition.
Both of them categorically rejected the orthodox conception
of woman as stated in the Smritis and as implied in the monastic notion of woman as the gate of hell. In its place they
shaped a conception which was extremely heterodox and re-
motely connected to Hindu religious tradition by the thread
of Tantrism. This was in its effects at least, seemed repug-

21

nant to many persons, but in the hands of Bankim and Vivekananda underwent a significant transformation.

The Tantrik conception of woman as the emblem of
power was expressly stated by Vivekananda, who derived the
notion from Ramakrishna, in whose eyes every woman was
the living embodiment of the Divine Mother. This was of
course a mystical doctrine not easily translatable in human
terms. Bankim paved the way for such a translation by his
emphasis on the heroic conception of woman. This is not the
place to discuss in detail to what glorious heights he raised
this conception in the delineation of the female characters
in his novels. In Bankim's novels (*Devichaudhurani, Sitaram,*
etc.) woman preponderates over the man by shedding a lustre
in the 'intensity of her vital energy' and in the 'vigour and
scope of her mind and character.' But this literary conception was accompanied by a serious re-examination of the conception traditionally accepted by Hindu society in Bankim's
essay on 'Draupadi',[36] in which he compared the heroic
queen of the Pandavas with the self-effacing Sita, the traditional idol of Hindu women. Bankim did not set out to
debunk Sita whose self-effacement in face of the tyranny imposed by a male-dominated society had passed the test of
sublimity and given her the status of the Hindu woman per
excellence. But he left no room for doubt that in the New
Hindu conception, the queen of the Pandavas, in whose making "the harder virtues of the female character" far outshone
the softer, was to be accorded a rank at least equal to Sita's.
The gigantic display of female pride and female courage in
Draupadi's vindication of her honour in the Kaurava Court
and her assertion of female independence in regard to the
husbands' will when that will clashed with woman's Dharma,
was Bankim's answer to social reformers and his own New
Hindu version of the doctrine of woman's emancipation.

But first and foremost it was a Hindu conception in
that it sought the fulfilment of the married woman's destiny
in marriage and marriage alone tied up the woman's search

for religion with her devotion to her husband. Bankim's addition to this traditional conception was this : he sought the traditional emphasis on female devotion to be supplemented by a reciprocal devotion on the husband's part; he conceived female devotion as a matter of gigantic self-assertion rather than one of kneeling self-effacement.[37]

Integral to Bankim's conception of the reciprocal devotion of husband and wife was his emphasis on the woman's role as 'Sahadharmini'—a helper in the husband's spiritual efforts. And Bankim was poetic enough to redeem this hackneyed notion from triteness by making it resplendent in the careers of his literary (masterful) heroines, who were portrayed as guides rather than as servile helpmates. Thus Santi in *Anandamath* and Prafulla in *Devichaudhurani* are shown as investing the lives of their husbands—no men of straw themselves—with a meaning that makes their existence glorious by taking radiance from a love, that could be mistaken for compassion but was in fact a species of womanly devotion so sublime as to make it a name for heavenly grace—sanctifying their brief hours of mortality.

It should be clear from all this that Bankim wanted to raise the status of women in Hindu society by raising the conception of womanhood but without violence to traditional laws or time-honoured social customs. His treatment of the "woman question" was very different from that of the reformers, whose position was that these laws were obsolete, and needed thoroughgoing reformation. Vivekananda, however, whilst he held the poorest opinion about legal reformation,[38] met the reformers half way, not actually in joining the legal reform campaign,[39] but in vigorously affirming that the condition of woman in Hindu society was absolutely scandalous.[40] Like Bankim's, his own answer to the problem lay essentially in raising the conception of womanhood in Hindu society but with a difference. In the first place, he generalised the heroic conception of womanhood in Vedantic-Tantric terms ; in the second place, he gave practical effect

to the Vedantic equality of man and woman by leaving the
ground prepared for starting women on careers that would
exclude marriage and thereby give freer and larger scope for
the development and expression of their powers.

To take the second point first, Vivekananda was the
first Hindu leader to recognise Hindu woman's right to monastic life, so long enjoyed by men alone. This right, allowed,
since the earliest times, in Buddhism and Roman Catholicism
alike, may not strike one as so very revolutionary after all,
but in orthodox Hinduism with its insistence on marriage
and devotion to the husband as the only expression of a woman's piety, this was an innovation of the most daring kind.
It is true that he did not found women's monasteries towards
the implementation of that idea. In fact, the significance of
this idea is symbolic. It was the first step towards recognising
women' right to any avocation whatsover, secular or religious.
When Vivekananda found fault with the reformers' scheme of
emancipating women by changes in marriage laws, he said in
effect that their programmes were no more conducive to
female freedom in any fundamental sense than the existing
laws in Hindu society were. "Liberty is the first condition
of growth. It is wrong, a thousand times wrong, if anyone of
you dares to say 'I will work out the salvation of this woman
or child."[41] "Educate your women first and leave them to
themselves ; then they will tell you what reforms are necessary for them. In matters concerning them, who are you ?"
Such words clearly indicate that what Vivekananda was
aiming at was women's right to mould their lives according
to their own lights without waiting for the lead given by male
busybodies. In an age when men were crying themselves
hoarse over the fate of widows, and when people could not
think of any measure for improving the lot of women except
within the fetters of marriage, Vivekananda sounded a most
refreshing note.

As regards the first, it is necessary first of all to remove a popular misconception regarding Vivekananda's idea

of womanhood in the context of the revitalised Hinduism of
which he was the apostle. Quite a few writers have been
misled by Vivekananda's many admiring references to Sita
into a conclusion that he was proposing that symbol of sublime self-effacement as the prototype of future Hindu women
as of those of the past. "The women of India must grow and
develop in the footprints of Sita, and that is the only way"[42]
—such a sentence is certainly apt to strengthen that misconception. But, Vivekananda's references to Sita, worshipful
as they are, are completely overshadowed by his numerous
references to the women of America, who in their courage,
in the complete uninhibitedness of their movement, in their
receptivity to new ideas—in a word, in the amenity of the ad-
venturousness that marked their every gesture, created in him
a wistfulness, when he compared the lot of India's woman
with those of America, which is the surest indication of the
way in which his mind was working in his conception of the
Hindu woman of the future. "If I can make a thousand such
women in India, I shall die in peace,"[43] he wrote to his brethren. The Swami was a hero if ever there was one, and in
women as in men, what he valued most was the heroic fibre.
But it should be noted at once that in the impulse the heroism he sought in the future women of India he (like Bankim)
sought essentially in Hindu sources, even though—unlike the
latter—he did not appeal to the Queen of the Pandavas as
the idol to inspire the women of his own epoch.

Vivekananda derived the heroic conception of womanhood by combining the doctrine of the sexlessness of the God
who pervaded all creation with the Shakti cult of the Tantras.
"When you will realise that all illuminating truth of the
Atman, then you will see that the idea of sex-discrimination
has vanished altogether, then only will you look upon all women as the veritable manifestation of Brahmin"[44]—this was
the first half of a conception of which the second half was
supplied by the notion of "an all-pervading power of which
women were the special manifestation."[45] The first half de-

clared the fundamental equality of men and women and by implication, conceded to women the freedom of self-expression customarily granted to men alone. The second half went a step further and placed women on a pedestal that was higher yet. It is interesting that Vivekananda was unconsciously making a concession to Dualism by recognising the nature-soul duality preached by the Sankhyas and the Tantras alike, the latter of which systems sought to build a half-way house between the Sankhyas and the Vedantas by glorifying Nature as Power and placidly treating her as one with the Divine Soul without troubling to mitigate the logical gap separating these very distinct categories.[46]

"Ya devi sarvabhutesu saktirupena Samsthita",[47] say the Tantras and in the same breath declare—

"Ya Srih Swayam Sukritinam bhavanesu",[48] as though womanhood was a special dispensation of that Shakti. Vivekananda quoted both these verses while praising the women of America and unconsciously betrayed the real reason behind his predilection for the Tantras. Actually, Vivekananda was no more an adherent of the system of the Tantras than Bankim was—or, for the matter of that the Brahmos were.[49] "I have preached nothing but the Upanishads and of the Upanishads I have preached nothing but that one word—Strength." This was a far closer approximation to Vivekananda's theological stand than his praise for any non-Vedantic system would indicate. But, in seeking scriptural sanction for a heroic conception of womanhood Vivekananda was not content to appeal to the Upanishads, which recognised for woman, her equality (with men) in the Atman, but did so only by implication and nowhere directly sang the glory of womanhood. The Tantras alone, of all Indian systems, recognised and preached Female Power as the root of creation and sang the praise of womanhood with a delight which was totally absent from all other systems of Hindu religious thought. This was why Vivekananda, the Vedantist, appealed to the Tantras ; when the point at issue was glory of womanhood, he was certainly the last man to be deterred by any consideration of theological consistency[50] from singing that glory at its loudest.

It was from the Tantras again that Vivekananda derived inspiration when he made the famous distinction between 'wifehood' as glorified by the Western nations and 'motherhood' as glorified by Hinduism. From the viewpoint of traditional Hinduism this was not strictly correct even though the Smritis preached divine status for both the parents inside the family (Manu called the parents—'Divinities in person'). But even this divine status traditionally applied in the case of father much more effectively than in the case of mother as is proved by the popular verse :

"Pita Svargah Pita dharmah, Pita hi paramamtapah." The scriptural verse quoted by Vivekananda in which a mother is said "to excel a thousand fathers of glory" was exceptional ; at all events the traditional glorification of motherhood in Hinduism was not effective enough to inspire the greatest poets of India to give literary immortality to a single representative of motherhood, all the well-known heroines of Sanskrit literature—Sita, Damayanti, Draupadi, Sakuntala and the like—being great as wives rather than as mothers. It is true that the popular mind in India has, through the ages, been unanimous in sanctifying the names of these heroines as the common mothers of the nation, but neither literature nor the scriptures give sufficient warrant for the assumption made by Vivekananda that the Indian tradition glorifies motherhood at the expense of wifehood. The Tantras alone speak of the mother-Power as the guiding hand shaping the destinies of men. Vivekananda gave a vital, down-to-earth meaning to this mystical doctrine and sought the source of power in women in their motherhood. Even in the celibate Nivedita he wanted her 'hero's will' to be combined with a 'mother's heart.' With Vivekananda these two went hand in hand and one was barren without the other.

CONCLUSIONS

Before concluding this section, we must answer the modern critics' persistent assertion that Bankim's and Vivekananda's social ideas had the stamp of 'revivalism' about them, and consequently these thinkers were instrumental in hampering Hindu society's steady progress towards 'modernisation' and enlightenment heralded so gloriously by the genius of Rammohan Roy and since his time, assisted largely by the spread of Western learning in India.

We have produced enough evidence in this chapter to show that such charges stem from a mistaken conception of reform which would confine the application of that term to measure such as were agitated for by Vidyasagar and Malabari. That conception fails to see that the method of 'regeneration' as pleaded for by Bankim and that of 'growth' as advocated by Vivekananda were no less potent instruments for the ends aimed at by reformers of the earlier generation. Actually they were better instruments for those ends ; if only because they did not strike at the very root of the society they were trying to reform as Vidyasagar's and more disastrously, Malabari's preachings did. But the critics of Bankim and Vivekananda might protest that in opposing legislative reform, they were only replacing the most practical mechanism for reform by a mass of high sounding, if well-intentioned verbiage whose action was at most educative. Let us examine the force of this argument :

(1) As regards the claim that legislative action is the most practical mechanism for reform we need only consider the fate of Vidyasagar's Widow Remarriage Act, which has remained virtually a dead letter for more than a century since its promulgation. This law was passed amidst great fanfare. It had the backing of the most enlightened members of the Hindu community. It had as its father a man who bestrode the narrow 19th century world of Bengal like a colossus—a man who in courage and loftiness of character has had few

compares in India during the whole course of her history. Yet this law has failed to make the slightest impression on Hindu Society.

(2) As regards the 'caste question', the treatment of Bankim and Vivekananda was again different from that of the reformers who would solve the question by 'interdining', 'shedding the sacred thread' and 'inter-marriage', the last mentioned item being in the best tradition of what we have called 'matrimonial reform'. We have examined Bankim's and Vivekananda's attitude to these reforms. We have seen that they would gladly accept them without making a fetish of them in the manner of the reformers.[62] It is not clear whether the critics who accuse Bankim and Vivekananda of being 'revivalists' (meaning 'social reactionaries') have this point in mind. But these critics should remember that many an Englishman in India, who had the greatest contempt for 'Natives', had never had any scruple about interdining with them ; also there have been Brahmins like Bhaktaprasad—the hero of Michael's farce "Buro Shalikar Ghare Ro"—who abominated Mussalmans, but nevertheless coveted the embrace of a pretty Muslim girl. Reforms like interdining and intermarriage are in fact double-edged weapons which often accentuate caste-animosity, rather than promote caste amity. Bankim and Vivekananda were therefore right in emphasising the Hindu doctrine of 'non-discrimination' when speaking of these reforms rather than rigidly harping on the mere forms of these reforms.

Far more important was the fact that Bankim and Vivekananda treated the caste question as one of which the solution lay in raising the lower castes by education and by working for their economic equality with the upper classes. We have already referred to Bankim's famous essay on the peasants of Bengal where he analysed the causes of India's downfall and sought it not in the gradual degradation of the religion of the Hindu but in the Brahmanical Smritis which shut out from the lower classes all avenues of education and economic

22

and political power. Reformers on the other hand put the emphasis rather on the deprivation of the lower classes as regards marriage (with upper class women), the sacred thread (which distinguished the upper castes as a class apart) and intercaste dining. In an essay entitled—'Lokashiksha', Bankim chided the educated community for their indifference to the question of the education of the lower classes. He mentioned Rammohan and the Brahmos by name and pointed out that their reform programmes nowhere dealt with the question of bringing education to the masses. Vivekananda's language was harsher. He accused all the reformers of being busy in putting their own house in order and remaining totally indifferent as to the fate of the masses. It is true that Bankim's and Vivekananda's concern for the masses was never given a practical shape, Vivekananda's dream of constructing a huge monastic organisation from which monks would be sent out to give education to the people being nowhere near fulfilment to this day. But it must be remembered that they were the first thinkers to rouse the national consciousness to a basic problem of India and shake the reformers out of their fond day-dream of setting India on the path of glory and grandeur by marrying widows and arranging huge intercaste diners after the Puri fashion. If we ignore for a moment the modern critics' clamour against 'revivalism' (by which term they mean 'social reaction') and listen to a contemporary reformer's impression as to the impact on the reform scene of that movement of revival, which, since Vivekananda, swept over the whole of India like a tempest, we get a very different picture from the one conjured up by the labours of the belittling critics of to-day.[53]

Charles Heimsath concludes on the basis of his study of contemporary opinions : "The advancement of the lower classes in society called for an enlargement of the 'meaning and scope of social reform', as Chandavarkar expressed it in a message to the conference of 1919, to include "such questions as the education of the masses, the sanitation of the country, the housing of the poor, the care of the sick and feeble, the employment of labour......, and rural education, instead of confining social reform as we have hitherto confined it to female education, widow remarriage, removal of caste restrictions and such other items," The Conference of that year responded to this new definition of social reform and K. Natarajan introduced a resolution incorporating Chandavarkar's new vision of the social progress of India.

(3)   There is, however, another argument, perhaps the strongest one urged by modern critics, which would find fault with the very basis of Bankim's and Vivekananda's social ideas.   In the opinion of these critics, the association of religion with social ideas was the most objectionable feature of Bankim's doctrine of 'regeneration' and Vivekananda's doctrine of 'growth.'   According to this view, such questions as the position of woman in society or the raising of the lower classes could as well be met by secular programmes.   We shall see in a subsequent chapter that the so-called Hindu Nationalism—the political side of the New Hindu doctrine of regeneration and growth—has, in our times, been subjected to the most violent criticism owing to belief that the alienation of the Muslims during the national struggle leading to partition and the bitter communal discord that has persisted to our own times, was due to this brand of Nationalism. We shall discuss this criticism in its proper place. Here let us try to answer the criticism insofar as it applies to the purely social teachings of the New Hindu thinkers.

It is notable in this connection that most of the reform schemes in the 19th century were associated with religion, and in this regard the New Hindu thinkers were merely following in the footsteps of the Brahmo Samaj, the Arya Samaj and many other lesser religious organisations.   Even Vidyasagar, for all his agnosticism, derived all his reforms from the so-called Dharma-Shastras.   B Malabari, was possibly the only social reformer of any consequence, who agitated for reforms on secular lines. But even this Parsi reformer is said to have appealed to those scriptures whenever a particular verse came in handy for this purpose. In fact, India in the 19th century was a much more religious country than she is now, and the demand that she should have consented to reform programmes simply because there were good secular reasons for doing so had as good a chance of success as the demand that Europe in the 16th and 17th centuries should have done likewise.

NOTES AND REFERENCES

1. "Many of us believe that a reformer is an ideal man ; and to be an ideal man, Krishna should have been a reformer like Malabari. This evil of child marriage should have been abolished. But we do not recognise Malabari style as the quality of an ideal man. So we do not think it necessary to answer this question." "Krishnacharitra" *Bankim Rachanavali* (Samsad). Vol. II, p. 503

2. *Ibid.*

3. "If these customs get a wide acceptance in any society, then the destiny of that society will become deplorable. In the past some of these customs were prevalent in India, and some of them are prevalent now. This was and is the reason of India's degradation." *Vividha Prabandha—Bahu Bibaha.*

4. "School reform is nothing but a craze and craze is a kind of fun." *Krishnacharitra*, Chapter IV, Sec. IV.

5. Quoted in Charles Heimsath : *Indian Nationality and Hindu Social Reform.* p. 150.

6. The remark about Malabari's gushing sentimentality is no attribution of ours. Even Heilmsath has been forced to comment : 'Malabari did not rely only on considered argument to support his case but allowed his pen to flow freely.'

7. That Malabari was not in possession of a very considerable body of facts to support this extravagant assertion is clear from the following passage of Heimsath's book : "On several important factual questions raised by Malabari opinions varied. No agreement was apparent on whether or not child marriage was followed by premature consummation." (Heimsath, p. 154).

8. Note on the Bill to amend the Indian Penal Code and the Code of Criminal Procedure, 1882—Quoted in Chandicharan Banerjee's *"Vidyasagar"*, p. 343, 4th edition.

9. Vidyasagar while agitating for legislation against Kulin polygamy, had objected to the marriage prevalent amongst Kulin women on the ground that such late marriage was condemned by the Shastras. He had quoted with approval such verses as :

   "Piturgeha Ca Ya Kanya rajah pasyatyasamskrta
   Bhrunahatya pitustasyah sa Kanya vrsanismrita."

   ("The maid who attains puberty (lit. sees her first menses) at her father's house brings into him the sin of abortion and herself becomes as good as a Vrsani.") *Vidyasagar Rachana Sangraha*, Vol. I, p. 188. Vidyasagar quoted many other verses to that effect.

10. Charles Heimsath : *Indian Nationality and Hindu Social Reform.* p. 173.

11. Preface to *Bibidha Prabandha*. Vol. II. Published in 1892.

12. "I read in the organ of the social reformers that I am called a Shudra and one challenged as to what right a Shudra has to become a Sannyasin." *(My Plan of Campaign.)*.

13. "Some of these societies, I am afraid, try to intimidate me join them." *(Ibid)*.

14. *Ibid.*

15. Vivekananda's attitude to the Vidyasagar school of reformers is no less emphatic. "The question of widow marriage would not touch seventy percent of the Indian women." *Ibid.* Also see later.

16. Manu enumerates 8 kinds of marriage : (1) Brahmas, (2) Daiva, (3) Arya, (4) Prajapatya, (5) Asur, (6) Gandharva, (7) Rakshasa, (8) Paishacha. Every varna is not entitled to the above eight kinds of marriage. According to Manu (chapter III), for the Kshatriyas four kinds of marriage are permissible ; they are (i) Asura (ii) Gandharva, (iii) Rakshasa and (v) Paishacha. Again, Manu opines, two kinds of marriage—(a) Paisacha (b) Asura, are to be discarded by all varnas. (Shloka 25). So, for the Kshatriyas, only two kinds of marriage, (i) Gandharva and (ii) Rakshasa, are proper. Mutual love leading to marriage is known as 'Gandharva' marriage whereas marriage by abduction is called Rakshasa marriage.

17. *Krishnacharitra. Chapter-IV.* Sahitya Samsad.

18. *Complete Works of Vivekananda* : Vol. III. 'My Plan of Campaign'.

19. It may be noted incidentally that the popular notion that the orthodox Hindus were always inimical to all types of social reforms is totally belied by the aforesaid movement which was sponsored by the Sovabazar Raj family, the supposed citadel of orthodoxy. According to Heimsath, it was the only Bengali social reform movement of the last quarter of 19th century Bengal. The leadership of the movement came neither from the Brahmos nor from other types of reformers, but from the much vilified Sovabazar family.

20. Sinha, Pradip : *Nineteenth Century Bengal* (Aspeets of Social History). Cal. 1965. Appendix C.

21. *Complete Works of Vivekananda*. Vol. III. "My Plan of Campaign."

22. *Ibid.*

23. *Ibid.*

24. *Dharmatattwa.* Chapter-XIX, p. 643.

25. *Dharmatattwa.* Chapter-X, p. 618.

26. *Bibidha Prabandha.* Vol. 2, p. 269.

27. '*Reminiscences of Vivekananda*'. His Eastern and Western Admirers : Advaita Ashram. Calcutta-1964. pp. 237-38.

28. Bankim has been the victim of much progressive indignation due to suppression (by himself) of his work on 'Equality' in the later years of his life. It seems to us that the indignation has been utterly wasted, because, Bankim took care to reprint that part of the essay which dealt with political and economic inequality (in *Bangadesher Krisak*), thereby indicating that he was dissatisfied only with the part that discussed social reform and toed the contemporary 'progressive' line on that topic. He has veered to the position of 'regeneration' and it was but natural that he would repudiate his earlier assent to 'reform'. Progressive critics have failed to see this.

29. Vide *Bankim's Commentary on the Gita* (1/4).

30. *Sreemadbhagbadgita.* p. 759. *Bankim Rachanavali*, vol. 2. Sahitya Samsad.

31 Chandicharan Banerjee. *Vidyasagar.*

32. And such a sentence as—"If a Hindu girl is kept unmarried even in an advance age, she will feel attracted towards a particular youth." *Krishnacharitra*, Chapter-IV, Sec. III.

33. In the reprint of *The Peasants of Bengal.*

34. *Dharmatattwa.* Chapter-XXIII.

35. *Samya.* Section-V.

36. 'Draupadi'. *Bankim Rachanavali.* Vol. II, Sahitya Samsad. pp. 194-200.

37. In the New Hindu novels, *Devichaudhurani* and *Anandamath* Bankim illustrates this self-assertion in the characters of 'Prafulla' and 'Santi' who are conceived in the genuine heroic mould but their heroism is shown to be a manifestation of their devotion to their husbands.

38. *Vivekananda Centenary Memorial Volume* edited by Dr R. C. Majumdar. 'Sociological Views of Swami Vivekananda' by Dr Roma Chowdhury, pp. 347-432.

39. *Ibid.*

40. "In India, there are two great evils : Trampling on the woman and

grinding the poor through caste restrictions." *Ibid*, p. 400. "We are horrible sinners and our degradation is due to our calling women 'despi cable worms', 'gateways to hell' and so forth." *Ibid*. p. 401.

41. *Ibid*. op. cit. p. 405.

42. *Complete Works of Vivekananda*, Vol. III. p. 256.

43. *Vivakanander Bani O Rachana* : Vol. VI.

44. *Vivekananda Centenary Volume*, vide essay by Dr Roma Chowdhury, p. 402.

45. *Vivekanander Bani O Rachana* : Centenary Volume (VI), p. 388. Letter to Haripada Mitra, December 28, 1895, from Chicago.

46. It is of course well known that the Vedantas do not recognise Nature as a distinct category but explains 'creation' as unreal—as the work of Maya.

47. 'The Divine Soul who as Power pervades all creation'.

48. 'She who in honest men's houses shine as Lakshmi in the form of their wives.'

49. The Brahmos abominated the Tantras.

50. The worship of Kali, as practised by Vivekananda, the Vedantist, has struck many a commentator as a mystery which failed to be wholly resolved by so worthy a disciple as Nivedita herself. Vivekananda himself refused to be explicit. "That's a secret that will die with me"—he is said to have remarked on one occasion. The fact, however, that the worship of Kali was no essential part of Neo-Hinduism, the Hinduism he preached in public is made clear from his assertion in a letter to Mary Hale. "Kali worship is my special fad." he wrote in that letter, thereby indicating that it was a private affair of his own. The conception of womanhood as derived from the Tantras was, however, no private revelation. He preached it as an article of the revitalised Hinduism of which he was the apostle.

51. Roma Chowdhury. *op. cit*. p. 402.

52. Vivekananda is silent on intercaste marriage, but we know from "The Dialogue of the Swami with his Disciple" that he did not recognise the three thousand and odd castes prevalent in India, and would have them reduced to the four castes recognised in the Vedas. To the extent that this reduction implies he must have contemplated inter-marriage amongst the Brahmanical castes, the Kshatriyas castes and so forth.

53. K. Natarajan (Editor of the Indian Social Reformer) wrote in 1911, in *Hindusthan Review*, XXIII, 13 : Revivalism has had a wonderfully steadying effect on the national character. It has made us more deliberate and self-respecting in our progress...and has invested the work of reform with a dignity which does not belong to mere imitation.

grinding the poor through caste restrictions", Ibid., p. 400. "We are horrible sinners and .... due to our calling women 'despicable'........", quoted .... Ibid p. 401.
41.   Ibid, op. cit., p. 40.
42   Complete Works of Vivekananda, Vol. III, p. 25.

<h1 style="text-align:center">CHAPTER- VIII</h1>

<h2 style="text-align:center">NEW VISTAS IN INDOLOGY</h2>

IN CHAPTER-II, we saw how the vision of a glorious ancient civilisation of India was conjured up in the pages of *Vanga-darsan* and sought to be established by the historical method without any attempt at rigorous historical research. In the *Vangadarsan* articles, the evidence furnished to prove the existence of such a civilisation was rather general and referred to no single historical epoch. Also the *Vangadarsan* approach was universalistic in the sense that the highest glories of the Indian civilisation discussed by the Vanga Darsan writers emphasized no special feature of that civilisation which could set it apart from the historical civilisation of the West. We shall see how this approach was modified by Vivekananda and Rabindranath Tagore. In this chapter we intend to describe the Indological thoughts of Bankim Chandra, Vivekananda and Rabindranath Tagore.

But first of all it will be in order to discuss the Indological work of Bankim Chandra. His post-Vangadarsan excursus into Indology was aimed at discovering a specific historical epoch in ancient India, thereby giving the Vanga Darsan vision a definite historical shape and illuminating an unwritten chapter of Indian history with the torchlight of genuine historical research.

The epoch selected by Bankim Chandra for his historical research was the epoch supervening between the Vedic age and the age of Buddha. To this day this has remained perhaps the darkest epoch of Indian history and Bankim Chandra's is perhaps the only serious work that helps us to gain some positive information regarding the nature of the civilisation obtaining in India during that epoch. It would be important to study how Bankim sought to answer two related questions :

1)   What was the nature of the religion prevalent in

India during the epoch ?

2) What were the characteristics of the secular civilisation prevalent in India during that epoch ?

It is only necessary to add that Bankim Chandra's answer to these questions was inspired by the desire to set off the New Hindu ideas against an epoch of true history so as to render the New Hindu vision something more than a vision—in other words, something that could serve as a gospel of future action by furnishing inspiration from a glorious series of past action.

(A) THE AGE OF THE MAHABHARATA

It would be relevant here to examine the authenticity of the sources on which Bankim's answers were based. The result of the researches he embodied in his famous work *Krishnacharitra* can be considered on two levels : (1) the actions of certain mythical heroes as described in the *Mahabharata* ; (2) the civilisation of a certain epoch as narrated in the same work. On the first level, Bankim claimed that the Kauravas, the Pandavas, and above all Shri Krishna were historical characters. On the second, he asserted (or rather implied) that the *Mahabharata* in point of its main story was a pre-Buddhistic work, and could be used as a source of historical information if carefully handled.[1] Bankim Chandra's claim as regards the first level can hardly be sustained in the absence of archaeological evidence regarding the historicity of the mythical heroes. His sources (apart from tradition) were literary—the *Vedic* literature, the *Mahabharata* and the *Puranas*. These works unanimously treat the Mahabharata story as historical. The *Puranas* and the *Mahabharata* even assign a date for the main event of the Mahabharata story—namely, the Kurukshetra war—which Bankim Chandra calculated to be 1430 B. C. (Circa). The unanimity of all these works regarding this date is indeed a striking discovery ;[2] but even so, Bankim Chandra's claim has to be viewed against the general untrustworthiness of purely literary sources as dependable

23

authorities regarding India's past. It however, remains a bold hypothesis, which, for all we know, may yet be proved to be true, if archaeological evidence turns up in its favour. After the discovery of Troy, and—coming nearer home—after the discovery of the Indus Valley Civilisation, it can hardly be reckoned a wild hope to believe that Bankim Chandra's hypothesis regarding the historicity of the Pandavas and Krishna may yet come true.

Coming to the second assertion of Bankim Chandra we are on a surer ground. Bankim Chandra took his stand against the bulk of European Indologists who had decided that the existing text of the *Mahabharata* was a later work, the original *Mahabharata*, as mentioned in the Vedic literature, being irretrievably lost. Bankim Chandra examined the arguments advanced in favour of this assertion and pointed out how unsound they were. A number of the Mahabharata heroes were mentioned in the *Satapatha Brahmana* (Dhritarastra, Parikshit, Janmeyjay, Arjun), the epic itself was mentioned in *Asvalayan* and *Sankhyana Grihya-Sutras*. Krishna's name occurred again and again in the *Rigveda Samhita* ; Krishna Debakiputra was mentioned in the *Chhandogya Upanishad* ; Kaushituki Brahmana omitted the epithet Devakiputra, but, like Chhandogya, mentioned Krishna's name in connection with one Chora Angirasa. All these were parts of the Vedic literature, most of them definitely pre-Buddhistic. Coming to post-Vedic literature, Bankim Chandra showed that the aphorisms of Panini not only mentioned the Mahabharata, and most of the Mahabharata heroes, but actually referred to Arjuna and Basudeva (a name of Krishna) as deities receiving worship. The Buddhist literature in its earliest phase as given in the Sutra-Pitaka itself mentioned Krishna as Mara,—thereby indicating that the Krishna cult was the most formidable adversary Buddhism had to reckon with.

These are formidable arguments, and on the strength of these arguments alone, Bankim was entitled to claim that the existing text of the *Mahabharata* contained its original text including "the Pandava story and the story of Krishna" in their bare outlines. But Bankim Chandra did not stop here. He considered Lassen's hypothesis regarding the original text of the Mahabharata and showed how that hypothesis did not contradict his own. Lassen (and some other European scholars) had noticed the early Vedic mention of the term *'Kuru-Panchala'* and hap come to the conclusion that the original text must have narratep a war between Kurus and Panchalas, but as the existing text narrated a war between Kauravas and Pandavas, the original text must have been lost. Bankim pointed out that the war mentioned in the existing text was essentially a war between the Kurus and Panchalas since the bulk of the Pandava army consisted of Panchalas and Srinjayas (a clean related to the Panchalas). Not only that, the Pandava general was a Panchala hero, namely, Dhristadyumna, the Panchala Prince. Also the *Mahabharata* was full of references to the conflict between Kurus and Panchalas. Bankim pointed to the fact of Bhisma's and Drona's joining the side of the unprincipled Duryodhana, and suggested that this was explicable only on the hypothesis that the Mahabharata was a Kuru-Panchala war, since, to these highminded heroes, Pandavas were dearer than the unprincipled Duryodhana. Bankim concluded that the Krishna-Pandava story in its essentials was what constituted the original *Mahabharata.*

It need only be added that when a work is mentioned again and again in the pre-Buddhistic literature, when the names of most of its permanent heroes happen to occur in the Vedic literature; when its existing text becomes as a 'fleshless skeleton' without the Pandava story and the Kurukshetra war—the European Indologist's repudiation of even this story as having formed the core of the original text appears plainly fantastic. Bankim's findings, on the basis of this story alone, therefore, seems to be a most dependable source of information regarding the post-Vedic and the pre-Buddhistic civilisation of India. To Bankim's interpretation of this civilisation we turn now.

(B) THE DAWN OF HINDU CIVILISATION

The character of the civilisation portrayed in the earli-est portion of the Mahabharata is definitely pre-Buddhistic. This comes out most clearly if we examine the nature of the religion prevalent in that epoch. The Vedic religion is pre-dominant; *Yagnas* or sacrifices are mentioned again and again; Vedic deities are paramount.   Tribal concepts of justice and fairness are prevalent.   Thus Arjuna is bent upon killing his elder brother Yudhistira for the sake of a pledge he had un-dertaken to kill anyone who should speak ill of his bow Gandiva.   But new ideas on religion are set afloat by the my-thical Krishna (whom Bankim took for a historical hero). Krishna combats the traditional ideas and pleads for a rational basis of religion and morality without violence to the tradi-tion. He says to Arjuna : "There are certain definite charac-teristics by which one can discriminate between religion and irreligion. In certain cases where the religious issue is extreme-ly complicated, we have to fall back upon Reason to decide."[4]

This is not all. Krishna says quite clearly that the tra-ditional Vedic religion is incomplete : "Many people say that the Vedic Revelation is the basis of religion. I do not cond-emn that belief but not all truths are stated in the Vedas."[5]

What then is the non-Vedic basis of religion by which Arjuna's tribal notion of truth (which instigates him to kill Yudhisthira for its sake) is to be replaced ?   Krishna says : "Religion is religion because it holds all creation. Therefore, that alone is religion which conduces to the well-being of all creation."[6]

This is revealing. It shows clearly that in the age of the Mahabharata a new foundation of religion was being laid by the mythical Krishna with emphasis on reason and the 'well-being of all creation' as surer guides to the truths of reli-gion. The relation of this new religion to the Vedic religion is shown in clearer light by Krishna's re-interpretation of the doctrine of action (Karma). Traditionally the doctrine of Karma inculcated the so-called "Kamya Karmas" or Vedic sacrifices aimed at the attainment of heavenly pleasure after death. But Krishna puts the whole emphasis on actions aiming at the "well-being of all creation." This is made clear in his speech to Sanjaya. Sanjaya is trying to construct a specious argument in favour of Duryodhana's usurpation of the Pandava kingdom. He is trying to put off the warlike Pandavas by an appeal to pacific sentiments inculcated by traditional religion. He is pleading for inaction as action in this case would mean war. Krishna says : "According to some, it is action alone that leads to salvation ; according to others, Vedic learning alone does so. But (I say) : Just as no one can know the taste of food without actually partaking of it, no Brahmana can possibly attain salvation by means of Vedic learning alone without engaging himself in action. Those actions are therefore to be performed which lead to *results in this very life* in the manner of a man's quenching his thirst by partaking of water."

Thus activism aimed at the "well-being of creation" was the essence of the new religion that was being formulated during the age of the Mahabharata. Also the air was thick with Vedantic ideas, Krishna himself taking a leading part in the propagation of the doctrine of an "all-pervading God" who was to be realised, not by taking to a monastic life but by trying to change the direction of desire from worldly pleasures to things of the soul—in other words by selfless action (Nishkam Karma).[7] This was of course the doctrine of Impersonal Pantheism (Nirguna Brahmavad) preached in the Upanishads. But side by side with this Impersonal Pantheism the doctrine of Personal Pantheism (Sagun Brahmavad) was being developed with Krishna himself beginning to be worshipped by certain of his admirers as the world-soul made of flesh. Bankim himself has left the question open whether the cult of Krishna as described in the existing text of the Mahabharata formed part of the original text. But it is clear

that the idea of a God-like men being worshipped as an Incarnation was already in the air.[8] In other words the doctrine of *Bhakti* was taking shape.

Coming to the secular civilisation as portrayed in the
Mahabharata we are again face to face with a tribal society
in the process of reconstruction by means of newer and loftier ideas.   The casteless Vedic society has given place to the
caste-ridden society of the later ages but caste in the Mahabharata epoch is by no .means rigid. Intercaste marriage is
prevalent.   There is no restriction on the intermingling of
castes on the social plane—interdining as amongst men of
different castes is the rule rather than the exception.[9]

As regards social customs tribalism is by no means
extinct. Marriage amongst Kshatriyas usually takes place by
abduction of the bride. But the romantic custom of Swayam-
vara where the bride chooses her own groom is also mentioned
again and again. For Kshatriyas it is actually considered
the best custom.

Women are by no means subservient to menfolk. Thus
Draupadi, the common wife of the Pandavas, breathes pride
and loftiness in every word she utters. Bankim quotes with
approval her words : "It is no less a sin to withhold death from
a man who deserves it than to murder one who does not."

In politics, the main activity is war. The Kshatriyas
are extremely war-like. Even Brahmanas excel in the art of
war. But already Brahmanas participating in war are under
severe social censure.[10] The Kshatriya ideal is death in the
battlefield. But even in peace as well as in exile the Kshatriya creed is lofty and generous. In the words of Krishna :
"Heroic people suffer the greatest tribulation or enjoy the
loftiest happiness. It is only sensual people who are satisfied
with the middle station which is the source of all unhappiness. Real happiness consists in conquest or in exile."[11]

These words of Krishna set the tone for a new drama
of ideas, directed by Krishna again, which aim at the establishment of a "Kingdom of righteousness" (Dharmarajya)

by enlarging and broadening the prevalent Kshatriya ideal.
Yudhisthira is a righteous king. But his notions of righteousness are traditional.   He thinks it part of his royal duty to
accept the challenge of Sakuni in a gamble in which he stakes
his kingdom, his brothers and even his wife.   When he is
finally exiled for thirteen years along with his brothers and
wife he lives out the term with unfliching determination. but
he is at a loss how to recover the lost kingdom.   Most of his
friends advise war.   War, in fact, is the traditional mode of
resolving political disputes. But Yudhistira recoils at the idea
of war amongst blood-relations. His traditional notion of
righteousness makes him fall between two stools. On the one
hand are the war-hungry kshatriyas of the Pandava camp ;
on the other his fear of the sin of killing his own kindred.
Krishna points out the way to found the kingdom of righteousness. He chides Yudhisthira for his chicken-hearted irre-
solution unbecoming of a Kshatriya and emphasises the im-
morality involved in not striving to recover his usurped kingdom.[12]   He says that the annulment of usurpation is a moral
duty. It is as imperative as the duty of avoiding war in resolving political disputes. These two—and not traditional Kshatriya ideal of war nor the traditional fear of sin in spilling the
blood of kinsmen—are the basic moral principles involved in
the matter.   But how should one reconcile these ideals when
they become contradictory ?   Krishna's suggestion is to strive
to the uttermost for peace by fixing the Pandava claiming to
only a half of the lost kingdom. He offers to act as a go-
between Pandavas and Kauravas for negotiating a reconciliation on such terms.   He himself would not participate in the
war and asks Arjuna to choose between his single unarmed
self and a big regiment of skilful soldiers. When Arjuna se-
lects for his unarmed assistance he hands over the regiment
to Duryodhana. He travels the whole way to the Kaurava
capital and does his best to prevent bloodshed.   He fails but
before clearly enunciating his doctrine of "righteous politics"
to all concerned.   After the holocaust he guides Yudhisthira

to found a kingdom of righteousness by learning the art of statesmanship from the oldest and the wisest of the Kauravas.

The idea of "righteousness statesmanship" attributed to Krishna, runs like a silver thread through the original version of the *Mahabharata* as conceived by Bankim. According to Bankim, Krishna's direction of the ethics of the Kurukshetra war as also his guidance in making Yudhisthira's kingdom a kingdom of righteousness is only the final act of a long life devoted to the cause of righteous statesmanship. Bankim has illustrated this with the Jarasandha episode. Jarasandha was the most powerful monarch of the Mahabharata epoch. He was an unrighteous ruler forcibly holding as many as eighty-six kings whom he intended to immolate before the God Siva by adding another fourteen to the number. Krishna advised Yudhisthira to subdue him, and, to prevent unnecessary bloodshed, took Bhima and Arjuna with him to the capital of Jarasandha and challenged the latter to engage in fight with one amongst the three. According to Kshatriya custom Jarasandha had to accept the challenge. He fought with Bhima and was killed by the latter. Krishna got all the eighty-six kings released and desisted from usurping Jarasandh's kingdom. Thus at one stroke he relieved the world of a scourage with the minimum of bloodshed and furthered the cause of 'righteous statesmanship' by making friends of as many as eighty-six monarchs.[13]

This summary in bare outlines, of the pre-Buddhistic and post-Vedic civilisation of India could be reckoned a valuable contribution to Indian history. European Indologists have all along doubted the authority of the Mahabharata as a historical work. We have admitted the validity of this doubt as regards the historicity of the characters portrayed in the epic. But just as the Rigveda Samhita is treated as a most valuable source book of Indian history, so the main story of the Mahabharata, denuded of all its miraculous trappings can form a significant source of historical information regarding the epoch supervening between two ages of the

Vedas and that of Buddha. Bankim was a pioneer in this direction with hardly any successor but that does not detract from the merit of his great work.

But Bankim's interest in the Mahabharata epoch was not merely antiquarian. Nor was it actuated by the desire to locate the shimmering Vangadarsan vision of a glorious Indian past at a definite historical epoch and thereby to give the vision a definite shape and form. No doubt this second was a most powerful motive behind his work. But this motive was indissolubly linked with his desire to justify his rationalist exposition of Hinduism (as given in (*Dharmatattwa*) by a historical precedent. Krishna's approach to Vedic revelation which Bankim discussed in such detail was identical with his own. His interpretation of the activism preached in the *Gita* was vindicated by Krishna's discourse to Sanjaya. Above all the concept of 'Dharmarajya' (kingdom of righteousness) was one which was intended to supplement that activism with a political programme. In the event, this concept was to play the most momentous role in the Nationalist Movement of the succeeding decades. Mahatma Gandhi modified the concept into that of Ramrajya which in English must be rendered by the same phrase "Kingdom of righteousness."[14] The Mahatma of course denuded the concept of its associations with war, but it must be remembered that in Bankim's work it was, the non-violence of Krishna, and the latter's emphasis on it to the uttermost limit, which was sought to be established against the popular notion of a war-hungry Krishna. Bankim's emphasis on Kshatriya ideal was perhaps one that the Mahatma would not accept, but it was echoed by Vivekananda with his cult of the 'rajaguna' and taken up enthusiastically by the Bengali youth during the Swadeshi struggle.

It should only be added that Bankim, in *Krishna Charitra*, discovered what may truly be called the Dawn of Hindu Civilisation. Its main features were, in the first place, the religion of the *Vedanta* and the *Gita*, in the activist sense of

Vivekananda, since Krishna, the supreme activist, was its exponent. In the second place, this Vedantism was merged with the incipient Bhakti Movement, in the sense that Krishna was already being worshipped. In the third place, this civilisation in its secular aspect, was characterised by a loose and intermarrying caste system in which Brahamanas like Drona could take up war as their profession ; but the Brahmanical ideal was already being emphasized as pacific and non-violent pursuit of religion and scholarship. The Kshatriya ideal was proclaimed in all its glory and violence, but already Krishna was shaping it in the direction of a "Kingdom of righteousness." The glory of Indian womanhood was being vindicated in such women as Draupadi, whose lofty spirit shone forth in all its splednour and eclipsed all the male heroes in the court of Dhritarastra, when her husbands stared helpless at her molestation owing to a superstitious adherence to the traditional religion which could not prevent them from gambling away their wife and yet disabled them from coming to her rescue by a foolish adherence to the laws of gamble.[15]

(C) CANONS OF CIVILISATION

Neither Swami Vivekananda nor Rabindranath Tagore was an Indologist. But they supplemented Bankim's findings by two important additions. Vivekananda defined the place of monasticism in Hindu civilisation and society, and Rabindranath revived the ideal of the forest. In Bankim's historical research into the dawn of Hindu civilisation the question of the monastic ideal was touched upon in passing, but its place in the civilisation of Ancient India was not determined. Actually the Mahabharata epoch does not seem to have been conspicuous in upholding the monastic ideal. Tapovans or forest settlements containing marrying as well as celibate Brahmans are mentioned in the Mahabharata, but the pre-Buddhistic Mahabharata does not seem to contain any reference to monks and monasteries. The Upanishads, of course, extol the Sannyasin ideal as the highest, but even the Upanishads do not mention monasteries, but describe the Yatins or Sannyasins taking up the pursuit of personal illumination (Moksha) individually rather than as members of a monastic organisation. To see how Vivekananda settled this question, it would be necessary first to examine his special approach to the civilisation of India.

Vivekananda was not an Indologist, but he was the first among Indians to start a comparative study of civilisations by emphasizing the distinctive feature of the civilisation of India. We say, "distinctive" because all other Indian thinkers before Vivekananda, who had taken note of the East-West conflict in contemporary India, had taken pains to emphasize the universal elements of the civilisation of ancient India. Thus Bankim was as much a universalist as Rammohan was. It is true that Rammohan's universalism had taken little (if any) notice of the secular civilisation of ancient India. But in his exposition of Vedantic monotheism, the impulse was supplied by his desire to look for a common basis of the three great religions—Hinduism, Christianity and Islam. Bankim had rejected monotheism, in favour of personal Pantheism but he too had emphasized Bhakti as the common basis of these three world religions.[16] We saw in Chapter-II that Bankim's universalism had extended to the sphere of secular civilisation. This same impulse had actuated him to glorify the Kshatriya ideal—a Kshatriya ideal by all counts—described in the Mahabharata with the modifications proposed by Krishna. This was, of course, the ideal of contemporary Europe, though according to Bankim, the European ideal lacked the modifications proposed by Krishna, who according to Bankim, was the ideal man amongst Hindus. Bankim admitted that this Kshatriya ideal, with the modifications supplied by Krishna was the ancient Hindu ideal, not to be found in contemporary Hinduism, just as the Christian ideal was the ideal of ancient Christians not to be found in contemporary Europe. The point, however, was that Bankim wanted the ancient Hindu ideal to be revived by contemporary India, which, in his opinion, was in a state of decline. In a brilliant passage of *Krishna Charitra* he discussed how India's decline was due to the loss of the ancient ideal which, in his opinion, was a complete ideal. To him this ideal was superior to the monastic ideal of the Buddhists and the Christians. He pleaded for the revival of the ancient ideal in language that was as noble as the ideal was glorious : "For us to-day it has become imperative that we understand the complete Hindu ideal as distinct from the incomplete ideal of the Buddhists and the Christians. For, there is a surprising thing involved in this lack of our understanding of our own ancient ideal. In Christian Europe as well as in Hindu India things have taken a turn quite contrary to the original ideal. The ideal Christian was modest, meek, pacific and monkish ;—the modern Christian is just the opposite. What is modern Europe but a sprawling camp of armed warriors totally given to earthly pleasures of the senses ? The ideal Hindu was a man of infinite activity ;—the modern Hindu glories in total inaction. How then to account for this total reversal of ideals ? The answer is simple : In both the countries the ancient ideal has vanished from the minds of their inhabitants. Since the day in which the ancient ideal vanished from the Hindu heart, since the day in which we lowered the ideal of Krishna's character we have been in a continuous state of decline. Everyone imitates the sensual Krishna of Joyadeva Goswami—no one remembers the Krishna of the Mahabharata. But now we are at the dawning of a new epoch in which the national mind must remember, once again, its original ideal. And it is my modest hope that this exposition of Krishna's character will be an aid to that task.[17]

This was Vivekananda's point of departure. It is clear that Vivekananda was profoundly influenced by this passage of *Krishna Charitra* for it occurs almost verbatim in his 'Prachya 0 Paschatya."[18] But he was too much of a disciple of Ramakrishna to subscribe to the Kshatriya ideal as the highest ideal of the Hindus. Bankim had studied only an epoch of

Indian history, Vivekananda viewed Indian history in its totality and examined the whole field of Indology by a canon of
civilisation instead of cannons of mere scholarship.

The cannon was what Vivekananda called the "aim of
national life." "Every nation has a national aim"[19]— this was
Vivekananda's postualte on the basis of which he undertook
to study the civilisations of India, Britain and France. On the
strength of this postulate and his application of it Vivekananda
must be pronounced a pioneer in the field of comparative study
of civilisations—a study since undertaken by Oswald Spengler
and, in times near our own, by Arnold Toynbee. Without
waiting to consider the special results of his study in regard
to Britain and France, let us see how Vivekananda applied his
canon (or postulate) to the civilisation of India and of the West.

The national aim of the West was Dharma in the sense
of the Mimansaka School of Philosophers.[20] The national aim
of India was Moksha or liberation or personal illumination.
"Dharma taught one to seek for happiness in this world and
the other. It was based on action." Moksha taught one "to go
beyond the bondage of nature, beyond the bondage of flesh",
beyond happiness. "This path of Moksha was to be found in
India alone and nowhere else," though, it was Vivekananda's
hope that the path would be taken up by other countries too.
This was therefore the distinctive feature of Indian civilisation
and the aim of India's national life.

But if this was so, should India not devote herself
wholly to the "path of liberation" (Mokshamarga) and leave
Dharma aside ? If Dharma in the Mimamsaka sense meant
"the path of happiness" and if this path did not serve India's
national purpose, should it not be left alone to make room
for a whole nation of Sannyasins who would devote themselves wholeheartedly to the path of liberation ? Quite the
contrary, said Vivekananda. This seems to contradict his own
postulate, though the contradiction was not real, for he wanted a balance between the two paths. He accepted Bankim's
Kshatriya ideal wholeheartedly by tracing the decline of India

from the age of Buddha who made the path of liberation the
only expression of national life.[21]   But he pointed out that
the Mahabharata epoch was not an epoch of the Kshatriya
ideal alone but of a balance of the Kshatrya ideal with the
monastic [22]   With this correction of the one-sided view of
Bankim the householder, the monk emphatically took the
householder's side, and, in language that sets the reader's
blood on fire sang the praise of the Kshatriya.[23]

Thus Vivekananda preached a balance between the
ideal of the Kshatriya and the ideal of the Sannyasin. But
was it a true balance when the Sannyasin ideal was asserted
to be the "aim of national life" and the householder was
asked to uphold the Kshatriya ideal to the uttermost but not
as something that could be included within that lofty designa-
tion namely, "the aim of national life." We know that Vivekananda's hesitancy was resolved by Mahatma Gandhi who
emphasized the Sannyasin ideal as the alpha and omega of
India's civilisation and modified Bankim's Kshatriya conception of the 'Kingdom of righteousness' into one that was
thoroughly monastic. But meanwhile Rabindranath Tagore
was striking a middle path of effecting a marriage between
the monk and the householder.

The word marriage in this connection is strictly appropriate, for Tagore interpreted the marriage between Siva, the
Sannyasin, with Parvati, the householder (which formed the
theme of Kalidas's great poem *Kumarsambhavam* as symboli-
sing the true course of India's civilisation. That marriage had
led to the birth of the hero Kartikeya. Tagore indicated that
the true Kshatriya was born by uniting the spirit of monasticism with the daily avocations of a householder's life.[24]

But how did this allegory symbolise the true course of
India's civilisation ? Vivekananda would, of course, have
laughed the idea of a marrying monk to scorn ; but Tagore
with true insight, was drawing attention to another distinctive
feature of Indian history, which had not been taken note of
by any of his illustrious predecessors. Like Vivekananda

he was examining the field of Indology by a canon of civilisation and like Vivekananda he was emphasizing a distinctive feature of Indian history but the feature discovered by the poet was enlivened by a historical insight as true as that of the monk.

Tagore pointed out that the distinctive feature of India's civilisation was a traffic of ideas and ideals between the forest and the city, between the forest-dwelling Rishis and the householders of the city. "It was the forest that cradled the civilisations of the two great epochs of ancient India —the Vedic and the Buddhistic. Not only the Vedic Rishis, but Buddha also, gave out his teachings in so many mango-groves and bamboo-forests. His spacious teaching could not be propagated within the narrow confines of palaces—it needed all the breadth of the wide-ranging forests."[25]

How did these forests give a distinctive expression to the civilisation of India ? According to Tagore the forests gave that civilisation its distinctive ethical tone. The men who inhabited these forests were not confined within the hard walls of a prison built of wood, brick and iron. The place where they dwelt connected them with the far-flung stream of life that flowed around them. These forests gave them shade, gave them flowers and fruits, supplied them with fire-wood and Kusa grass. The forest played a vital role in their lives—their work no less than their leisure was intimately affected by it. This was how they felt in their own lives a unity with a broader and larger life around them. All that they received from nature—light, air and food—all these were instinctively felt by them to have their origin in a well-spring of bliss that was infinite and full of consciousness rather than in earth, trees and vacant space. This is why India's distinctive contribution to civilisation was a consciousness of unity—the unity of the individual self with the whole universe in a fellowship that was at once the fellowship of the soul, of the heart and of the mind.[26]

This was of course a restatement of the Vedantic tea-

ching of love for all creation preached so eloquently by Bankim and Vivekananda.   But Tagore's restatement is original
in the very proper sense that neither Bankim nor Vivekananda had noted the sylvan setting in which the teaching had its
birth.   That the relation between the two,—the teaching and
the setting—was a fact of true history and no mere figment of
Tagore's poetic imagination was proved by him with a wealth
of detail which left little room for skepticism.   He pointed to
the well-known fact that the places of pilgrimage in India
were those "where nature was revealed in some special glory."
He mentioned the custom in India according to which even
kings and emperors took pride in tracing their ancestory to
some forest-dwelling Rishi of venerable name.   He pointed
out that in all the great works in Sanskrit literature down to
the age of Hindu decline the forest played a part that was of
the greatest literary and spiritual significance.   Thus in Valmiki as in Kalidasa, in Bhababhuti as in Banabhatta the forest
was the leaven that went to the making of the characters of
the heroes and heroines of their works ; it was the background that set off their passions and by intensibly working
its own influences rescued those passions from the utter nak-
edness displayed in some of Shakespeare's plays ; it was the
paradise that revealed the unutterable gloom of unmerited de-
sertion by spreading an atmosphere of peace and holiness.[27]
      This indeed was the most substantial point made by
Tagore—this insight into the nature of Indian civilisation with
the help of the light supplied by the role of the forest ideal
in India's ancient literature.   This role was something very
different from that played by the forest in the literature of
Europe.   Tagore mentioned three plays of Shakespeare.   In
"As you Like it", as in "The Tempest" and "A Midsummer
Night's Dream", "we are face to face with a spectacle in
which man is out to lord it over nature and not to allow his
passions to be mellowed by the fellowship with nature."
Even in "Paradise Lost", which was supposed to indicate
humanity in an ideal fellowship with nature in the garden of

Eden, there was hardly any trace of this fellowship. "Bird, beast, insect or worm // Durst enter none, such their awe of man"—this was how Milton described the relationship of man with nature.[28] Tagore compared this with Kalidasa's treatment of nature in *Kumar Sambhabam* and *Shakuntala*, and, in unforgettable language pointed out the special role of the forest ideal in the literature of India.

Let us now examine the implications of Tagore's discovery and its place in the New Hindu Movement. To take the second point first, Tagore would probably not agree with the view that the emphasis on the forest ideal had anything to do with the New Hindu Movement. According to his own statement, his predilections for the forest ideal originated from his father's construction of the hermitage at Santiniketan as a place for meditation. But as against this fact we have to consider Tagore's treatment of the Vedantic teaching of love for all creation as the ethical expression of his forest ideal. The unity with nature and all creation was, of course, the essence of Vedantic Pantheism as explained by Vivekananda. It was certainly no part of the Brahmo creed with its emphasis on Monotheism. It is true that, like all true Brahmos, Tagore repudiated the monastic ideal preached by Vivekananda. But the forest ideal was not accepted by any section of the Brahmo Samaj even in the form of hermitages intended to give the best type of religious education from the Brahmo viewpoint. The operative part of Tagore's emphasis on the forest ideal as a most important factor in the civilisation of India was the proposal to construct such hermitages in the form of educational centres, but Tagore took care to repudiate any creed that was specifically Brahmo in the religious teaching of such centres. It is however unnecessary to labour the point whether the forest ideal was Brahmo or New Hindu in origin. The New Hindu Movement was not a centralised movement led by a single leader and guided by a rigid system of ideas. The rationalist approach to Hinduism, the ethical teaching of the *Gita* and the *Vedantas*, the activism associated with that

25

teaching, the search for personal illumination through mystical experiences, the doctrine of Hindu universalism—all these certainly defined a new movement ; but just as Vivekananda, without being a disciple of Bankim, could justly be said to have been adding, with far greater vigour and far more sureness of purpose, to the impulse put forth by his predecessor, —Tagore, in like manner, and without being a disciple of either, was adding to their search for material ideals by a study of the national civilisation. In this broad and comprehensive sense, Tagore was as much a New Hindu as Bankim and Vivekananda before him.[29]

The implications of the forest ideal preached as a distinctive feature of the civilisation of India were profound and far-reaching. Though Tagore took care to emphasize that the forest ideal was not monastic, and though, in his view, the true Kshatriya was born of a marriage between the monk and the house-holder—the whole emphasis of "the religion of the forest" (as he later named the ideal) was necessarily in the direction of monasticism, or at any rate, pacifism. Tagore never preached the doctrine of absolute pacifism which was Mahatma Gandhi's version of Hindu ethics. The Mahatma took up the idea of forest hermitage but associated it with total pacifism.[30] Tagore himself had written that forest hermitages were abodes of peace,[31] and indicated that the idea of unity through pacifism was India's special message to the world. Bankim's emphasis on the Kshatriya ideal in search of a 'kingdom of righteousness', Vivekananda's modified version of the same and Tagore's forest ideal—viewed as an ideal of education and as a valuable factor in civilisation—all these ideas floated side by side, nerving the rising Bengali youth to new heights of imagination and new modes of expression in secular civilisation. These we shall describe in the Chapters that follow.

NOTES AND REFERENCES

1. *'Krishnacharitra'* : Chapter I, Sec III : *Bankim Rachanavali* : Sahitya Samsad, p. 412

2. *Krishnacharitra* : Chapter I, Sec. V : *Bankim Rachanavali* : Sahitya Samsad, p. 416.

3. *Krishnacharitra* : Chapter I, Sec. XI : *Bankim Rachanavali* : Sahitya Samsad, p. 429.

4. *Krishnacharitra* ; Chapter VI, Sec. VI : The original verse (not quoted by Bankim) is : Tatra te laksanoddesah Kascidevam bhavisyati Duskaram paramajnanaja tarkenanuvyavasyati.

5. *Ibid* : Srute dharma iti hyeke vadanti vahavo janah
    Tat ten pratyanuyami na ca sarvam vidhiyate.
    —Both these verses occur in the Chapter Karnavadha, *Mahabharata*, Gita Press.

6. *Krishnacharitra* : Chapter VI, Sec. VI.

7. *Krishnacharitra* ; Chapter-XI : Bankim quotes in full the religious discourse Kamgita addressed to Yudhisthira dissuading the latter from renouncing the world, and shows the simplicity of the religious ideas discussed in the discourse with the ideas of the Gita.

8. Cf. Bankim's discussion in *Krishnacharitra,* Chapter-IV : Section IX.

9. *Krishnacharitra,* Chapter-V.   Footnote of Section VI.

10. *Krishnacharitra* : Chapter-VI.   Section V.

11. *Krishnacharitra* : Chapter-V.   Section VI.

12. *Krishnacharitra* : Chapter-V.   Section II.

13. *Krishnachritra* : Chapter-IV.   Sections VI-VIII.

14. We have already referred to Mahatma's acquaintance with *Krishachritra* in a Gujrati translation.

15. Bankim's essays on 'Draupadi' : *Vividha Prabandha* : Part I.

16. *Dharmatattwa* : Chapter XI.

17. *Krishnacharitra.* Chapter-IV. Section VII.

18. "See the fun ! Jesus advises, "Invite no enmity. If any one slaps you on a cheek, turn to him the other, Stop working." And our saint says, "work with all enthusiasm, kill your enemies, enjoy the world". But they took the reverse. The Europeans did not care to follow what Jesus said. They are enjoying the world exhibiting their strength (rajogun), activity and enthusiasm. And we are resigning ourselves to fate and thinking of Death. Who follow the advice of the Gita ? —The Europeans. And who are following Christ's advice ? —The follower of Krishna." 'Prachya O Paschatya,' *Vivekananda Bani O Rachana* Vol. VI.

19. *Ibid.*

20. Dharma is the subject of inquiry in Mimamsa. Jaimini defines dharma as a command or injunction which impels men to action. Dharma and adharma deal with happiness and pain to be enjoyed or suffered in the life beyond. Actions performed here produce an unseen potency (apurva) in the soul of the agent which yields fruit when obstructions are removed and time becomes ripe for its fructification. The earlier Mimamsaka believed only in dharma (and not in moksha) and their ideal was the attainment of heaven (svarga). But later Mimamsakas believe in moksa and substitute the ideal of heaven by that of liberation (apavarga).

21. "The decline of the country became imminent when in the Buddhist empire every temple had a following of one lakh of monks." 'Prachya O Paschatya'.

22. "Once there was a balance between religion and salvation (Moksha) in India. Then the Kshatriyas like Pandavas, Kauravas, Bhisma and Karna lived together with saints like Vyas, Shuka and Janaka." 'Prachya O Paschatya'.

23. *Ibid.*

24. *Creative unity*, p. 53. Macmillan, 1971. Creative Unity was first published in 1922, but the essay "Religion of the Forest" from which we have quoted was a free translation of an earlier essay *Tapovan* first published in B. S. 1316, 1909-10 A. D.

25. Tagore : *Tapovan* : *Siksha* p. 80.

26. Tagore : *Tapovan* ; *Siksha* p. 79-80.

27. *Ibid.* p. 89.

28. *Ibid.* pp. 91-92. *Creative Unity*, p. 61.

29. Tagore's *Tapovan* as also the books through which he interpreted the civilisation of India to the West, were published many years after Vivekananda's death.

30. It is doubtful whether the Mahatma was indebted to Tagore for the idea. He had started forest hermitages in South Africa much before his actual acquaintance with Tagore or his writings.

31. 'Tapovana Santa rasaspada.'

CHAPTER—IX

RELIGION AND POLITICS

THE NEW Hindu Movement aimed at being a movement of social regeneration by giving new vitality to the religions of the Hindus. In Vivekananda's formulation, its aim was to create a new India by educating its women and the poorer classes and raising them by preaching the Vedantic divinity inherent in all creation. But in Bankim's formulation a political programme was added to the social ; in his words the aim of the movement was to effect a "moral and political regeneration" of the land and raise a "kingdom of righteousness" (Dharmarajya). Also both these thinkers envisaged a cultural regeneration by harnessing the religious impulse to the rejuvenation of the arts and literature. In the next Chapter we shall sum up the nature of the impact of the New Hindu Movement on arts, literature etc. In this Chapter we shall concentrate our attention on what Bankim called 'political regeneration.'

THE FACTORS LEADING TO THE SWADESHI MOVEMENT

That the Swadeshi Movement of 1905-11 owed considerably to the New Hindu Movement becomes clear if we study its programmes and the pronouncements of three of its greatest leaders—Aurobindo Ghose (1872-1950), Bepin Chandra Pal (1858-1932) and Rabindranath Tagore (1861-1941). Before discussing those programmes and pronouncements we must note that they were the direct offshoots of the ideas of Bankim and, to a lesser extent, those of Vivekananda. It is relevant here to examine the claim of other factors and other personalities to count as the 'makers' of the movement in the sense that these thinkers were.

(1) The first factor is patriotism and its glorification. The patriotic impulse which found its ultimate fulfilment in 1905 was a direct consequence of the introduction of English

education in India and had found its expression in poetry as
early as the 1920's, when Derozio published what was probably the first patriotic poem in praise of India. Bankim's
'Bande Mataram', which served as the 'Mantra' of the Swadeshi Movement, actually came last in a series of moving
poems. To put the argument more baldly, the outburst of
patriotic sentiment we designate by the expression Swadeshi
Movement, had its origin in the cult of patriotism that had
come in vogue in the early years of the Hindu College (founded in 1817) and had gathered momentum during the period
1817-1905 ; the New Hindu contribution to that cult did not
begin to make its impact felt before the publication of Bankim's *Anandamath*, which was published in 1882 ; thus, so
runs the argument, the movement of 1905 could hardly be
called a New Hindu achievement.

The argument, plausible as it seems, fails to bear closer scrutiny. The patriotism of 1905 had little resemblance
to that in its pre-Bankim phase. This becomes clear from the
analysis given of the nature of the two varieties of patriotism by
Bipin Chandra Pal, one of the foremost leaders of the Swadeshi Movement. Bipin Chandra's article was written in April
1905, just four months before the beginning of the Movement
(August 1905) and is thus of the highest importance in throwing light on the matter,

As regards patriotism of the pre-Bankim variety Bipin
Chandra writes : "There was patriotism of a kind among the
educated classes thirty or forty years back. It was, however,
inspite of its sincerity and exuberance,...something positively
more outlandish than indigenous, and decidedly more sentimental than real. English literature, European and American history, stories of the fights for freedom among western
nations, these were the principal sources of our patriotic inspiration in those days ..... In the name of India we loved
Europe, and therefore, we fed our fancy not upon Indian but
European ideals. We loved the abstraction we called India,
but, yes, we hated the thing it actually was. Our patriotism

was not composed of our love for our own history, our own literature, our own arts and industries, our own customs and institutions, nor even was it allied to any affection for the masses of our people, even as they are...our love for our people was something like the pious love of the Christian missionaries for the heathens, for whose salvation they are so anxious."[1]

This according to Bipin Chandra was patriotism in its pre-Bankim phase. What then was the nature of the "New Patriotism" which was in the air in 1905 and whence did it originate ? According to the same writer : "The one great good that the *social and religious reactions of the last twenty years* have done is to cure us, to a very large extent, of this old, this unreal, this imaginary and abstract patriotism. Love of India now means a loving regard for the very configurations of this continent,...a love for the flora and fauna of India, an affectionate regard for its natural beauties,...a love for its sweating, swarthy populations, unshod and unclad ;...a love for its languages, literature, its philosophies, its religions, a love for its culture and civilisation ;—this is the characteristic of this new patriotism. And we owe it, it must be said, to a very large extent to the *religious and social reactions of the last twenty years*."[2] (emphasis added).

The only comment we need to make upon this passage is that Bipin Chandra, who was a Brahmo, and could hardly be called a *friend* to the New Hindu Movement, characterised that Movement as the "social and religious reactions of the last twenty years."[3] But the admission that the New Patriotism was largely a creation of those reactions, coming as it does from a Brahmo, carries added conviction and confutes the view that the political movement of 1905 owed its origin to the sort of patriotic sentiment that began to gain currency since the foundation of the Hindu College.

(2)   The second factor is the long series of political agitations that started with Rammohan himself, were taken up with enthusiasm on almost a nation wide scale through

the labours of Surendranath Banerjee, and culminated in the
foundation of the Indian National Congress in 1885. Actually
Surendranath was the fourth great leader of the Swadeshi
Movement apart from the three we have already mentioned.
But without underestimating the role of Surendranath and
that of the Congress (in its pre-Gandhian phase),in the nationalist movement it may be asserted that the Swadeshi Movement derived little inspiration from their work. The Congress
in those days was an upper middle class organisation protesting its loyalty to the Government during each of its session
with a constancy that was as pathetic as it was wearisome. In
the words of Aurobindo : "The Congress in Bengal is dying
of consumption ; annually its proportions sink into greater
insignificance ; its leaders, the Bonnerjis, Banerjis and Lal-
mohan Ghoshes, have climbed into rarefied atmosphere of the
Legislative Council and lost all hold on the imagination of
the young men. The desire for a nobler and more inspiring
patriotism is growing more intense."[4]

These words occurred in Aurobindo's memorial essays
on Bankim, written shortly after the latter's death in April
1894, in which Aurobindo asserted that the sort of "more inspiring patriotism" of which he was speaking was to be derived from Bankim's writings. We should only add that neither
'boycott' nor 'Swadeshi'—nor 'national education', nor 'militant nationalism',—in other words, not a single feature of the
Swadeshi Movement was foreshadowed in the sort of political work the Congress in those days was engaged in. And,
as for 'patriotism' the Congress brand of patriotism was, at
its best, the 'outlandish patriotism' of which Bipin Chandra
spoke, and at its worst, it was what the same writer described
as 'loyal patriotism'.[5]

(3) The third factor is the Hindu Mela founded by
Naba Gopal Mitra in 1867 and which held annual sessions at
least upto 1880.[6] Naba Gopal also founded a journal named
"National Paper," in which he described the Hindus as a
'nation.' The Mela itself was designed to unite Hindus on a

social plane by preaching self-help and patriotism and patro-
nising Vernacular literature and indigenous crafts and industries.[7]

It cannot be denied that the Hindu Mela was the first
institution to foster the Swadeshi idea and thus to foreshadow
the Swadeshi Movement insofar as the encouragement to
indigenous industries was an essential part of the latter. But
recent writers have been led or rather misled by the terms
'nation' and 'Hindu nation' to exaggerate its importance. It
is notable that the Mela was essentially a social gathering as
the organisers themselves were quick to emphasize : "The
Indian association in political affairs and this Hindu Mela
in matters of unity in a general sense has become like straw
to us in a drowning state."[8] This separation of 'political
affairs' from 'unity in a general sense' is significant. To view
the Hindu Mela as a precursor of the Swadeshi Movement
would be unhistorical. It is extremely doubtful whether the
Mela ever attracted any more than a handful of spectators in
or around Calcutta. Admittedly, both Rabindranath Tagore
and Bipin Chandra Pal, two of the leaders of the Swadeshi
Movement, have referred to the Mela in terms of affection as
due to a sweetly cherished event of adolescence, but they have
furnished no evidence that it is possible to trace in the Mela
the first murmurings of the great political upsurge that con-
vulsed Bengal in 1905. At least one contemporary observer,
Nabin Chandra Sen, who was reckoned a great 'national'
poet of the day refers to the Mela as the place where he made
his acquaintance with Rabindranath Tagore, but is absolutely
silent on its achievements.

(4) The fourth factor is the influence of Tilak, the
Chapekar brothers and Vasudeo Balwant Phadke (1945-83).
This alone is the most substantial factor apart from the teachings of Bankim and Vivekananda that may be said to have
moulded the Swadeshi Movement. Tilak's "No Rent Campaign" of 1896, was the first genuinely nationalist movement
In India and foreshadowed the boycott as nothing else did.

26

The Ganapati festival as organised by him in 1893, with overt nationalist overtones was an indication of similar festivals in Bengal during the Swadeshi days. The Shivaji festival organised annually since 1895 in Maharashtra was taken up in Bengal and was the occasion of Tagore's celebrated poem on the Maratha hero. In all these Tilak profoundly influenced the Swadeshi Movsment.

The cult of political murder and political robbery which were the most obvious features of the 'militant nationalism' associated with the Swadeshi Movement was a legacy of the Chapekars, who committed the first political murder (1897) in modern India and of Phadke, who committed the first political robbery.

BANKIM AS "PROPHET OF NATIONALISM"

The ideas of Bankim which supplied the Swadeshi Movement with an ideology should be considered under four heads : (i) Criticism of political 'medicancy', (ii) Historical consciousness regarding the Hindus' political prowess in the past and their possible resurgence in the future, (iii) A new conception of patriotism with its place in religion, (iv) The notion of Dharmarajya. These four formed the ideology of the Swadeshi Movement, though some of them were misunderstood by the agitators who made a mockery of Bankim's lofty conception.

Regarding political 'mendicancy' it must be remembered that it was on this ground that during the nineties the Congress (in those days run by loyalists like W. C. Banerjee, Surendranath Banerjee, Dadabhai Naoroji, Pherozeshah Mehta and the like) was judged to be utterly unfitted to give the country the proper guidance in political matters. The Extremist Party within the Congress was formed with the specific aim of replacing that policy ; and the history of the Congress till 1907 was largely the history of a tussle between the Moderate and Extremist wing as to which policy—that of mendicancy or that of courageous political action—should prevail in the Congress. In Maharashtra and Bengal, the initiative in every political move during this period was with the Extremists. The Moderates ultimately won in the sense that the Extremists were ousted from the Congress after the fiasco of Surat. But even as they won, the importance of the Congress dwindled, and initiative in politics remained with the partyless followers of the extremist line, till a reconciliation was patched up in 1916. It was an uneasy reconciliation and could hardly last. The rise of Mahatma Gandhi clinched the issue in favour of extremism though on considerably different lines. In the history of the Congress as well as in the history of the national struggle in India, the criticism of the policy of 'mendicancy' is therefore of the highest importance. This criticism started with Bankim.

Bankim's criticism was couched in two satirical pieces within the years 1880-1885. One[9] of them referring to the Local self-Government Act of 1884, and the other[10] being a scornful denunciation of the sort of politics pursued by the English-educated Indians of the time. The essays, it is true, preceded the Congress by a few years but as the Congress only pursued, on an all-India scale, the sort of agitation made popular by petitioning bodies such as the British India Association (founded in 1851), the Indian Association (1876) and other organisations of the same type, they applied to its policies as much as they did to those of the earlier bodies.

In the *Lokarahasya* piece Bankim satirizes an English-educated Baboo gloating over the charity of local self-Government made by the administration of Lord Ripon. The Baboo is clad in a dress which is the most monstrous Anglo-Bengali hybrid imaginable in sartorial fashion. He speaks English with a pertinacity that refuses to give way except under the strain of imminent strangulation. The mythical monkey-hero, Hanuman, with whom he converses on the merits of self-Government at first takes him for a fellow citizen, an inhabitant of Kishkinda, the monkey-land. But on being informed as to his Bengali descent, and his grotesque pride at his English masters belonging to a race of 'free-born' citizens he is provoked to much merriment mingled with not a little scorn. The Baboo mouths the words "Independence" and "Liberty" with considerable unction, but in the same breath glories in his British masters "bestowing in their bountifulness, some part of the country's administration" on the worthy hands of politically conscious Indians like him as a sort of recognition of their love for liberty and self-Government. Hanuman finds some difficulty in reconciling the two sentiments—the Baboo's proud assertion of self-Government and his no less proud enumeration of his master's bestowal of the same on his worthy hands. Much amused, he remarks that the Baboo's notion of self-Government strikes him as being self-Government of the monkey-land. The Baboo pities Hanuman on his failure to comprehend his lofty political notions and actually says so with some disdain. Hanuman, who understands perfectly well which of them is actually in need of pity, offers the Baboo a large supply of bananas and asks him to a generous helping. The Baboo does so with alacrity, and is no less well pleased with the toothsome monkey-gift of bananas than he was earlier with Ripon's gift of local self-Government.

This is violent satire, but Bankim's comic talent, which was of the highest order, dished the satire under the garb of uproarious fun ; and his own spokesman being a monkey he left it to the reader's intelligence to infer that the contemporary political agitations led by the anglicised Indians of his time, were, in his opinion, so many instances of monkey politics. In the *Kamalakanta* piece, however, he took care to make the satire more biting and to render his meaning perfectly obvious. In this piece he compares the political agitations of the day to the manoeuvres of a famished dog who, crouching before a ten-year old boy at his meal, gives him many piteous looks of supplication and prayer. As the boy is eating a rather hearty meal he is not averse to rewarding the servile dog with a wellsucked bony remnant of a fish.

After this initial success of his "political agitation", the dog is induced to make a "bold move" ; which takes the shape of a stealthy approach nearer to the boy's dish, followed by a renewal of the same piteous looks. Again the boy is moved to pity and to reward the dog—this time with a handful of rice. But at this juncture appears the boy's mother, who is so much incensed at the dog's audacity to sit so near her son and dine from almost the same plate with him, that she picks up a piece of brick and throws it at the insolent dog. The politician is however roused to the gravity of the situation in time and all but defeats her move by beating a hasty and political retreat.

It is unnecessary to add that this was perhaps the most violent satire ever directed at the sort of political agitations mounted by the Anglicised Baboos who, within a year or two, were going to form the Congress to pursue that servile political line from a national platform. Its lessons went home and Aurobindo, as early as 1894, was to notice its implication —the need for a "surer and more inspiring patriotism" to "hold the imagination" of the younger generation—in the columns of the Bombay journal *Induprakash*. And in 1907, he wrote : "(Bankim), first of our great publicists, understood the hollowness and inutility of the method of political agitation which prevailed in his time and exposed it with merciless satire in his *Lokarahasya* and *Kamalakanter Daptar* . He saw that force from above must be met by a mightier reacting force from below,— the strength of repression by an insurgent national strength. He bade us leave the canine method of agitation for the leonine."[11]

(2)   The second great contribution of Bankim to the Swadeshi Movement was the awakening of that historical consciousness which was on the look out for evidence to represent Hindu history or the history of a political or rather martial race.   Strictly speaking, Bankim did not make any original historical discovery apart from his conception of India's pre-Buddhistic age as described in his *Krishnacharitra,* As

we saw in an earlier Chapter that work was devoted to the
study of a lofty Kshatriya ideal expressing itself in a tale of
conquest leading to the establishment of a "kingdom of righteousness." But, this, though Bankim's most original contribution to Hindu history, was not the only nor even the most
important when viewed merely as an essay on the martial
achievements of the Hindus. For such achievements, Bankim
drew mainly upon British as well as Muslim sources, and with
unerring instinct, extracted from what was, to all appearances, a hopelessly hostile array of facts narrated by hostile
witnesses, a wealth of information regarding the martial glory
of the Hindus.

In Chapter-II we discussed Bankim's essay entitled—
"The Infamy of India" published in the first number of
Vanga Darsan. We saw there how the negative evidence of
the Muslim conquest of India being spaced over five hundred
years was used by him to prove the material glory of the
Hindus. In his view the length of the time span over which
the conquest of India was achieved by the Muslims indicated
the superiority of the Hindu arms over the 'invincible
Arab legions'. But apart from the facts mentioned by Bankim, this essay mapped out a definite outlook which would
rescue Hindu history from being misrepresented by British
writers from whose writings in the first place Hindus had to
know of such a thing as their past history. Elphinstone, for
example, had noticed the length of the time span required for
the Muslim conquest of India, but in his view this was due to
the Hindus' deepseated attachment to their religion. Bankim
pointed out that if this were the reason, the conquest would
have remained an impossibility even when it did occur, because the attachment to religion was as strong in the 19th
century (not to mention the 12th) as in earlier times.

This was a wholly new approach to the history of the
Hindus, who, according to most European writers, were an
'effeminate' race, but Bankim did not stop here. He pointed
out that the slur of effeminacy was uncalled for as the decline

of the Hindus was quite explicable from other causes which did not include any deficiency in their martial fibre. The causes were in the first place the total absence, in the whole of Sanskrit literature, of any reference to love of Independence as distinct from martial prowess as an end in itself; in the second place, the non-existence amongst Hindus of any desire to found a national kingdom. Thus in India, it was only the kings who sent soldiers into the battle-field ; the people themselves never took arms either for love of Independence or to found a kingdom. There were three notable exceptions to this rule. The Rajputs of Mewar were fired by a spirit of Independence with the result that they remained invincible even to Mogul arms. The Marathas and the Sikhs sought to found a kingdom each, and they succeeded magnificently. In other words, when martial prowess, which amongst the Hindus was of the highest order was conjoined with love of independence and the desire to found a national kingdom, the Hindus performed feats which did not fall short of similar feats performed by other nations. Thus with a single stroke —with a change in outlook as to how well-established facts of history should be viewed, Bankim gave Hindu history a significance that was totally new and that could be used as a mighty weapon of national self-consciousness.

It must be asserted that, apart from this new historical outlook—this way of viewing the chronicle of a whole millennium of defeats as in no way detracting from the Hindus' martial prowess—Bankim was not a pioneer in the field of writing or rewriting individual chapters of that chronicle to represent the heroic fibre of the Hindu race. Colonel Tod's *Annals and Antiquities of Rajasthan* (1829) which was published many years before the publication of *Vanga Darsan*, had already become a classic with English-educated Hindus. But it was Bankim who was primarily responsible for quickening the historical consciousness in Bengal, partly through essays like "The Infamy of India" but chiefly through the medium of his historical novels. His novels chronicled stories of Rajput chivalry and tales of heroic exploits performed by Hindu heroes. These were, of course, works of imagination, but so great a historian as Sir Jadunath has testified to the accuracy of their historical setting, if not to the accuracy of the facts described. These novels were immensely popular, so much so indeed that following in Bankim's footsteps, a whole line of novelists appeared in Bengal, amongst them Ramesh Chandra Dutt whose *Maharastra Jivan Prabhat* and *Rajput Jivan Sandhya* narrated respectively the story of Sivaji and of Rana Pratap. It must be admitted that the device of awakening the historical consciousness of a people by means of historical romances was not without its pitfalls, and a palpable one in the Swadeshi days was the idealization of Siraj-ad-daulha as a national hero, thanks to the labours of romance writers. But they gripped the imagination of the people. Thus, Bipin Chandra Pal, speaking of the impression made upon his mind by the reading of *Durgeshnandini*, Bankim's first-historical novel wrote : "*Durgeshnandini* quickened my earliest patriotic sentiments. Our sympathies were all entirely with Birendra Singha and the court scene where the Muslim invader was stabbed through his heart by Vimala (widow of Birendra Singha) made a profound impression on my youthful imagination."[12]

Bipin Chandra's testimony may be read in the context of Sir Jadunath's summing up of the influence of Bankim's historical novels in 19th century Bengal. Sir Jadunath, quoting from a review published in the *Times Literary Supplement* (June 30, 1945) which was discussing Prof. Gooch's views regarding historical novels used the following assertion of the latter to indicate Bankim's influence : "Historical fiction (according to Dr. Gooch) has played an active part in reviving and sustaining the sentiment of nationality, which for good or evil has changed the face of Europe in the nineteenth centuries."

In Sir Jadunath's view, Bankim's historical novels went to show that this opinion of the scholars of English was "rigorously and absolutely true."[13]

(3)   The third contribution of Bankim was a new conception of patriotism arrived at by defining its place in religion and rendering it a most powerful sentiment expressible in great poetry as well as evocative of the highest idealism. Bankim was in fact the maker of what Bipin Chandra called the "New Patriotism" of the Swadeshi days, and Aurobindo proclaimed him as such. But since Aurobindo coined the phrase "religion of patriotism" to denote Bankim's great service to his country, historians for over fifty years have been parroting that phrase with endless repetition indicating that Bankim preached the 'religion of nationalism'. In actual fact, Bankim not only never used the word 'nationalism', but was very careful to distinguish his brand of 'patriotism' from the Western variety and would have his patriotism governed by religion, rather than make his religion synonymous with his patriotism. It is time one should let Bankim speak for himself, rather than make others—even if those others include so worthy a disciple as Aurobindo—do so.

If patriotism was Bankim's religion, then the humanistic exposition of Hinduism, of which we gave an account in the earlier Chapters could hardly have been that, for no man, within his senses, preaches two different religions simultaneously. The expounders of Bankim's thought have been led astray by the fact that he made his patriotism a part of his religion ; they, on the other hand, have confounded the part with the whole. To understand the true import of Bankim's teachings we must view the part in relation to the whole, and for that we must turn to his systematic exposition of religion as given in *Dharmatattwa* (1888), rather than begin with *Anandamath* (1882), as most writers have hitherto done.

As noted earlier Bankim's conception of religion required the highest development of all the human faculties—physical, intellectual, active and aesthetic—in a state of balance which was to be attained by governing the other faculties by Bhakti (i. e., devotion to that God who pervaded all crea-

27

tion). Now, of the active faculties, love came only second to Bhakti and 'its highest' development was the love that embraced all humanity, nay all creation. But humanity included one's own country besides including one's own self, one's family and one's kindred, and the development of the faculty of love would require love for all these smaller portions of humanity to the extent *that those smaller loves* did not militate against love of humanity. Also, of these smaller loves, love of one's country ranked as the highest, and was one's best means to serve humanity by making that love God-directed—in other words, making it self-less (Nishkam) and pure. This love of one's country would extend upto laying down one's life for it, but never in bringing evil to other countries, except possibly in its defence from the attack of those other countries. It was in this sense alone that Bankim's patriotism was religious. Bankim was not preaching the gospel of the 'religion of nationalism' ; he was only defining the place of nationalism (his own word was 'Swadesh Priti' 'love of one's country') in religion, which was a very different thing from preaching nationalism as a sort of religion.[14]

To render his meaning perfectly obvious Bankim contrasted his notion of patriotism with the 'religion of patriotism' as understood in the West.[15] In the words of the Guru, the mouthpiece of his systematic exposition : "The conception of patriotism I have expounded to you is not the patriotism of Europe. European patriotism is a monstrous sin. The teaching of European patriotism consists in enjoining on its adherents the duty of exploiting other societies for the benefit of their own; of glorifying one's own land at the expense of others. It was this terrible patriotism of Europe that led to the destruction of the primitive races of America. Would pray to God that such patriotism may never be taught to the inhabitants of India."[16]

From the above exposition it should be clear that Bankim's patriotism was most austere conception satisfying the strictest canons of morality and forestalling modern criti-

cism by imposing on it limitations so as to make it perfectly
consistent with the claims of humanity. It was religious in
the sense that religion was to guide it and include it as a part
—and a most important part at that but never in the sense
that patriotism was to be a substitute for religion. Bankim's
Anandamath, which came to be held as a sort of holy scripture in the Swadeshi days, has to be read in the light of this
conception of patriotism, and a close reading of that book
will convince anyone that, in that work, Bankim was not
formulating a conception of patriotism that violated the limitations discussed in *Dharmatattwa*, but merely restating the
earlier results in the language of poetry and eloquence, and
invoking the muse of tragedy for the vindication of a sentiment that had deeply touched his soul.

The story of *Anandamath* is simple. It is the story of
Satyananda, the leader of a band of monks who have dedicated their lives to the service of the mother-land in the anar-
chical days following the battle of Plassey and preceding the
Governor-Generalship of Warren Hastings. The Nawab is
yet the nominal ruler of Bengal, but his rule consists in allowing Reza Khan, an official deputed by the English to bleed
his people white by extorting a land tax which was exorbitant
by any standard but, at this moment, when a terrible famine
has gripped the land, was nothing less than monstrous.
Satyananda and his monastic band, who have vowed life-long
celibacy and dedicated themselves to the deliverance of their
motherland from Mohammedan misrule have raised the ban-
ner of rebellion to fight the Moslems and have actually freed
the northern part of Bengal by achieveing two remarkable
victories against soldiers sent by Warren Hastings. Satyananda is under the impression that the English soldiers are mere
auxiliaries to the Nawab's battalions. But even as he has
completed the deliverance of a part of Bengal, his mysterious
teacher brings him enlightenment as to the real political situation in his country. He tells him of the invincibility of the
English; of their supremacy over Nawab; of their intention

to take over the administration from the hand of the worth-
less Muslim ruler; of the impossibility of Hindu restoration
before Hindu society, bogged in ignorance and superstition,
has acquired sufficient knowledge of matter and the physical
world from the English to enable itself to make its own spiritual knowledge shine forth in purity and splendour. This is
heart-breaking news to Satyananda. His rebellious spirit refuses to take up the life of meditation his teacher proposes for
his remaining years. He refuses to lay down arms before his
work is finished. But he is now alone. His most valiant
commanders have disappeared—Bhabananda, by sacrificing
himself in the battle-field to atone for his hopeless and sinful
passion for another man's wife, and Jivananda, by retiring to
a life of meditation and chastity guided by his heroic wife.
A terrible gloom comes upon Satyananda. Slowly, he is led
by the teacher to a Himalayan retreat leaving his life's work
unfinished. The curtain of Renunciation shuts off the glorious image of Restoration.

It has been suggested that in *Anandamath* Bankim proposed a new cult—the cult of worshipping the Motherland as
the Goddess Kali, and propitiating that terrible deity by sacrificing Englishmen (and Moslems) at her altar. This is
certainly the most monstrous perversion of the teaching of an
author, who even in his novel has taken pains to insert a discourse on the relation between religion and patriotism. The
deity of Satyananda and his disciples is not Kali, but Vishnu
—not indeed in His aspect of God of Love but without any
suggestion of blood thirstiness. Satyananda worships Vishnu
as God of war—the war against evil and against demons who
symbolise evil; but Satyananda is careful to emphasize that
his brand of Vaishnavism is only half the religion, for religion in its completeness mut comprehend both aspects of Divinity—that of love as well as that of fight against evil.[17]

As for worship of the motherland as Kali, Bankim has
given clear indication that, in his view, worship must not
outstrip the worshipper's pre-eminent duty to his God. The

Mother is not God, She is a Child-goddess in the lap of Vishnu—eclipsing, indeed, in her radiance, the other gods and goddesses of the Hindu pantheon, but meriting her sons' worship only as the nursling of Vishnu and in no other capacity. She is not Kali, not at least till the depradations of foreigners and the failure of her unworthy sons to protect her from molestation, have led her reveal in her person that terrible Epiphany.[11] Originally she was the mother of the Universe (জগদ্ধাত্রী) incomparable in her beauty, complete in the fullness of her limbs and perfectly happy in the abundance of her wealth. She will again assume that shape, but with this difference that, with her sons rising to the duty of protecting her motherly form from molestation by invaders, her splendour will grow, and, whereas, in her original form she only radiated peace and wealth, in her transformation she will inspire victory and knowledge, and beauty and assume a shape that will be glorious, triumphant, radiant.

What then is the teaching of *Aanandamath* ? Is it an apology for blood thirsty nationalism in the garb of religion ? Is it a tract of jingo patriotism impressioning on its readers the necessity of slaughtering Moslems and Englishmen in order to found a Hindu kingdom ? *Anandamath* is a work which is primarily a product of the literary art and only secondarily concerned with questions of religion and politics. *Anandamath* is a product of the tragic muse, dealing indeed with the theme of Hindu restoration, but demonstrating the futility of sheer patriotism, however lofty, to attain that end ; it sings the glory of patriotism but only when patriotism subserves the cause of religion and is not made a substitute for it ; it glorifies Bhakti even above laying down one's life ;[19] it finds fault with even so austere a character as Satyananda for securing money by plundering the agents of tyranny ; [20] it deals death, even if that death be of his own seeking, to Bhabananda for his surrender to his hopeless passion ; it sends Jivananda to life-long exile and asceticism ; even if that exile and that asceticism be made bearable by the companionship

of his heroic wife ; it conjures up the vision of the Mother—
the Mother that is triumphant, radiant, glorious—but
conjure up, withal, the 'purification by fire' her sons will have
to undergo, before they are made worthy of that vision.

It must be admitted that this interpretation of *Anandamath* and its conception of patriotism as a lofty emotion inspiring one to dedicate one's best in the service of the country,
was not its only legacy to the Swadeshi Movement : by a
strange misreading of its meaning it was harnessed to aims
which were far less admirable. It is true that the best patriotic poetry of the Swadeshi days—that of Rabindranath,
Dwijendralal, Rajani Kanta and Atul Prasad—derived its tone
from *Anandamath*, which, in the words of Aurobindo, for the
first time revealed the Motherland "as something more than
a stretch of earth or a mass of individuals,—as a great Divine and Maternal power in a form of beauty that can domi-
nate the mind and seize the heart." To show this, it is only
necessary to compare the patriotic poems of Hem Chandra
Banerjea, with their stilted rhetoric juxtaposing the glories of
India against those of Greece and Rome, with the poems of
these later authors to understand the transmutation caused in
the Bengali heart by such a song as 'Bande Mataram'. Hem
Chandra set out to sound the bugle of eloquence but ended
with the mock-heroic 'shinga' ; whilst, these later poets,—
shunning eloquence and tuning their modest bamboo-flute
with the cadence of paddy-fields, rivers, and the trees of
Bengal produced a crop of ageless songs. Years ago Rangalal
had sung a truly martial song but had failed to enlist a single
soldier in the war of independence. But when these later
authors, in whose hands even martial themes were denuded
of militarism, put forth songs of prayer and worship, their
words took wings, and, all on a sudden, a nation was born.
This prayer and this poetry—these were *Anandamath*'s best
legacy to the Swadeshi Movement.

But side by side with this, the Swadeshi fighters sought
in *Anandamath* a meaning that was quite different and a coun-

sel of political action that was little short of the cult of head-
hunting.   Secret societies were formed in the model of the
Abbey of Bliss ; political robberies were committed in the
manner of the one committed by Bhabananda and his followers ; political murders were organised by those secret societies though the novel itself never mentioned such murders
even by way of condemnation. As for political robbery, the
mysterious teacher of Satyananda had expressly stated this
as a point against Satyananda's notion of patriotism.   All
this was a perversion of Anandamath's teaching.

(4) Bankim's fourth   contribution to the Swadeshi
Movement was the notion of Dharmarajya (kingdom of righteousness) of which we gave an account in an earlier Chapter
while discussing the contents of *Krishnacharitra*. As we saw
in that Chapter, Krishna's, according to Bankim, was the
guiding hand that used Yudhisthira as an instrument for the
founding of a 'Commonwealth of righteousness' by winning
the Kurukshetra war.   That this commonwealth was not a
fact of remote history but that Bankim very much wanted it
to be realised in contemporary India, is clear from his reference to Krishna's work of national regeneration as a sort of
rebuttal of contemporary Indian reformers' argument that
social reform was the most pressing need of 19th century
India.   To quote Bankim's exact words :

"The mission of Krishna is the Moral and Political regeneration, preaching of Religion and the establishment of a
Righteous Kingdom.   If this can be done, social reform will
be automatic, if it does not so happen, social reform will
never be possible.   So, the ideal man did not try to be a
Malabari."

Thus Dharmarajya was Bankim's utopia, the goal of
Hindu restoration conceived in Satyananda's mysterious teacher's concluding peroration.   In the above extract it is explicitly stated as an ideal of the future and not merely as a
sort of romantic glorification of a remote past.

What was the shape of this Commonwealth ? Actually

Bankim never gave a full-length blue-print of his Dharmarajya.
It was not a state, such, for example, as the one portrayed in
Bhudeb's "Swapnalabdha Bharatbarser Itihas." In fact Bankim's Dharmarajya was not a Utopia in the sense Bhudev's
Hindu Kingdom was one. Bankim's picture carefully left out
details and confined itself to the discussion of the righteousness of a war of restoration (such as Kurukshetra war) and
the righteousness of a scheme of legislation (such as the legislation prescribed according to Krishna's advice by Bhisma for
Yudhisthira's benefit). Bhudeb gave full-length picture of
Hindu monarchy, but Bankim spoke of a war of restoration
and of a scheme of legislation. If Bhudev's picture was that
of a Utopia, Bankim's was that of the landmarks that separated the Utopia from the reality of India under British rule.

In the event, this deficiency in detail was a virtue rather than a defect. In the Swadeshi Movement, the idea of
a Dharmarajya served the same purpose as Mahatma's Ram-
rajya did in later years. Both these conceptions had the merit
of vagueness so necessary in a political struggle that sought
to unify men and groups of the most diverse persuasions.
Dharmarajya was a symbol of restoration—not an outline of
the restored kingdom as that of Bhudeb, which by the very
definiteness of its structure was apt to repel the majority of
English-educated Indians by its suggestion of going back to
the middle ages. Dharmarajya was an idea with a ring of
universality in it ; the war that was to precede it invested it
with all the romance surrounding a war of Independence ;
and the universality of the idea served to give it a meaning
that rendered the war something more than a mere fight with
the British.

VIVEKANANDA AND THE SWADESHI MOVEMENT

Vivekananda's contribution to the Swadeshi Movement was in the direction of (i) emphasizing the idea of restoration first conceived in Bankim's *Anandamath* and *Krishnacharitra* and (ii) restating the idea of Dharmarajya—though

Vivekananda never used that word—by preaching India's special mission in the world as that of a religious teacher. Both these ideas were directly connected to Bankim's notion of 'Dharmarajya', but Vivekananda's preaching gave added significance to the notion by his concept of 'aggressive Hinduism', of which a foretaste was given in his success in carrying the message of Vedanta in the West. It is easy to see now, with the historical hindsight of over seventy and odd years that have elapsed since Vivekananda's death, that his work in the West was an achievement of very modest proportions. Actually the Swami himself had no illusion regarding the solidity of his work in America. He himself never claimed to have done anything more than 'sowing a seed or two'. But his reception in India in 1897, as some sort of a world conqueror was indicative of the way in which his countrymen were viewing his work. They were viewing it as the first step in the imagination of India's Dharmarajya that would one day embrace the whole world in its sweep. It is easy to ridicule this notion with the advantage of historical hindsight but the Swadeshi doctrine of Swaraj, which was an ideological doctrine rather than a mere formula for India's independence from British rule, was formulated in the shadow of Vivekananda's triumphal procession in India. We need not wait to consider Vivekananda's specific utterance which contributed to giving the doctrine the characteristic shape it assumed in the hands of the Swadeshi leaders ; but a discussion of the doctrine itself will bring out the measure of that contribution. "Swaraj" was in fact the Swadeshi variant of Bankim's Dharmarajya and the ideas of Vivekananda combined together.

THE SIGNIFICANCE OF THE SWADESHI MOVEMENT

But before discussing this doctrine it would be in order to recall the events that led to the Swadeshi Movement and the forms—political and social—through which the movement took shape. Curzon's scheme of partitioning Bengal into two provinces was broached in 1903. This led to public demons-

28

trations against the scheme on a scale unprecedented in the history of India. The scheme was shelved for a time but was announced as a settled fact on July 20, 1905.[21] The Swadeshi movement was formally launched in Calcutta on August 7, 1905, in the historic Town Hall meeting with the programme of boycotting British manufactures so long as the Partition Resolution was not withdrawn. Boycott led to Swadeshi—the setting up of indigenous industries with indigenous capital. Actually modern Indian Industry was born during the Swadeshi days.[22] The National Council of Education was started in 1906. In 1906, again, the Congress so long following the policy of medicancy, began to be dominated by extremist ideas and took up the restorations of Swaraj, Boycott, Swadeshi and National Education. This was the signal for making the movement India-wide as also making it wider in implication. What started as an anti-Partition movement now became a movement for India's independence. Actually it purported to become more : it proposed a total reorganisation of national life on the lines suggested by the three ideas— Swaraj, Swadeshi and National Education, boycott being the form in which the war of restoration was to be waged. The narrower aim with which the Movement had begun—that of annulling the partition was achieved in 1911.

THE DOCTRINE OF SWARAJ

It is usually supposed that the term 'Swaraj' was a formula for independence if not for the sort of colonial self-government which was the goal of politicians of the Moderate Camp. In fact, the great Tilak himself, who was the first to use the term, is not known to have employed it before the Swadeshi Movement, except in the rather restricted sense imparted to it by the Moderates. The Congress, which, under Swadeshi pressure was forced in 1906 to accept it as its goal, used it in a sense so vague that, immediately after the session of that year, the Extremists and the Moderates divided to put their own interpretations on it. Independence was the sense accepted by the former, and it was Aurobindo who was the first to enunciate this sense in the columns of his journal 'Bande Mataram'.[23] As he put it "There are at present not two parties in India, but three—the Loyalists, the Moderates and the Nationalists (i. e., the Extremists).   The Loyalists would be satisfied with good government by British rulers and a limited share in the administration ; the Moderates desire self-government within the British Empire, but are willing to wait for it indefinitely ; the Nationalists would be satisfied with nothing less than independence whether within the Empire if that be possible, or outside it."[24]

Again : "Our ideal is that of Swaraj or absolute autonomy free from foreign control.   We claim the right of every nation to live its own life by its own energies according to its own nature and ideals."[25]

Similar statements about the meaning of Swaraj occur in Bipin Chandra Pal's speeches.

It is thus clear that Swaraj in the sense of independence or absolute autonomy was an idea that has to be traced to the Swadeshi leaders.   But the Swadeshi employment of the word signified much more. It meant nothing less than a theory of state. This is how Bipin Chandra Pal explained the theory in his Madras speeches : "The ideal of Swaraj that has revealed itself to us is the ideal of Divine Democracy.   It is the ideal of democracy higher than the fighting, the pushing, the materialistic, I was going to say, the cruel democracies of Europe and America. There is a higher message still. Men are gods ; and the equality of the Indian democracy is the equality of the divine nature, the divine possibilities and the divine destiny of every human being, be he Hindu, or Muhommedan, Buddhist or Christian."[26]

This extract is extremely revealing. Bipin Chandra's coinage of the term Divine Democracy clearly harks back to Bankim's Dharmarajya. But the sentence "men are gods, and the equality of the Indian democracy is the equality of the divine nature" clearly bears the impress of Vivekananda. Actu-

ally Bipin Pal is trying to combine Bankim's political concept of state with Vivekananda's Vedantic conception of human nature in a fuller political ideal.   Incidentally, the concept of democracy is his own addition but Bankim's and Vivekananda's writings are full of references to Western liberalism
and its political form.   Liberal Democracy of the Western
type was, in fact, the ultimate goal of the moderates, but
Bipin Chandra's doctrine of Swaraj was an attempt to trans-
late it in Indian terms and thereby render it the vehicle of a
'higher message'.

Compare this with Aurobindo's essay in *Bande Mataram* (November 25, 1907), entitled 'Srikrishna and Autocracy'.   Krishna, the greatest hero of his time, was the counsellor of Kings but himself neither assumed kingship nor
ceased to remain a man of the people till the end of his days.
Aurobindo who closely followed the arguments given in Bankim's *Krishnacharitra* wrote : "Look at that one great divine
figure in the history of India—the God in man whose life and
teachings influence Hindu thoughts even to the present day.
The scourage of all tyrants, counsellor of kings, was brought
up amongst cowherds.   They were his playmates, his early
associates.   The great deliverer of mankind from despotism
of all types and degrees imbibed and strengthened his democratic tendencies by living and moving amongst people working in the humblest spheres of life."[27]

Aurobindo objected to British rule as an autocracy.
But even in this he did not fail to bring in the name of
Krishna :   "The nation that looks up to Sri Krishna as their
ideal hero and man of action can never submit to autocracy
in any form.   They will never insult the divinity in themselves
by bending their knees to an autocrat, however powerful."[28]

Thus in Aurobindo's hands too 'democracy' was being
interpreted in Indian terms and Sri Krishna was being held up
as an ideal democrat.   Needless to say, the pharse 'divinity
in themselves' came straight from the pages of Vivekananda.
Far more important than this essay however, is the essay

entitled "Asiatic Democracy".[29]   This is how Aurobindo criticises the European concept of democracy in this essay.   He
begins with a history of the concept :   "Democracy has travelled from the East to the West in the shape of Christianity,
and after a long struggle with the feudal instincts of the
Germanic races has returned to Asia transformed and in a
new body."

   According to Aurobindo, this new body though tricked
up with the (Christian) ideals liberty, equality, and fraternity
of the French revolution, those ideals—"were associated with
a fierce revolt against the relics of feudalism and against the
travesty of the Christian religion which had become an integral part of that feudalism."   In Aurobindo's eyes : "This
was the weakness of European Democracy and the source of
its failure.   It took as its motive the rights of man and not
the Dharma of humanity; it appealed to the selfishness of the
lower classes against the pride of the upper ;   it made hatred
and internecine war the permanent allies of Christian ideals
and wraught an inextricable confusion which is the modern
malady of Europe."

   What then is the remedy ?   It is in a higher sythesis of
the Western political ideals in the ideals of India's religion :
"(India's) mission is to point back humanity to the true
source of human liberty, human equality, human brother-
hood.   When man is free in spirit, all other freedom is at his
command; for the Free is the Lord who cannot be bound.
When he (man) is liberated from delusion, he perceives the
divine equality which fulfils itself through love and justice,
and this perception transfuses itself into the law of government and society...This is the Asiatic reading of Democracy
which India must re-discover for herself before she can
give it to the world."

   True Democracy is thus the democracy of the liberated
soul.   But can this (mystical) perception be translated in
political terms ?

   Aurobindo believes it can : "It has been said that

Democracy is based on the rights of man; it has been replied that it should rather take its stand on the duties of man; but both rights and duties are European ideals. Dharma is the Indian conception in which rights and duties lose the artificial antagonism created by a view of the world which makes selfishness the root of action, and regain their deep and eternal unity. Dharma is the basis of democracy which Asia must recognise, for in this lies the distinction between the soul of Asia and the soul of Europe."

It is clear that Aurobindo was not only combining Bankim's and Vivekananda's ideas but adding something more to reach a fuller conception of Dharmarajya.

SWADESHI

Next to Swaraj comes Swadeshi. Here again the popular notion falls far short of the conception actually arrived at by the Swadeshi leaders. Just as Swaraj, with those leaders, did not mean mere political independence, so did Swadeshi mean not merely a programme for setting up power looms for India-made cloths. As everybody knows, the Swadeshi Movement started with the boycott of Manchester cloths. To render the boycott effective, the setting up of Indian-owned power looms as well as a vigorous campaign for using hand-made clothings, was started in the early days of the Movement. However, as Dr R. C. Majumdar has pointed out : "(Very soon) Swadeshi completely outgrew the original conception of promoting Indian industry. It assumed a new form based upon the literal connotation of the word Swadeshi, namely attachment to everything Indian. This development was undoubtedly the result of the newly awakened patriotism which had been slowly gathering force during the 19th century."[30]

In confirmation of Dr Majumdar's words we need only consider Rabindranath Tagore's theory of what he called 'Swadeshi Samaj'—('national society'). Tagore's conception of Swadeshi had the hallmark of the true philosophic thinking on the point, because it was he alone who looked beyond the temporary expedient of defeating Manchester by setting up Indian industries and gave to Swadeshi a meaning that in its sweep included all the temporary measures and at the same time added something that was of permanent value. On the practical plane, the importance of Tagore's conception becomes appreciable if we remember that he anticipated Mahatma Gandhi's schemes of village development by a great many years.

Tagore started from the New Hindu position propounded by Vivekananda regarding the dissimilarity of canons by which civilisations of different nations are to be judged. In Tagore's opinion, no true conception of Swadeshi was possible so long as we did not take into account the basic differences subsisting between civilisation in India and that in the West. In Europe the operative instrument of civilisation was the State, but in India the instrument was religion in its social forms.

In Tagore's words : "The vitality of different civilisations runs along different channels. Where a nation's common weal is as it were, concentrated, there lies its nerve centre. If you strike at that centre, the nation as a whole is wounded fatally. In Europe while nations are endangered as soon as the political system gets disorganised;—this is why politics are so vitally important in Europe. But in our country the whole race is faced with catastrophe if the society gets somehow maimed or paralysed ... This is why the survival of the British people is tied up with survival of the British state, whereas in our case, the survival of the race is ensured by maintaining the religious order (which in our case, is tantamount to the social order.)"[31]

Readers of Vivekananda's "East and West" will at once recognise the Swami's influence in this extract. The reference to "concentration of commonweal in different nerve centres" as being the basic features of different civilisations is too Vivekanandian—to be missed by anyone. But Tagore is not merely echoing the Swami, whose concern was more with the ends of different civilisations than with the institutional forms through which those ends were expressed. Tagore's emphasis was on these very institutions, and, in order to arrive at a true conception of Swadeshi he laid his finger on the true seat of India's collective identity, namely her social order which again was the institutional expression of her religion. In India's case the seat of collective identity was not her 'state', which, from time immemorial was in a continuous condition of disarray.

With these premises, Tagore's conception of Swadeshi could be nothing less than the restoration of her social auto-nomy which in Tagore's opinion, was a matter of far greater moment than the restoration of political autonomy preached by Aurobindo and others.

What did this social autonomy consist in ? According to Tagore : "In Europe all public works starting with the giving of alms to the poor to the imparting of religious edu-cation to the public, were part of the State's duty : In India they formed part of the religion as practised by the masses."[32]

Also social and personal laws such as the laws of mar-riage and inheritance fell outside the purview of parliament or the king's legislative assembly. It was these duties and these rights that were being bartered away during British rule. Matters had come to such a pass that even Hindu social cus-toms were being legislated for or against by the British.[33] Tagore's suggestion was to redeem these rights and duties — this was his programme for regaining social autonomy. In effect, Tagore was proposing the construction, of a state with-in the state, a 'civil society'. His 'Swadeshi Samaj' was not indeed a political entity, but it sought to include within its scope the whole complex of social phenomena indicated by such headings 'social behaviour', 'education', 'sanitation', 'commerce and industries', 'arts and literature', and 'justice'.[34] It is questionable whether the construction of such a 'Samaj' was at all possible without destroying the political edifice

erected by the British.   Some of the items of his programme
clearly presupposed political autonomy and were plainly un-
realisable without seriously disturbing the existing political
order ; but when instead of considering the question of 'autonomy' in relation to society as a whole, we came down to its
smallest units, the villages of India, Tagore's conception not
only revealed a social programme of the deepest significance,
but laid bare a matter of life and death for the fate of India
as she was developing under British rule.

     From time immemorial, self-governing villages were the
smallest units of Indian society.   With the beginning of British rule had started a process in which villages were being
looked upon as mere sources of food supply for the consumption of the urban population, and the identity of the
village as the smallest unit of society was being lost.   It was
a tragedy of the greatest magnitude, because Indian civilisation was essentially rural just as Modern Western civilisation
was essentially urban.   The difference was no mere matter of
organisation but had deeper roots According to Tagore,
the real significance of the village as the smallest unit of society consisted in the "formation of ties of kinship between
man and man" rather than ties of work or organisation,—
and this was where Indian civilisation differed fundamentally
from that of the West.   The village was essentially the medium for the formation of such ties.   In Tagore's words :
"India's effort was ever in the direction of formation of ties
of kinship between man and man.   This kinship had to be
maintained with the most distant of relations (young and
old) ; it could not be allowed to grow thin even when the
child grew to manhood ; the guru and the disciple, the guest
and the beggar, the Zemindar and the tenant,—kinship was
prescribed for all.   Also these were no mere moral ties prescribed by the scriptures—these were ties of the heart....
Thus it is that in India, in virtue of the closest ties of the
heart that have always been recognised within and outside the
family, between the lowly and the highly placed, between the

householder and the stranger—society was never in want of means for the establishment and maintainance of 'tols', 'path-salas', 'aqueducts', 'guest houses', temples, and houses for the upkeep of the maimed and the disabled."[35] It was this feature, this essence, so to say, that was being lost with the gradual decline of the village. It was this tragedy that was to be averted, and Tagore's 'social autonomy' was aimed at averting it.

But Tagore was too much a man of his age to be satis-fied, with suggesting a village reconstruction programme along ancient lines. As he saw it, society in India was the institutional form of her religion and the village was the means to realise the aim of that religion,—the aim itself being noth-ing less than love for all creation—by allowing ties of kinship to grow amongst the inhabitants of each self-governing unit and to assume diverse social forms in education, in economic relationships and in works of charity. But the call in the modern age was in the direction of making larger units, in other words, merging small units in the larger entity of the nation. How was this merger to be brought about ?

By raising a leader for the whole society (Samajpati) through the elective principle, answered Tagore ; by organi-sing large fairs and rendering them great vehicles of mass education by means of newly constructed programmes of 'Jatra' (itinerant theatrical performances), 'Kirtan' (musical performances dealing in religious themes), 'Kathakata' (educa-tional lectures treating Puranic fables) ; by enlarging the con-ception of religious duty to man, to one's ancestors, to the sages, to the gods and to animals—so long practised by Brah-mos as five daily sacrifices—and instituting the practice of daily sacrifice to the motherland (Swadeshbali) in the shape of the tiniest fragment of one's money or food.

NATIONAL EDUCATION

The Debate on National Education is another instance of New Hindu impulse working behind the Swadeshi Move-

ment. This is all the more remarkable because, unlike Swaraj
and Swadeshi, which were not matters immediataly conditional on the partition of Bengal but had roots in the historical
situation prevailing in pre-partition days, the question of
National Education had no such background. For generations past English Education had been supposed to be the
only instrument for revitalising a decadent India, and even
our newly-awakened national consciousness owed much to
that education. It was only in 1892-93 (B.S. 1299) that
Tagore, following upon the lead given by Bankim's introductory *Vanga Darsan* essay[36] (1872), raised the issue of medium
of instruction, and showed how Bengali, rather than English,
was best suited to serve as that medium. But in pre-Swadeshi
days even Tagore had no criticism to offer regarding the content of the education imparted by English schools.[37] Bankim
and Vivekananda alone had pointed out the shortcomings
of that content years before the debate on National Education
started. Bankim's criticism (included in *Dharmatattwa* centred round a comprehensive conception of knowledge which,
in his opinion, was not satisfied by English education, while
Vivekananda criticised that education as being 'denationalising'.
Bankim accepted the conception of knowledge given in the
Gita, according to which knowledge aims at the perception
of the Unity of the whole creation with the knower as well as
God. To Bankim, such a conception of knowledge required
a combination of three things : (1) knowledge of the whole
creation which is obtained from physical sciences like Mathe-
matics, Astronomy, Physics and Chemistry ; (2) knowledge
of one's self which is obtained from sciences like Biology and
Sociology. ; and (3) knowledge of God which is best derived
from Hindu Scriptures : the Upanishads, the Purans, the
systems of Philosophy and most notably the Gita. In a word,
Bankim, the New Hindu, accepted English education in its
totality but wanted to supplement by a complete course of
religious education.[38] Bankim did not exactly find fault with
English education. Vivekananda followed Bankim in his

scheme of supplementing the secular English education by a study of the "true external principles of religion", by which expression he of course meant a study of the Upanishads and the Gita. But Vivekananda also pointed out the defect of the prevalent system of secular education. According to him[39] :

(1) "(The prevalent system) is wholly one of defects. Why, it is nothing but a perfect machine for turning out clerks."

(2) "We have had a negative education all along from our boyhood. We have only learnt that we are nobodies. Seldom are we given to understand that great men were ever born in our country."

In other words, Vivekananda objected to the excessive literary bias of the prevalent system (which rendered it a "machine for turning out clerks") and also to its un-Indianness.

It is unnecessary to elaborate further on Vivekananda's thoughts on education at this point. It is only proper to say that neither Bankim nor Vivekananda used the phrase 'national education', because both of them started from the position that 'man-making'—a phrase often employed by Vivekananda—rather than nation making was the proper business of education. As a matter of fact, the Swadeshi leaders, in their turn, accepted this Universal approach to the question of education, but circumstances supervening immediately after the start of the Swadeshi Movement made the emphasis on the 'national' aspect of their programme compelling.

The circumstances leading to the scheme of national education were briefly these : shortly after the start of the Swadeshi Movement (August, 1905), the Chief Secretary to the Government of Bengal issued a circular—the so-called Carlyle Circular (October, 1905)—prohibiting students of all schools and colleges from participating in any Swadeshi activity. As students constituted one of the chief sources of strength of the movement, the need was felt for immediately starting schools and colleges absolutely free from Government control. The National Council of Education was registered in June, 1906. It set up the Bengal National College on August, 1906, and also many primary and secondary schools with similar ideals. We need not stop to follow the career of these institutions— it was in fact a very short-lived one—but need only study the ideals inspiring the National Council of Education : they followed directly from the New Hindu educational thought of Bankim and Vivekananda.

According to the sponsor of the National Council :

"Education on National Lines should imply among other things :

(1) (a) Imparting of education, *ordinarily* through the medium of the vernaculars, English being a compulsory subject.

(b) The preparation of suitable text books, especially in the vernaculars.

(2) Promoting of Physical and Moral education and providing for denominational Religious Education out of funds specially contributed for that purpose and inspiring students with a genuine love for, and a real desire to serve, their country.

Such religious education is not to include the enforcements of religious rites and practices.

(3) Attaching a special importance to a knowledge of the country, its Literature, History, Philosophy and incorporating with the best oriental ideals of life and thought the best assimilable ideals of the West.

(4) Imparting of Scientific, Professional and Technical Education chiefly in those branches of Sciences, Arts and Industries which are best calculated to develop the material resources of the country and to satisfy its pressing wants.

(5) Inclusion in the scientific education generally of a knowledge of the scientific truths embodied in oriental learning and in the medical education especially of such scientific truths as are to be found in the Ayurvedic and Hakimi systems."[40]

Such were the educational programmes preached by the National Council of Education. It is unnecessary to point out the similarity of these programmes with the ideals preached by Bankim and Vivekananda. It is clear that they follow directly from those ideals.

It is however necessary to say a word about the educational thoughts of Rabindranath Tagore as embodied in his Brahmacharya Ashram at Santiniketan later reconstituted as the Visvabharati. It should be remembered that Tagore founded his institution in 1901, a year before Vivekananda's death. Vivekananda had emphasized one aspect of education — that of the strictest celibacy to be observed by students during the period of their studentship. The idea of studentship itself had, in India, during the whole course of her past history, involved a notion of spiritual culture under the direction of *Gurus*. The Gurus were no mere communicators of thoughts, but some sort of spiritual guides directing the pupil's studies by means of a relationship which was a personal one. It was Vivekananda's contention that these personal elements with its spiritual overtones were lost in the system of education popularised by the British. Tagore accepted both these ideas and to these he added a third. This was the Ideal of the Forest that we have disscussed in an earlier Chapter. Tagore wanted education in India to embody all these elements, and this was made the basis of his own educational experiments.

BOYCOTT

Boycott, as the very title implies, was not a New Hindu idea. The term itself was borrowed from the history of the Irish freedom movement. Ireland's own freedom efforts were on everybody's lips. Its sponsors harked back to the history of American Independence. Dr R. C. Majumdar has traced the origin of the boycott idea in the proposal in India, mooted during the 1870s, to renounce Manchester goods in favour of the incipient cotton industry of Bombay.[41] Neither

Bankim nor Vivekananda has ever been credited with the proposal in any form, and it does not appear that though Bankim was the first, and probably the harshest, critic of the policy of 'mendicancy' as pursued by contemporary Indian politicians, he, in one of his writings, proposed boycott of British manufactures as the answer to that policy. "The Kshatriya ideal of the Hindus", and "a war of restoration"—these were the ideas preached by him. The case of Tagore, who, after Bankim, was the most consistent critic of 'mendicancy' is interesting. He not only did not accept 'boycott' as the answer to the policy of mendicancy but opposed it with great vehemence, and actually cut off his connection, with the Swadeshi Movement on this very score. As for Surendranath Banerjee, the moderate leader, he was naive enough to consult his English friends before launching the boycott agitation, feeling no doubt, that boycott, whatever it was, was not war, and so could be reconciled with his moderate conscience. Moderate leaders like Dadabhai, who allowed the boycott resolution to form the operative part of the deliberations of the famous Calcutta Congress of 1906, were no doubt moved by similar considerations. The question is therefore relevant : was boycott a prelude to the war of restoration spoken of by New Hindu thinkers like Bankim ?

The answer to this question is that it was undoubtedly so intended—at least by leaders like Tilak and Aurobindo. Tilak's formula, "Militancy—not mendicancy", sums up the attitude of the Extremist faction led by himself and Aurobindo. Also the despatch with which the moderate leaders, who had espoused boycott in 1906, tried to relieve themselves of that dangerous responsibility within a year and thereby brought into the open the inevitable rift within the Congress on a question of fundamental principles, namely, whether the Congress would be a fighting machine or a merely constitutional body, leaves no room for doubt as to what shape the notion of boycott was taking in the hands of the Nationalist Party, otherwise called the party of the Extremists. Boycott as understood by Tilak and Aurobindo was the preparation for revolution—the war of restoration to realise the New Hindu idea of Swaraj. Two extracts from Aurobindo's writings will make this clear. Thus Aurobindo, on the eve of the second anniversary of the Swadeshi Movement, wrote in the *Bande Mataram* : "When we declared the Boycott on the Seventh of August, it was no mere economical revolt we were instituting, but the practice of national independence ; for the attempt to be separate and self-sufficient economically must bring with it the attempt to be free in every other function of a nation's life ; for these functions are all mutually interdependent."[42]

Again "We have repeatedly said that Boycott is not a gospel of hatred. It is simply an assertion of our independence, our national separateness. But neither do we pretend that we can ask the rulers to overflow with feelings of benevolence for the Boycott......Boycott has come among us not to bring peace but a sword."[43]

It is only necessary to add that 'national separateness' with Aurobindo was nothing less than the New Hindu notion of polity, to wit, the foundation of a 'kingdom of righteousness', a conception which he himself was trying to elaborate during the Swadeshi days and which we have clearly explained in Aurobindo's own language.[44]

Aurobindo's conception of boycott was therefore that of a 'sword' and not of a weapon of peace. The juxtaposition of the words 'peace' and 'sword' leaves no room for doubt that Aurobindo looked forward to nothing less than an armed struggle with the British. Or was he merely using a figurative expression in the manner of people who in Mahatma Gandhi's days called Satyagraha—a sort of non-violent war ?

The so-called theory of Passive Resistance which Aurobindo explained in the pages of *Bande Mataram* in April, 1907, is apt to lend credence to this view. Briefly the theory was one of obstructionism in order to bring the machinery of the Government to a standstill by 'non-co-operation' (Aurobindo actually used this expression, thereby anticipating Mahatma by a whole decade). As Aurobindo explained the theory again in 1909 : "Our methods are those of self-help and Passive Resistance. The essence of the policy (of Passive Resistance) is the refusal of Co-operation so long as we are not admitted to a substantial share and an effective control in legislation, finance and administration. Just as 'No representation no taxation', was the watch-word of American constitutional agitation in the 18th century, so 'No Control, no Co-operation', should be the watch-word of our lawful agitation."[45]

These words make it clear that Aurobindo anticipated Mahatma Gandhi's agitation, even though he did not actually start such a movement. But it would be far from true to say that he meant Passive Resistance as anything more than a prelude to an armed insurrection. The above words, it must be remembered, were written when the Swadeshi Movement was already a thing of the past. Tilak was in jail. Bipin Chandra Pal had exiled himself in England. Tagore had retired from politics. The movement had failed all along the line. Aurobindo himself had received a call, from the standpoint of which all mundane activities were useless without a communion with the "Life Divine". But, his lucubrations on the doctrine of Passive Resistance notwithstanding, he had already written an obituary of the 'Politics of Peace' and had announced his vision of the 'politics of the sword', which, in his opinion, was going to shape the future history of India. In 1908, he had written : "The grim forces that have been moving under the surface will now find the field upon to them by the shattering of the keystone of the old political edifice. The disappearance of the old Congress announces the end of the preparatory stage of (our) movement (and) the beginning of a clash of forces whose first full shock will produce chaos. The fair hopes of an orderly and peaceful evolution of self-government, are gone for ever. Revolution, bare and grim, is preparing her battle-field, mowing down the centres of

40

order— ......and building up the materials of a gigantic downfall and a mighty new creation. We could have wished it
otherwise, but God's will be done."[46]

These words, obviously written by a visionary, rather
than one who had any knowledge and mastery of the forces
that make a revolution indicate clearly why Aurobindo's
revolution even if "let loose to mow down the centres of
order" and 'build up a mighty new creation' was foredoomed
to inevitable failure. But no less clearly do they indicate the
climax to which the boycott agitation was inevitably heading.
It was heading towards revolution, a revolution that was to
be a 'war of restoration' to found a 'kingdom of righteousness' on the Indian soil. The nature of this revolution—the
so-called 'terroristic' agitation of the Swadeshi days—we
intend to examine now, in order to show how it was related
to New Hindu ideas and how in its failure, the whole New
Hindu movement, slowly and unobstrusively drained of its
religious life-blood by conspiratorial politics, was set on its
course of decline, and how the New Hindu dream of a 'kingdom of righteousness' ended in a tragedy of gloom and
inanity, only partially relieved by the martyrdom of a few
bold and fearless spirits who, even in the futility of their
death blazed a trail of dauntless courage and matchless self-
sacrifice.

'TERRORISM' OR 'WAR OF RESTORATION' ?

It is no part of our intention to give here even an outline of that tragedy. The task is indeed impossible in the
present state of our knowledge of the so-called 'terroristic
movement' of Bengal that started with the founding of the
'Anusilan Samity' of Calcutta in 1902.

The Anusilan Samiti was founded as an association for
training youngmen according to New Hindu ideas. The name
of the association was taken from Bankim's 'Dharmatattwa',
according to which religion consisted in the fullest development of (Anusilan in Bengali) of one's powers in a state of

balance,—the balance being attained by harnessing all these powers to the service of God who pervaded all creation. The association was intended to provide training on these lines, but it is clear that, from its very start, it emphasized the narrower conception of service to God, namely, the service to one's motherland. The association was thus a political organisation and its motto was again the New Hindi motto of founding a 'kingdom of righteousness'. The doctrine of self-less service for the country was re-emphasized, and Nivedita, who was associated with Samiti from its start, preached the Swami's cult of manliness as the essence of religion. Whether the Gita was prescribed for compulsory reading or not, it is clear that this work with the New Hindu emphasis on its teaching of self-less work and 'righteous war' formed the doctrinal basis of the conception of practical religion of its members. Such was what may be called the 'ideological background of the activities of the Samiti'.

From the very beginning Aurobindo was associated with the Samiti. He was, in fact, one of its Vice-presidents, the President being Barrister P. Mitra of Calcutta. But Aurobindo was also associated with secret societies, and his own group including his younger brother Barin and some of his friends inclined more towards 'conspiratorial' politics, than Mitra and some other leaders of the Samiti would allow. The Samiti's work in the three years of its existence previous to the start of the Swadeshi Movement seems to have been confined to the training of young men in humanitarian service and physical and mental culture. It is true that some members had committed one or two robberies by way of securing money for patriotic work, but these did not find favour with the majority of the members. With the start of the Swadeshi Movement, however, 'terrorism' began to be regarded as the first step towards gaining India's independence. Aurobindo's pamphlet 'Bhawani Mandir' published in 1905, did not preach violence and crime, but it was his group that was chiefly instrumental in propagating the cult of the bomb and the manufactures of explosives to murder obnoxious officials. Thus the cult of manliness and the cult of unprincipled violence were inextricably linked together, and, for this admixture, responsibility to a great extent must be laid at Aurobindo's door.

The tract 'Bhawani Mandir' preached manliness as a pre-requisite to India's freedom and proposed a scheme for training a band of volunteers in the manner of the disciples of Satyananda in *Anandamath*. The volunteers were to undergo the discipline proper to Sannyasins—they were to renounce worldly pleasures and devote themselves heart and soul to the inculcation of physical strength by worshipping Kali, the goddess of strength. Aurobindo was of course almost echoing Satyananda's scheme, but his alterations, were not without significance. Satyananda and his band, it must be remembered, were devotees of Vishnu who was the God both of love and strength ; even if Satyananda emphasized the latter aspect he was conscious of the incompleteness of his Vaishnavism. Aurobindo by opting for Kali instead of Vishnu set a seal of approval to the cult of force-worship. This aspect of Aurobindo's tract has to be emphasized ; because this worship of violence as an end in itself gradually came to be an article of faith with all 'terrorists'. Just as the conception of the patriot as one who must renounce worldly pleasures and conduct himself as one under the strictest monastic discipline found its way into the compulsory regulations of the Anusilan Samiti, so this cult of violence came to be a regular feature of all secret Societies.

But this cult of unprincipled violence was not the only rock on which Aurobindo's ship of 'revolution' foundered, and, to tell the truth, it was not even the hardest. The tricks of conspiratorial politics were imported wholesale from the supremely irreligious underworld of European insurrectionism and the revolutionists of Italy, the terrorists of Ireland and the Nihilists of Russia—all lent a hand in transforming the original religious programme of founding a kingdom of righteousness on the Indian soil and in rendering the Bengal terrorists immune to all considerations of forbearance and scruple in murdering officials and informers. "The juxta-position of names, (of) Hindu deities, and (of) Cromwell and Washington, and (of) celebrated (European) anarchists", which Valentine Chirol found so strange an element in the literature of Bengal terrorism, is explicable in the light of this change. A 'kingdom of righteousness' could scarcely rise from such a medley.

This was not all. The doctrine of 'self-less work' or 'work for its own sake', preached in the *Gita*, was perverted to the doctrine of slaughter for its own sake, and Krishna's insistence on the warrior's duty of not shrinking from righte-ous war on sentimental considerations was explained as a glorification of murder when murder was not committed in self-interest. This was, of course, the most flagrant violation of Bankim's teaching who had tried his utmost to show that Krishna was the supreme pacifist in an era of reckless Ksha-triya blood-thirstiness and that his exhortation in the Gita was to be viewed in that background. The perversion of the doctrine of the Gita actually started with Tilak who had sought justification for Shivaji's murder of Afzal Khan in the teaching of the *Gita*.[47] It is quite possible that the Bengal terrorists imbibed their interpretation of the *Gita* doctrine from Tilak ; for, the Chapekar brothers who had committed the first political murder and had thereby earned the distinc-tion of being the first terrorists in modern India, were supp-osed to have been inspired by Tilak's speech on Shivaji. It is possible that even Aurobindo, in those days, subscribed to this interpretation of Krishna's doctrine. But, whatever the source, this perversion, this glorification of murder for its own sake, came to be accepted by the terrorists as the true teaching of the Gita.

The career of Kanailal Dutta[48] can be taken as an illustration of the consequences of such a perversion. Kanai was a youngman who seems to have been within his teens.

He was in jail custody, being one of the accused in the Ali-
pore Bomb case of 1908, amongst many others of whom
Aurobindo was the most famous. It is not known whether
Kanai had manufactured a single bomb nor whether he was
capable of manufacturing any. He was probably arrested
on mere suspicion because of his association with Barin's
group. He was a generous lad, full of animal spirits and
thinking nothing of laying down his life for his country
which he loved with that youthful steadfastness which was
the characteristic of all youngsters who had met Aurobindo
or been influenced by his ideas. Kanai enlivened the dull
routine of prison-life by endless expressions of his bubbling
vitality. He was full of boyish pranks, and when most of
his associates in the jail fell asleep he along with four or five
youths of his age started ransacking the prison house in
search of biscuits, fruits and sweets. When that operation
failed, Kanai would tie the feet of one of the sleeping members with the ears of another by means of a rope and entertain his friends by many other pranks of similar nature.
Upendranath Banerjee, one of the senior members of the
group has narrated an incident in which Kanai was found
dancing with glee on a certain night at about 1 a. m. in cele-
bration of his securing a packet of biscuits from under the
pillow of one of the sleeping gentlemen. Kanai's dancing
roused Aurobindo who was promptly offered a handful of
biscuits to prevent his talking to others about the midnight
larceny. According to Upendranath, Aurobindo was so
pleased with the bribe that he shammed instanteous slumber
and Kanai was happily out of danger.

    It is not in reason to suppose that such a youngman
could commit murder in cold-blood, but in fact, this is exactly
what happened within a few days. Kanai, together with his
friend Satyen, planned, arranged and accomplished the murder of Naren Goswami in broad daylight inside the jail com-
pound and before the eyes of a host of dumbfounded spectators.
Naren was a member of the group but had turned a police

informer : in the terrorist code this was an offence punishable
with death.   In extenuation of Kanai's murder, it can only
be pleaded that Naren's death probably spared the lives of
some of the members of the group including that of Aurobindo. But even this argument is of doubtful validity.
According to Upendranath the police had unearthed most of
the facts regarding Barin's (and Aurobindo's) group, and
many of the youngsters in their inexperience had divulged a
great many secrets regarding themselves in the belief that
such confessions would exculpate the rest. So, Naren's death
probably achieved nothing ; and in the eyes both of law and
morality Kanai was a murderer and a cold-blooded murder
at that.

        This, however, is not the end of the story. Kanai was
promptly condemned to death by hanging. But the interesting
thing is that he not only did not make any fuss about the
sentence, but, in the interval between the passing of the sentence and the execution of the same, he actually began to gain
in weight; so that on the day of his hanging he weighed full
sixteen pounds heavier than on the day on which the sentence
was served.   A great serenity had dawned on him, and who-
ever looked at him marvelled at the change.   The jail authorities who hanged him were so much impressed by the change
in his countenance that they began to whisper in Barin's ears
enquiring if there were many other boys of the same stamp
amongst Barin's associates. In the words of Upendranath, to
whom we owe this description :

        "It was a countenance in which there was not a line
that betrayed anxiety, not a shadow that betrayed sorrow,
not a quiver that betrayed restlessness : it was like a lotus in
full bloom, irradiating joy and loveliness."

        It is only necessary to add that Upen calls Kanai a
"Yogi", and a supremely exceptional Yogi at that, since,
according to Upen, not even Patanjali could explain the
source of such serenity in a condemned criminal's face.

        The moral of this story is that the scheme of a kingdom of righteousness which Bankim envisaged as issuing out of a war of restoration and the 'mighty new creation' which Aurobindo visualised as being the result of a 'revolution, bare and grim'—both these versions of a vision, which were in fact identical in essence, failed tragically. They failed because the 'revolution' conceived by Aurobindo degenerated into a species of conspiratorial politics—in other words a form of death-dealing terrorism.

MOVEMENT KILLED BY ITS OWN POLITICAL PROGENY

Meanwhile the New Hindu Movement was subsiding all along the line. Both the Swadeshi Movement and its terroristic offshoot were of course great events inspite of their failure to achieve any momentous result. The annulment of the partition of Bengal, which occured in 1911, can be regarded as the immediate consequence of these events, but greater significance attaches to the 'political regeneration' of the whole country which was galvanised out of its torpor within a few years ; so that Mahatma Gandhi could declare as early as 1908 that the partition of Bengal was the prelude to the 'partition of the British Empire'.[49] To the extent that this was due to the Swadeshi Movement and its terroristic offshoot, the New Hindu Movement must be given its due in achieving the 'political regeneration' of India. But this 'political regeneration' was the signal of nothing less than the defeat of the parent movement. The New Hindu impulse was exhausting itself in the process of bringing about the political awakening which was only one of its aims. Its other aims—that of raising the lower classes and women through education and that of rejuvenating Hindu society by the new canons of civilisation as well as by spreading everywhere the light of our ancient civilisation, were imperceptibly relegated to the background. Here we must briefly analyse the causes that led to their decline—

Foremost among these causes was of course the overmastering passion for political independence, which, from the start of the Swadeshi Movement, gripped the youth of Bengal, and, within a few years, that of the whole country. The forty-two years from 1905 to 1947 were wholly devoted to the cause of political independence, and all other expressions of our national life were made absolutely subservient to it and other aspects of the 'Renaissance', which was considerably influenced by the New Hindu Movement itself, tended to be ignored. The later writings of Tagore, are full of lamentations, on this point. Tagore, who was essentially a product of our 'renaissance', saw more clearly than any other contemporary the shadow that was gradually lengthening over the finer expressions of our national life in the shape of an exclusively political movement. This also was the basic reason behind his own retreat from the political struggle which had drawn so much inspiration from his writings.

A second cause of this decline was the failure of the National Education Movement to replace the denationalising elements of the officially sponsored English education. The New Hindu Movement, if it were to hold its own against the all powerful Westernising process of the British regime, needed an intellectual backing from the educated classes, amongst whom the light of our ancient civilisation as well as that furnished by the new canons of civilisation discovered by Vivekananda and Rabindranath Tagore, began to grow dim as soon as the discussion of these topics which had started in the periodical press began to be replaced by the all-absorbing question of political independence. The only remedy for this state of affairs was to include those topics as an essential ingredient of our liberal education. The failure of the National Education Movement rendered this impossible.

A third cause of the decline was the failure of the Ramakrishna Mission to take up Vivekananda's programme of 'raising the lower classes' by the spread of the mass education scheme envisaged by the Swami. It must be remembered that the Mission was the only major non-political organisation thrown up by the New Hindu ferment. But while

31

it tried to work the humanitarian programme of Vivekananda in right earnest it never gave much thought to his scheme of raising a band of Sannyasins who would take education to the villages. The educational work undertaken by the Mission not only remained confined to the towns and the cities, but what was worse, this organisation never tried to mould the education imparted by it according to Vivekananda's New Hindu ideas. This failure on the part of Vivekananda's organisation contributed not a little to the precipitate decline of the New Hindu Movement.

As mentioned in the Introduction, if we are to assign a definite date to this decline, the year 1911 may be taken as the point from which the process started. This was the year which saw the annulment of the Bengal partition that had taken place in 1905, and thus, in a sense, it was also the year in which the Swadeshi Movement may be said to have run its course. But in a sense much deeper and more significant, Aurobindo's departure to Pondicherry, which took place in 1910, may be taken as a more symbolic event when viewed in the New Hindu context. Aurobindo was the leading spirit behind activating the half-hearted political agitations of contemporary India along New Hindu lines. It was Aurobindo again who developed the notion of Dharmarajya to a certain extent to render it an ideology of India's political reconstruction. Also the disastrous cult of terroristic violence in its heroic as well as its murderous aspect was due not a little to his inspirations. He converted Bankim's doctrine of 'patriotism governed by religion' into the 'religion of patriotism' of the Nationalist Party. Thus, Aurobindo was the greatest New Hindu 'activist' since Vivekananda. His departure from politics and retreat into 'mysticism', therefore, was a matter of the highest significance. It was a tale of 'dichotomy of the soul'—one part of it longing for participation in the 'war of humanity's liberation' and the other part hankering after that state of mystical communion with God. It was a dichotomy itself in the career of Vivekananda, with the highest tragic intensity leading to a premature death. The Swami, however, died in harness, whereas Aurobindo retired from the arena in the middle of the fray. This statement is not intended as criticism of the latter, whose retirement was actuated by high and noble motives.

APPENDIX TO CHAPTER - IX

IT IS relevant here to examine the views of some writers about the relation between Indian Nationalism, or a phase of it, namely, the Swadeshi Movement, and the New Hindu Movement. Some have generally ignored the impact of the ideas of the New Hindu thinkers on the development of political consciousness in India. Some again have viewed them as positive obstacles to its development. J.N. Farquhar considered the introduction of religious vocabulary, symbols and ideas into the nationalist movement prior to 1910 to be political tools and propaganda weapons used by unscrupulous politicians to inspire and inflame the masses. Valentine Chirol in his interpretation of the nationalist movement contended that it was the association of Hindu revivalist sentiment with political aspirations that generated the nationalist movement, and gave it a conservative or reactionary character. Coming nearer our own times, R. P. Dutt[50] opines that two factors— (a) the insistence on orthodox religion and (b) the affirmation of the supposed spiritual superiority of ancient Hindu civilisation to modern 'Western' civilisation "inevitably retarded and weakened the real advance of the national movement and of political consciousness." Anil Seal[51] again attempted to interpret Indian politics in terms of unevenness in Indian society and competition amongst the people guiding the politics of the time. Attempts have also been made to interpret nationalism as being no more than a realisation of selfish and narrow group interests. To him 'Extremism was less an ideology than a technique.'

It would be idle to answer all such criticisms author by author. We should concentrate on the points raised by

R. P. Dutt and Anil Seal. It is however pertinent to point out that while Farquhar criticises the New Hindu Movement, on the score of its supposed potency to inflame the masses, R. P. Dutt bases his indictment on its supposed incapacity to achieve that very end.

Anil Seal's book covers the period upto 1888 ; he has not studied the Swadeshi Movement. But by way of making some 'fresh approaches' to the history of Indian Nationalism after 1888, he indicates a line of argument which is relevant to our discussion. According to him, 'Extremism' was less an ideology than a technique. We have shown in Chapter-IX that the doctrines of Swadeshi, Swaraj and National Education which formed the programme of the Extremists in the Swadeshi Movement can be largely traced to writings and preachings of thinkers like Bankim, Vivekananda and Tagore. These three ideas formed an ideology by which a nation can be reconstructed ; only boycott could be called a technique. Bankim's conception of 'Dharmarajya' surely supplied a model ; Vivekananda's call for 'raising the masses and women of India' showed the way for removing the real malady in Indian Society and Tagore's 'Swadeshi Samaj' provided the framework to proceed on. These ideas exemplified a search for national identity and they countered the challenge of what they thought to be superficial Westernization of Indian life, thought and politics. These ideas derived from certain firm convictions. Even Anil Seal would agree that the Extremists had shown the seeds of the aim of complete national liberation and of determined struggle to achieve it.

R. P. Dutt's statement that "the insistence on orthodox religion as the heart of the national movement, and the proclamation of the supposed spiritual superiority of the ancient Hindu civilization to modern 'Western' civilization (what modern psychologists would no doubt term a compensatory delusion), inevitably retarded and weakened the real advance of the national movement and of political consciousness"[52] is plainly contradictory to his own subsequent admission that the Swadeshi Movement "achieved" "the permanent advance......in the stature of the national movement" which "was never lost."[53]

R. P. Dutt also states that from the Swadeshi "era dates the disastrous combination of political radicalism and social reaction in India."[54] He leaves little room for doubt that by "social reaction" he means the particular New Hindu attitude to contemporary social reformers. Dutt does not mention Bankim and Vivekananda by name, but bitterly criticises Tilak. He says, "The alliance of radical nationalism with the most reactionary forces of Orthodox Hinduism was signalised by Tilak when he opened his campaign in 1890 with a fight against the Age of Consent Bill, which sought to raise the age of consummation of marriage for girls from ten years to twelve years."

He did not take note of the fact that the Bill was a direct outcome of the campaign launched by Malabari, the Parsi, who represented the Hindus as a race of rapists and child-molesters. He ought to have noted the fact that Tilak never opposed the measure as such but wanted to get it accepted by Hindu society by propaganda and spread of education. He has concealed the fact that Tilak's campaign had the effect of greatly promoting the nationalist cause. It is by such omissions that R. P. Dutt has supported the thesis that the Swadeshi Movement (and in other words the New Hindu Movement) was associated with social reaction.

NOTES AND REFERENCES

1. Bipin Chandra Pal. *Swadeshi and Swaraj.* (pp. 17,19). Jugajatri Prakashak Ltd. 1951.

2. *Ibid.* pp. 19-20

3. It should be mentioned that under this title he also included the Arya Samaj Movement, Theosophy and the preachings of Sasadhar and Krishnaprasanna Sen.

4. Quoted in Dr R. C. Majumdar's *History of the Freedom Move-*

ment in India. (p. 373, Vol. I) from Aurobindo's *Essay on Bankim Chandra Chatterjee.*

5. Bipin Chandra Pal : *Swadeshi and Swaraj* : See "Loyal Patriotism" (pp. 24-29). This article was written in February 1905, i. e., six moths before the Swadeshi Movement came into being.

6. Jogesh Chandra Bagal : *Muktir Sandhane Bharat* : p. 88.

7. *Ibid* p. 91.

8. *Ibid.* p. 92.

9. "Hanumandbabu" *Lokarahasya* (1874), Second edition.

10. "Politics" in *Kamalakanta* (1875).

11. Sri Aurobindo : *Bankim-Tilak-Dayanand*, 1947, p. 10.

12. Bipin Chandra Pal : *Memories of my Life & Times*, Vol. I pp. 227-28

13. *Bankim Rachanavali* : Satabarsik Sanskaran, Bangiya Sahitya Parishad. Historical introduction to Sitaram.

14. Bankim Chandra : *Dharmatattwa :* Chapter-XXI and XXIV.

15. *Ibid.* Chapter-XXIV.

16. *Ibid.* Chapter-XXIV.

17. "Chaitanyadeva's Vishnu is only Love incarnate. Santan's Vishnu is only Might. Both of us are Vaisnavas, but half-vaisnavas." *Anandamath*, Part II, Section IV.

18. Brahmachari said, "See, what Mother has *become.*
    Mahendra said trembling : "Kali"
    Brahmachari : Kali—*Veiled* in darkness. She has become a destitute, so she is nude. To-day our country has heen reduced to a cremation ground. So Mother is wearing a garland of skulls. So her Shiva is lying under her feet—*Anandamath*, Part-I, Section XI.

19. *Anandamath* : "Upakramanika"

20. Vide last Chapter.

21. It was to take effect from October 16, 1905.

22. S. Sarkar : *The Swadeshi Movement* : Chapter III. A. Tripathi : *The Extremist Challenge* : p. 151.

23. *Bande Mataram*, April 26, 1907.

24. *Sri Aurobindo and the New thought in Indian Politics*" : Haridas Mukherjee and Uma Mukherjee. p. 117.

25. Quoted in *Freedom Movement in India* (Vol. II) R. C. Majumdar. p. 191.

26. Bipin Chandra Pal : "*Swadeshi and Swaraj*" : p. 207. The Reference to Muhammedans, Buddhists and Christians is important, because it contradicts the popular belief that the 'nationalism' of the wadeshi Movement was Hindu Nationalism. It was in fact religi-

ous Nationalism or rather Nationalism guided by Religion.

27. *Aurobindo and the New Thought in Indian Politics :* Haridas Mukherjee and Uma Mukherjee. p. 237.

28. *Ibid.* p. 238.

29. *Bande Mataram,* March 16, 1908.

30. Dr R. C. Majumdar. *History of the Freedom Movement in India.* vol. II, p. 33.

31. *Rabindra Rachanavali :* (centenary) volume published by Govt. of West Bengal, vol-XII. *Swadesh O Samaj :* p. 685.

32. *Ibid.* p. 685.

33. *Ibid.* p. 686.

34. *Ibid.* p. 775.

35. *Ibid.* pp. 690, 692.

36. In which Bankim had pleaded for the Vernacular as the best mass communication medium, and pointed out how English was driving a wedge between the masses and the educated community.

37. Tagore's second great essay on education was written as late as May 1905 (Baisakh 1312) during the hightide of the Swadeshi impulse. (The reader should remember that though the Swadeshi Movement was formally launched on Aug. 7, 1905 the Swadeshi impulse dates back to 1903, the year in which the proposal for partitioning Bengal was broached.)

38. *Dharmatattwa :* Chapter XV.

39. Quoted in *Vivekananda Centenary Volume,* p. 488 edited by R. C. Majumdar.

40. Haridas Mukherjee and Uma Mukherjee : *The Origin of the National Education Movement.* Jadavpur University, Cal, 1957. p. 45.

41. R. C. Majumdar : *History of the Freedom Movement in India,* Vol. II.

42. Haridas Mukherjee and Uma Mukherjee. *Aurobindo and the New Thought in Indian Politics.* p. 132.

43. *Ibid.* p. 135.

44. The section entitled, "The Doctrine of Swaraj."

45. "An open Letter to my Countrymen" published in the *Karmayogin* of July 3 , 1909.

46. Haridas Mukherjee and Uma Mukherjee : *Aurobindo and the New Thought in Indian Politics.* p. 382.

47. Tilak had said, "Did Shivaji commit a sin in killing Afzal Khan ? The answer to this question can be found in the Mahabharat itself. Shrimat Krishna's teaching in the Gita condones even the killing of one's teachers and kinsmen. No blame attaches to any person if he is doing deeds without being actuated by a desire to reap the

fruits thereof."—*Lokamanya Tilak* : Ram Gopal : p. 147.

48. Upendranath Banerjee : *Nirbasiter Atmakatha.*
49. *Hind Swaraj* : M. K. Gandhi.
50. Dutt, R. P. : *India To-day*, Manisha, (Second Indian edition, 1970).
51. Seal, Anil, : *The Emergence of Indian Nationalism*, Cambridge University Press, 1971.
52. R. P. Dutt : *India To-day*. p. 326.
53. *Ibid.* p. 331.
54. *Ibid.* p. 325.

CHAPTER- X

THE IMPACT OF THE NEW HINDU MOVEMENT

THIS STUDY is mainly concerned with the history of ideas — history of the growth of the ideas that constituted the foundation of the New Hindu Movement. It would be in order now to briefly indicate the actual effects of the New Hindu ideas.

First, the New Hindu thinkers discovered the essence of religion of Hindus as distinct from caste rules, pollution rules and innumerable lifeless ceremonials. They established that the Upanishads and the Gita were the basic scriptures of Hinduism ; they discovered the ethical doctrines of 'love for all creation' and 'Nishkam Karma.' They showed the way how to attain personal illumination through renunciation. It may be argued that the impact of such discovery was not much, the prevalence of materialistic ideas in our generation apparently justifying that assertion.

Secondly, the New Hindu thinkers conjured up the vision of an ancient Indian civilization and by an interpretation of India's past civilization, they both historicized the Indian past and stimulated a consciousness of history. By their rediscovery and revitalization of a Hindu golden age, they transmitted a new sense of identity to Bengalis and greatly contributed to modern India's cultural self-image.

The New Hindu Movement again provided the ideology of social and political actions. Bankim's doctrine of moral and political 'regeneration' and Vivekananda's doctrine of 'growth' were particularly effective in this regard. The New Hindu ideas like 'Dharmarajya', 'war of restoration', 'militancy as against mendicancy', 'swadeshi samaj', etc. undoubtedly influenced the course of the Nationalist Movement particularly the Swadeshi Movement.

The movement, on the plane of action, was only a

partial success.   This is evident from what is said in the previous chapter.   The reasons of this failure are complex in nature and their analysis is outside the purview of this study.
But it would be true to say that this failure was not due to
any inner inconsistency of the New Hindu ideas.   In brief,
the failure had much to do with the complex social and political conditions then prevailing in Bengal.

Against this failure has to be reckoned again the fact
that the New Hindu Movement considerably contributed to
the development of some aspects of Bengali culture—a glorious literature, a new school of painting, some fine music, and
a new type of monasticism in which the humanitarian
impulse merged with the search for spiritual illumination.
However, it would be misleading to offer a monocausal
explanation of the cultural efflorescence in the late 19th and
early 20th century, and to relate it entirely to the New Hindu
Movement.   For instance, it was mixed up with the general
background of growing nationalist feelings, which, contrary
to a dominant school of historiography, were not the results
of rivalry between elite groups competing for power and position.   While the New Hindu Movement promoted such feeling, the movement itself was considerably influenced by the
general climate of nationalism.   The changing cultural life in
Bengal should be studied in this wider background.

(1)   It is not generally recognised that the development of modern Bengali literature in the late 19th century
owes a great deal to the New Hindu Movement.   Admittedly, this literature as regards structure and form was wholly
an importation from the West.   Thus Michael's (1824-74)
literary medium was what may be called the heroic poem in
blank verse, both of which devices had good indigenous ancestry in Sanskrit, but were, in fact, in the way Michael used
them, much more closely related to the Western varieties than
to the Eastern.   Bankim's literary medium was the novel and
the essay (in such works as *Kamalakanter Daptar*), the latter
wholly deriving from the West, and the former only distantly

related to such indigenous forms as, for example used in *Kadambari*. Strictly speaking, Bankim's medium was not the novel as understood in the West. True, such an early work as *Durgeshnandini* (1865) closely followed the structure of Scott's historical romances ; but with *Vishabriksha* (1872) began a cycle of 'novels', 'historical' as well as 'domestic', the resemblance of which to the Western form was only superficial. This may be most easily judged by examining the structure of any 'domestic novel' of Bankim's in which the actions are regulated by a strict adherence to a plot very much in the manner of a Greek tragedy (or at any rate in the manner in which Aristotle understood that literary form). Also to be noted is the part played by the supernatural in the unfolding of that plot, with the incidents steadily leading to a climax, in the manner of the tragic drama rather than that of the novel. Bankim's literary form is really one of his own creation but if we analyse its elements the influence of Western forms has to be recognised as the dominant one.

A similar remark applies to the literary forms adopted by Tagore. The lyrical form was indeed nothing new in Bengali literature : Chandidas's poems—some of them among the greatest love songs in the world—were cast in the lyrical mould. But our older poets knew nothing of the infinite variety of lyrical forms such as found in English literature. Tagore adopted them all along with the short story, verse, drama and the novel.

When we come to the content of all these works,—as distinct from their forms—we are face to face with a very different state of affairs and one can trace here the influence of some New Hindu ideas. This does not mean that the writers preach New Hindu ideas, though such a tale as Bankim's *Devi Chaudhurani* certainly does that. But some of their works are New Hindu in their treatment of Hindu society, not as an accretion of customs to be blindly accepted or blindly rejected, but as a certain special configuration of human relationships which, in its very restrictiveness, especially in female characters, shows the way to a higher fulfilment. They are New Hindu because they sing the heroic glory of Hindus, and seek to recapture the ancient light of a civilization characterised by charity and renunciation rather than by war and conquest. They are New Hindu, because by emphasizing the Sanskritic element of a language, which in the most impressive of its achievements gained hitherto, was essentially feminine and lyrical, they seek to fashion another, which without losing its identity, is suddenly roused into a state of masculine vigour, rendered nervous and stately, and made capable of the loftiest human emotions.

This Sanskritization of diction is important, for, it anticipated the general cultural movement which started soon and this was pioneered by Michael who wrote before the New Hindu Movement became a force to reckon with. It is certainly one of the greatest puzzles of 19th century Bengali literature that Michael, who was the most Westernized man of letters of his time, should have opted for a pre-eminently Sanskritic diction as the surest means to divest his vernacular of what was so long considered its native femininity. Despite his superior admiration for the literature written in English and the classical languages of Europe, despite the fact that in blank verse he took Milton for his model, he took his story from Valmiki and he not only did not attempt to Hellenise or at any rate, to Anglicise his diction, but took infinite pains to Sanskritise it. An an exercise in the reform of verse and diction, his poem stands out supreme, even after a lapse of a whole century, as indicating what a man of superior genius can do in the way of raising his vernacular from the status of a rustic language to one that is capable of expressing the noblest and the loftiest sentiments in verse.

If Michael's greatest achievement was his language and his blank verse, that of Bankim was a bounteous crop of the most unforgettable characters in Bengali literature. The most astonishing thing about these characters is their variety— astonishing because apart from Bankim, our literature has all along been strangely deficient in this regard. Bankim's world stands out as the vastness of the Himalayan landscape stands out aginst the scenery of a beautiful Bengali village. His is not a world of tearful women wasting their lives under the grip of cast-iron social customs, with their highminded lovers looking helplessly on. His is a world of action on the heroic scale, with soldiers clanking their swords in restless frenzy, statesman scheming the destruction of kingdoms, women rushing on horseback to meet their lovers or destroying themselves and their lovers too by the very intensity of their passions, men of vision sacrificing their lives and all else for the sake of their vision, passionate youngmen moving from sin to sin and then to God to seek solace for their lacerated souls —in a word, a world as large as life itself and actions as big as literary art could make them. Bankim is indeed the poet of great actions worthly attempted by heroes who fail to attain their goals. But even in their failure they vindicate his dictum about the great man as being the sort of man who cannot help gambling for mighty sorrows or mighty pleasures, because, without these, his faculties, ever hungry for more and more expansion, refuse to grow and develop.

When we say that this world of action and strife is a New Hindu one what we mean is this : Most of Bankim's heroes are cast in the mould of Kshatriyas —being consumed with a desire for expansiveness, sometimes fighting for the realisation of a definite political vision characteristic of the true born Kshatriya (Rajsinha, Satyananda, Bhawani Pathak, Sitaram), sometimes fighting their own passion with Kshatriya manfulness (Pratap, Bhavananda)—but always (with the exception of Rajsinha) destroying themselves tragically by the very magnificence of their desire, which inevitably precludes a lesser end. It is of course arguable that there is nothing specifically Hindu about such writing ; just as on the strength of the evidence furnished by the Hindu-Muslim political strife depicted in most of Bankim's historical novels, it has been argued by latter day detractors of Bankim that these novels are Hindu in the narrower sense, that of invidious political propaganda. But to a discerning reader it should be clear that Bankim's heroes are Hindu in a larger sense : they are a literary expression of regenerative elan which breathed through the whole New Hindu Movement. A brief glance at the historical development of our literature since the 1820s and a comparison with the religious history during the same period (i. e., the period 1820-70) strengthens the same view. As in religion the pre-Bankim period was characterised by Brahmo Reformism, so in literature the period was one of reformistic propaganda starting with such works as *Naba-Baboo-Vilas*, Michael's farces, Dinabandhu Mitra's *Sadhabar Ekadasi*, Tekchand's *Alaler Gharer Dulal* and so forth. Just as in religion and social customs the earlier period was characterised by Hindu College Westernization, so in literature it witnessed Michael's attempt at Hellenising the heroes and heroines of Hindu epics. It is against this background that the heroes of Bankim's historical novels are to be viewed.

When we come to Bankim's female characters this conclusion gets strengthened. It is well known that Bankim's female characters—all (or at any rate most of them) exhibit a Hindu virtue which in English can only be rendered by such terms as 'faithfulness' or 'chastity', but which is in fact based on a far nobler idea than what these strictly limited words imply. The Sanskrit word 'Satitva' stands for whatever is glorious in a married woman's existence. Sexual fidelity to the husband is only part of that glory, 'Satitva' means a lot more. It includes a married woman's dignity— the dignity, that is to say, which demands of the husband an equal fidelity and of society the respect which is a married woman's due ; it includes her religious initiation, the sort of initiation that prepares her for illumination by absolute devotion to the husband and necessarily implies heroic efforts when the husband is a poor creature and has to be led by the hand to be made worthy of that devotion ; it includes motherhood, the sort of motherhood that looks upon the work of child bearing as a sort of worship. By the term 'Satitva' is thus implied an austere doctrine with all its component parts ; and Bankim leaves no room for doubt that his heroines are portrayed as embodiments of these virtues. Thus Bhramar stands for the wifely dignity, and would rather seek death than cohabit with a lecherous husband ; the weak and irresolute Roma for the social dignity that is a married woman's due, and to regain which the weak and irresolute bride would be suddenly transfigured into a stern crowd-daring woman of steel ; the mirth-loving Labanya for the hard-hearted punisher of sacrilege, who would think nothing of writing 'thief' in letters of red-hot iron on the back of her lover who was not her husband but for whom her whole soul yearned ; and would brush out but for her superhuman self-control ; and lastly the heroic couple Shanti and Prafulla for the devotion that would not serve passively but would lead their husbands by the hand to the path of transcendent glory. This also explains the reason why the vital Saibalini, having fallen from 'Satitva', has to undergo a system of penance as excruciating as hell-fire while still in her earthly frame. It is possible that here for once Bankim the moralist has got the upperhand of the literary artist ; but it is a measure of Bankim's genius that consciously conceived as embodiments of a Hindu virtue as they are, his female characters are no lay-figures, but are in fact the well-springs of vitality in all his novels.

Coming to Tagore, we are faced with the initial difficulty of deciding how much of his writings were inspired by the New Hindu impulse. Tagore's literary output is so vast and so various that any attempt to include it all within a single scheme would be misleading. But here our task is simplified by the time limits imposed on our work. His output after 1911, is automatically excluded from consideration here. But even so we must guard agaidst attribution of a New Hindu inspiration to any work of Tagore. In Tagore's case this is all the more necessary because as we saw earlier he was on many points a staunch Brahmo and this has also influenced some of his writings.   Take for example, such an early work as 'Visarjan' whose central idea is that the worship of Kali by offering animal flesh at her altar is a vile and cruel practice.

But there can be little doubt that a considerable part of Tagore's works during the closing years of the 19th century and the first decade of the 20th shows influence of some New Hindu themes.   This is especially true of the poems of *Chaitali*, and *Naivedya*, where the forest ideal of ancient India was the dominant theme.   These are poems with an obvious message.   However, dignity and loftiness of diction has saved these poems from being mere vapourings of high minded idealism (as in the case with most works of Hemchandra Banerjee).

There are, however, two works belonging to this period *Katha O Kahini* and *Kahini*—where the New Hindu impulse is not merely one that adds to neutral material a new dimension and thereby heightens its intensity and deepens its significance, but is directly concerned with New Hindu themes. The first is a collection of ballads—the sort of historical or semi-historical tales in which Bankim would have been in his element, but which Tagore made his own by his very special way of treating them.   These are not poems of action in any sense but a series of intense moments in the lives of certain Hindu and Buddhist heroes (and heroines)—moments mostly of self-inflected martyrdom in a blinding flash of self-expansion, described in the fewest of words and with hardly any adornment of language. There are some other poems in which the power of renunciation is described by way of dramatising a single unassuming action of marvellous power. 'Katha O Kahini' is religious poetry of a new kind, a kind that has no parallel in word literature.

'Kahini' is a work having little resemblance to 'Katha O Kahini'.   It is collection of five poems in dialogue, three of them adapted from the Mahabharata—but each[1] dealing with a religious theme. Of the five 'Gandharir Abedan' is the longest and calls for special notice.

'*Gandharir Abedan*' is one of the noblest poems in our language.   Its subject matter is the infructuous appeal made by Queen Gandhari to her husband Dhritarastra, the king of the Kurus, to exile their son Duryodhan for the monstrous sin he (Duryodhan) had brought upon the illustrious house of the Kurus by deceitfully depriving his cousins of their kingdom, and bringing dishonour on their noble queen Draupadi in an attempt to disrobe her publicly in front of her oath-bound husbands and all the nobles in the kingdom. The story is almost exactly as told in the Mahabharata and the characters exactly as drawn by the ancient author. Tagore has scrupulously followed in the footsteps of the great predecessor.

'Gandharir Abedan' is unique in being an epitome of the whole Mahabharata within the smallest possible compass, the whole poem occupying no more than a thousandth part of the space covered by the gigantic epic. It is unique in describing within its compass the Mahabharata theme of Dharma in distress pronouncing its fearful triumph through the person of a mother who in her terrible spiritual isolation contemplates the chaos that is slowly going to engulf her house even as the kingly glory sought by her evil son was apparently achieved. The evil son in the stateliness of his self-destructive pride, the infatuated father in complete awareness of the approaching doom but in his infatuation powerless to avert it, and above all the righteous mother in the profound dignity of her sorrow—all these have been portrayed through a few short speeches of unequalled nobility and an unrivalled balance of style.

The above is an all-too-brief account of our literary achievements during the last half of the 19th century and the first decade of the 20th. We have had no occasion to go into details and have left out some works of outstanding merit—among them Tagore's earlier short stories, in some of which

33

(such as 'Dristidan', 'Megh O Raudra'), the influence of New Hindu ideas is evident. Also we have left out 'Gora'—possibly Tagore's greatest achievement—in fiction, in which the hero, a New Hindu character, towers above the goody-goody Paresh Babu, whose Brahmoism has in the end, been shown to score a victory over Gora's New Hinduism by a device which convinces nobody and Gora's New Hindu image continues to haunt the reader. But the little we have written amply shows that the greatest achievements of our literature owe not a little of their greatness to the New Hindu afflatus.

(2) *Painting* : It seems to us that the painting of this period is not as great as its literature. But it is universally recognised that the Neo-Indian school of painting founded by Abanindranath Tagore and his disciples, is the only style of painting created in modern times which can be credited with originality and some amount of excellence. It is also recognised that the excellence of this style derives not a little from Neo-Indian painters' successful attempt at breaking away from the practice of imitating Western form. This does not necessarily imply that the new paintings were New Hindu : at best, they were 'national'. But Abanindranath's Krishnalila paintings, his illustrations of certain scenes taken from Kalidas's *Meghduta* and *Ritu Samhara*, his 'Buddha and Sujata'—all these are New Hindu in the sense that they derive their life from the visionary harking back to an ancient Indian civilization, which was one aspect of the New Hindu Movement. But Abanindrnath's interest in ancient India was romantic and lyrical rather than religious. Thus his 'Buddha' (in Buddha and Sujata) inspite of his serene countenance and the traditional posture reminds us of Tagore's Upagupta and his own Kacha (in the picture entitled 'Kacha and Devyani')—both of them romantic heroes rather than givers of a 'peace that passeth understanding'. Abanindranath's paintings are to be judged within these limitations, but once we recognise these limitations we are struck with the variety of artistic expressions of which the New Hindu

impulse was capable.

(3) *Ramakrishna Mission* : How potent the New Hindu formula of uniting humanitarian service with the search for spiritual experience was, can be judged from the fact that very many respectable religious missions founded in India since Vivekananda's death have combined both these aims and have closely resembled Vivekananda's organisation in this respect. In humanitarian service, indeed, the record of some of these missions does not compare unfavourably with that of the Ramakrishna Mission. But the Ramakrishna Mission was the pioneering body in such service and we shall content ourselves by recording some of its achievements.

If the mission founded by Vivekananda did nothing but undertake the many acts of service it performed by establishing hospitals, relief centres and many other charitable bodies over the length and breadth of our land, it would have nevertheless earned our undying gratitude. In this respect, the record of our religious bodies in the past was far from admirable. Hundreds of religious bodies has flourished in our country previous to the establishment of the Ramakrishna Mission, but none of them was ever known to take up humanitarian service as part of its work. Nivedita, in emphasising the epoch-making nature of Vivekananda's mission, when considered from this angle, has tried to gloss over the deficiency in this respect, of earlier religious bodies, by remarking that : "In India the head and front of the demand made on a monastic order is that it produces saints" ; but such a charitable view hardly takes account of the fact that the number of saints born in India has never been proportionate to the number of its *maths* or monasteries. However, the impact of Vivekananda's mission is evident from the fact that there is hardly one respectable religious order in the country which does not at least pay lip service (if no more than that) to the now well-established custom that a religious order must justify its existence by taking up humanitarian work in the first place. In this respect the founding of the Ramakrishna

Mission was a truly 'epoch-making' event.

But humanitarian service is after all secular work, and one can argue that such work could as well be performed as satisfactorily by a secular body and even by a department of the State. The significance of the humanitarian work performed by Vivekananda mission is that it prevented charity from being polluted with the stink of the work-house and the soullessness of unemployment doles, and raised it to the level of a sacrament.

Sir Jadunath Sarkar, the great historian, who was an eye-witness of work performed by Nivedita and some of Vivekananda's disciples, on the occasion of the plague which broke out in Calcutta in 1891 has written : "When the sweepers had fled away, (I) chanced upon a white woman one day clearing the streets with broom and basket in hand. This was none other than Nivedita" ;

Again, "If the stench of garbage accumulated in a narrow lane repelled even the practised sweepers, (another disciple) would nonchalantly snatch the basket and spade from one of them and set about removing the decomposed heap till the sweepers too would step forward...At the end, he would congratulate them and embrace them warmly, regardless of their social distance or dirty bodies. Or if there was an uncared for patient he would hug him and nurse him to recovery." The disciple referred to was Swami Sadananda.

These two examples give us some idea of the glory with which Nivedita and Sadananda had invested their humanitarian work. Unfortunately, this aspect of the matter has received little notice in official histories of the Ramakrishna Mission. Even Swami Gambhirananda's 'History' gives one the impression that the Mission's achievement consisted in the bigness of the tasks it undertook ; as if the institution founded by Vivekananda in the name of his Guru would justify itself by the number of hospitals and schools it founded. The examples we have given, few as they are, should make it clear that at least in the case of Nivedita and

Sadananda a higher justification of 'service' was operative. That this justification was by no means absent from the 'service' undertaken by some other monks is evident from the following statement made by Nivedita, who however withheld the name of the 'Sanyasin' in question. As she put it : "I know of one disciple, who, in the early days of the Order, was so filled with the impulse of this reverence (for work as worship) that he sucked the sores of the lepers to bring them ease."[2]

The mission founded by Vivekananda is the only offspring yet in existence of the New Hindu Movement. The year 1911 saw the death of Nivedita, who was in some sense the closest spiritual heir of the great Swami. The continued existence and the gradual expansion of the activities of the Ramakrishna Mission after 1911, admirable and wholly praiseworthy as those activities are, are no refutation of our statement that the New Hindu Movement became moribund with the dismantling of the Swadeshi Movement, when politics tended to overshadow the religious impulse of the movement. It would be churlish to harp on the failures of so great an institution as the Ramakrishna Mission but it can hardly be denied that since 1911, this institution has not even attempted to take up the two outstanding schemes of Vivekananda. First, the 'raising' of the masses through religious education spread by itinerant monks all over the country and the devising of methods by which these masses could be helped in their problem of subsistence ; and secondly, the 'raising' of our women.

NOTES AND REFERENCES

1. With the possible exception of *'Karna-Kunti-Sambad'* which narrates the personal tragedy of the heroic son of Kunti who, having been early deserted by his mother and remained unknown to his brothers turned down his mother's request to go over to their side at the last moment, and faced death in their hands—unknown, unhonoured and unsung.

2. Nivedita : *"The Master as I saw him,"* p. 41.

SELECT BIBLIOGRAPHY

ENGLISH PERIODICALS AND NEWSPAPERS

The Hindoo Patriot, Mookerjee's Magazine, Bande Mataram, The Indian Mirror, The Bengalee, The Indian Nation, The Indian Social Reformer.

BENGALI NEWSPAPERS AND JOURNALS

Somprokash, Vangadarsan, Sadharani, Bandhab, Sanjibani, Nabyabharat, Nabajiban, Prachar, Udbodhan, Tattvabodhini, Brahman Samaj.

BOOKS : PRIMARY SOURCES

Banerjee, Surendranath : *A Nation in Making* (London. 1925).

Banerjee, B. (edited) : *Letters by Bankim on Hinduism* (Calcutta, M. M. Bose, 1940).

Basu, Dr Prem Sundar : *Life and Works of Brahmananda Keshub Chandra Sen,* (Calcutta, 1940, Second edition).

Basu, Sankari Prasad and Ghosh, Sunil Behari (edited) : *Vivekananda in Indian Newspapers* (Calcutta, 1969).

Chatterjee, Bankim Chandra : *Bankim Rachanavali* (edited by Jogesh Chandra Bagal ; Sahitya Samsad, Calcutta, 1969).

Collet, S. D. : *The Life and Letters of Raja Rammohan Roy* (edited by D. K. Biswas and P. C. Ganguli, Calcutta, 1962).

Chintamani, C. Y. (edited) : *Indian Social Reform in four parts*—a collection of Essays, Addresses, Speeches etc. (Madras, 1901).

Gandhi, M. K. : *Hind Swaraj or Indian Home Rule* (Navajiban Publishing House, Ahmedabad, 1938).

Ghosh, Aurobindo (Sri Aurobindo) : *Bankim Chandra Chatterjee* (Pondicherry, 1954) ; *The Renaissance in India* (Chandernagore, 1927) ; *Bankim-Tilak-Dayananda* (2nd edn., 1947) ; *The Doctrine of Passive Resistance,* (2nd edn., Pondicherry, 1952) ; *The Foundations of Indian Culture* (Pondicherry, 1959) ; *Essays on the Gita* (Pondicherry, 1952) ; *Sri Arabinder Patra* (Pondichery, 1952).

His Eastern and Western Disciples : *The Life of Swami Vivekananda,* (Advaita Ashram, Calcutta, 1961).

His Eastern and Western Admirers : *Reminiscences of Swami Vivekananda.* (Advaita Ashram, Calcutta, 1961. Being memories of thirty-four admirers—compiled from 'Prabuddha Bharata' and 'Vedanta Kesari').

Majumdar, P. C. : *The Life and teachings of Keshub Chandra Sen.*

Marshall, P. J. (ed.) : *The British Discovery of Hinduism in the eighteenth century* (Cambridge University Press, 1970).

Max Muller : *India : What can it teach us ?* (Oxford, 1882).

Mukherjee, Haridas and Uma : (ed.) *Bande Mataram and Indian Nationalism* (1906-1908 ; Calcutta, 1957) ; *Sri Aurobinda and the New Thought in Indian Politics.* (Calcutta, 1964—contains 106 editorials from the daily edition of 'Bande Mataram' and three editorials from the Weekly edition) ; *Sri Aurobindo's Political Thought* (1893-1908, Calcutta, 1964 ; Includes selections from the 'Indu-Prakash' : "New Lamps for Old", and selections from the 'Bande Mataram').

Nivedita, Sister : *The Master as I saw Him* (Calcutta, 1910).

Nevinson, H. : *The New Spirit in India.* (London, 1908).

Pal, Bipin Chandra : *Memories of My Life and Times* (vol. I & II ; Calcutta, 1932, 1951) ; *The Soul of India* (Calcutta, 1911) ; *The Spirit of Indian Nationalism* (London, 1910) ; *Saint Bijoy Krishna Goswami* (Calcutta, 1964 ; *Character Sketches* (Calcutta, 1957) ; *Swadeshi and Swaraj* (Calcutta, 1954) ; *Speeches of Bipin Chandra Pal* (Madras, 1907) ; *Nationality and Empire* (Calcutta, 1916).

Ray, Rammohan : *The English Works of Raja Rammohan Roy*, 7 parts in one ; edited by K. Nag & D. Burman (Calcutta, 1958).

Sastri, Sibnath : *History of the Brahmo Samaj,* (2 vols., Calcutta, 1911, 1912).

Sen, Keshub Chandra : *Jeevan-Veda* : translated by Jamini Kanta Koar (Nababidhan Trust, 3rd edition, 1969).

Tagore, Rabindranath : *Creative Unity* : (Macmillan, 1971).

Vivekananda, Swami : *Complete Works of Swami Vivekananda* : 8 vols. (Mayavati Memorial Edition, Advaita Ashram, Calcutta, 1962).

SECONDARY SOURCES

Banerjee, S. K. : *Bankimchandra : A Study of His Craft* (Calcutta, 1968).

Bose, N. S. : *The Indian Awakening and Bengal,* (Calcutta, 1969).

Burke, Marie Louise : *Swami Vivekananda in America ; New Discoveries* (Calcutta, 1958).

Chaudhuri, Nirad, C. : *The autobiography of an unknown Indian,* (Macmillan, 1951) ; *Life of Max-Muller.*

Chirol, Valentine : *Indian Unrest* (London, 1910).

Cotton, H. J. S. : *New India* (London, 1907).

Christopher Isherwood : *Ramakrishna and His Disciples* (Advaita Ashrama, Calcutta, 1969).

Chakravarty, B. C. : *Rabindranath Tagore : His Mind & Art* (New Delhi, 1970).

Chakravarty, Ramendranath : (edited)—*Abanindranath Tagore : His Early Works* (Indian Museum, Calcutta, 1964).

Datta, Bhupendranath : *Swami Vivekananda—Patriot-Prophet* (Calcutta, 1954).

Dodwell, H. H. (edited) : The Indian Empire 1858-1918 ; *The Cambridge History of the British Empire* vol. V (Cambridge, 1932).

Datta, K. K. : *Renaissance, Nationalism and Social Changes in Modern India* : (Bookland Pvt. Ltd. 1965) ; *Dawn of Renascent India* : (Allied Publishers, 1964).

Dutt, R. Palme : *India To-day*. (2nd Indian edition, 1970.)

David Kopf : *British Orientalism and the Bengal Renaissance*. (Calcutta, 1969).

Farquhar, J. N. : *Modern Religious Movements in India* (New York, 1915).

Gambhirananda, Swami : *History of the Ramakrishna Math and Mission* (Calcutta, 1957).

Gopal, Ram : *Lokamanya Tilak* (Asia Publishing House, 1956).

Ghosh, J. C. : *Bengali Literature*, (London, 1948).

Gupta, Atul Chandra (edited) : *Studies in the Bengal Renaissance*—In connection to the Birth Centenary of Bipin Chandra Pal (Cal., 1958).

Gordon, Leonard A. : *Bengal : The Nationalist Movement* 1876-1940, (Delhi, 1974).

Heinsath, Charles H, : *Indian Nationalism and Hindu Social Reform* (Princeton, New Jersey, 1964).

Johnson, David L. : *The Religious Roots of Indian Nationalism* (Calcutta, 1974).

Majumdar, R. C. : *Glimpses of Bengal in the Nineteenth Century* (Calcutta, 1960). *History of the Freedom Movement in India :* 3 vols. (Calcutta, 1962-64). (ed.) *Swami Vivekananda—Centenary Memorial Volume,*(Calcutta, 1963) ; *Swami Vivekananda—A Historical Review,* (Calcutta, 1965) ; (ed.) *British Paramountcy and Indian Renaissance*, Pt. II (vol. X of the Bharatiya Vidya Bhavan's History and Culture of the Indian people, (Bombay 1965).

Majumdar, B. B. : *History of Political Thought from Rammohan to Dayananda* (Calcutta University, 1934) ; *Militant Nationalism in India* (Calcutta, 1966).

Marshall, P. J. (ed.) : *The British Discovery of Hinduism in the eighteenth century* (Cambridge University Press, 1970—for the Introduction).

Mukherjee, Amitabha : *Reform and Regeneration in Bengal*, 1774-

1823, (Calcutta, 1968).

Mukherjee, Haridas and Uma : *India's Fight for Freedom or the Swadeshi Movement* 1905-1906, Calcutta, 1958. *The Growth of Nationalism in India 1857-1905*, Calcutta, 1957. *The origins of the National Education Movement* 1905-1910, Calcutta, 1957.

Mukherjee, S. : *Sir William Jones : A study in Eighteenth Century British Attitude to India*, Cambridge, 1968.

Nirvedananda, Swami : *Sri Ramakrishna and Spiritual Renaissance*, Calcutta, 1940.

Nikhilananda, Swami : *Vivekananda : a Biography*. New York, 1953.

Philips, C. H. (ed) : *The Evolution of India and Pakistan, 1858 to 1947*. Select Documents on the History of India and Pakistan IV. London, 1962.

Parliament of Religions (1963-64) : *Swami Vivekananda Centenary*, Calcutta, 1965.

Romain Rolland : *The Life of Ramkrishna*, Advaita Ashram 1929. *The Life of Vivekananda and the Universal Gospel*, 1931.

Ranade, Eknath : *Rousing Call to Hindu Nation*, Calcutta, 1963.

Sarma, D. S. : *Studies in the Renaissance of Hinduism*, Benaras, 1944.

Sarkar, Sumit : *The Swadeshi Movement* 1903-1908.

Seal, Anil : *The Emergence of Indian Nationalism—Competition and Collaboration in the Later Nineteenth Century*. Cambridge, 1968.

Sen, D. C. : *History of Bengali Language and Literature*, 2nd edition, Calcutta, 1954.

Sen, S. : *History of Bengali Literature*, New Delhi, 1960.

Sen, P. R. : *Western Influence in Bengali Literature*, Calcutta, 1932.

Sinha, N. K. (edited) : *The History of Bengal*, Calcutta University, 1957.

Sinha, Pradip : *Nineteenth Century Bengal—Aspects of Social History*, Calcutta, 1965.

Tripathi, A. : *The Extremist Challenge* : Calcutta, 1967.

V. Bengali : Primary

Bandyopadhyaya, Brojendranath : *Sambadpatre Sekaler Katha* (3rd edition), vol. I, II, Calcutta, 1949, 1950. *Bangla Samayik-Patra* (1818-1868), Calcutta, 1948.

Bose, Rajnarain : *Atmacharita* (autobiography), Calcutta, 1909. *Sekal ar Ekal*, Calcutta, 1358, B. S. *Hindu Dharmer Srestatha*, Calcutta, 1873.

Banerjee, Upendranath : *Nirbashiter atmakatha*, 7th ed., Calcutta, 1960.

Bandopadhyay, Chandicharan : *Vidyasagar*, 3rd ed., Allahabad, 1909.

Bedantabagish, Kalibar : *Sri Sasadhur Tarkachudamoni Mahasayer Baktritar Samalochana*, Vedanta Press, Calcutta, 1291 B. S.

34

Bisi, Pramathanath (edited) : *Bhudev Rachanasambhar*, Calcutta, 1962. *Kanta Kabi Rachanasambhar*, Calcutta, 1967. *Michael Rachanasambhar*, Calcutta, 1961.

Chatterjee. Bankim Chandra : *Bankim Rachanavali*, 2 vols. Sahitya Samsad, Calcutta, 1954.

Chattopadhyay, Shachis : *Bankim-Jibani*.

Gandhi, M. K. : *Gandhi Rachana Sambhar* (Gandhi Satabarsiki Samiti, Paschim Banga), 6 vols-

Gupta, Bipin Behari : *Puratana Prasanga* (First series), Calcutta, 1913. *Puratana Prasanga* (Second series), Calcutta, 1923.

Ghose, Benoy (edited) : *Samaikpatre Banglar Samajchitra*, in three volumes, Calcutta, 1962-64.

Ghose, Ajit Kumar (edited) : *Rammohan Rachanavali*, Calcutta 1973.

Kar, Bankabehari : *Mahatma Bijoy Krishna Goswamir Jibanbrittanta*. (Second ed., 1328 B. S.)

Krishnananda, Swami : *Paribrajaker Baktrita* : A compilation of lectures delivered by the Swami.

Mukhopadhyaya, Bhudeb : *Paribarik Prabandha*, Hooghly, 1882. *Vividh Prabandha*, Chinsura, 1905. *Samajik Prabandha*, Calcutta 1937.

Pal, Bipin Chandra : *Nabayuger Bangla*, Calcutta, 1955. *Sattar Vatsar* (Atmajibani), Calcutta, 1962.

Roy, Upadhaya Gour Gobinda : *Acharya Keshub Chandra*, Keshub Centenary, Allahabad.

Sastri, Sibnath : *Ramtanu Lahiri O Tatkalin Banga Samaj*, Calcutta, 1903. *Atmacharit*, Signet Press edition, Calcutta, 1359 B. S.

Sasadhar Tarkachudamoni : *Dharmabakshya*, Calcutta, 1806 Saka.

Sen, Nabin Chandra : *Amar Jiban* (Autobiography).

Sengupta, Amritlal : *Sri Madacharya Prabhupadha Bijoy Krishna Goswami : Sadhana O Upadesh*.

Sri 'M' : *Sri Sri Ramakrishna-Kathamrita* (5 vols.) : Calcutta 1 59 B. S.

Tagore, Debendranath : *Atmajibani*, Calcutta, 1962.

Tagore, Rabindranath ; *Rabindra Rachanavali* (14 vols) : Tagore Centenary, West Bengal.

Trivedi, Ramendra Sundar : *Charit Katha* (7th edition), Calcutta, 1365 B. S.

Vivekananda, Swami : *Swami Vivekanander Bani O Rachana* : Centenary volumes (8), Udbodhan, Calcutta.

Vidyasagar, Iswarchandra ; *Vidyasagar Rachana Sangraha* : 3 vols : Calcutta, 1972.

VI. *Bengali : Secondary*

Bagal, Y. C. : *Radhakanta Deb, Sahitya-Sadhak-Charitmala Series*,

Kalikata, Bangiya Sahitya Parisad, 1957. *Debendranath Thakur* ; *Sahitya Sadhak-Charitmala* Series. *Unabinsa Satabdir Bangla,* Calcutta, 1348 B. S. *Muktir Sandhane Bharat*, Calcutta, 1940 ; *Jagriti O Jatiyata*, Calcutta, 1959.

Basu, Pramatha Nath : *Swami Vivekananda,* 4 vols.

Chakraborty, Chintaharan : *Bangla Sahityer Sanskrita Pandit Samaj,* (Bangiya Sahitya Parisad, Calcutta, 1972).

Chaudhuri, Nirad, C. : *Bangali Jibane Ramani.* Calcutta.

Datta, Bhabatosh : *Chintanayak Bankim Chandra*, Calcutta, 1961.

Datta, Hirendranath : *Darsanik Bankim Chandra.*

Gupta, Sushil Kumar : *Unabinsa Satabdite Banglar Nabajagaran,* Calcutta, 1959.

Ghosh, Pranab Ranjan : *Unabimsa Satabdite Bangaleer Manan O Sahitya*, Calcutta, 1968.

Ghosh, Benoy : *Banglar Nabajagriti,* vol. I, Calcutta, 1948.

Majumdar, Satyendranath : *Vivekananda Charit,* Calcutta, 1919.

Majumdar, Mohit Lal : *Banglar Nabayug* : (New edition), Calcutta, 1879 Sakavda.

Mitra, Haraprasad : *Bankim Sahityapath*, Calcutta.

Mukhopadhyay, Prabhat : *Rabindra-Jibani* (Visva Bharati, 1954).

Poddar, Aurobindo ; *Bankim-Manas*, Calcutta.

Raichaudhury. Girija Sankar : *Sri Aurobindo O Banglay Swadeshi Yug,* Calcutta, 1956.

Roy, Alak : *Rajendra Lal Mitra,* Calcutta.

Sarkar, J. N. : *Historical Introduction* : *Bankim Rachanavali* : Satabarsik Sanskaran, Bangiya Sahitya Parisad.

INDEX